COCOA® PROGRAMMING FOR MAC® OS X

SECOND EDITION

COCOA® PROGRAMMING FOR MAC® OS X

SECOND EDITION

Aaron Hillegass

✦Addison-Wesley

Boston • San Francisco • New York • Toronto • Montreal
London • Munich • Paris • Madrid
Capetown • Sydney • Tokyo • Singapore • Mexico City

Many of the designations used by manufacturers and sellers to distinguish their products are claimed as trademarks. Where those designations appear in this book, and Addison-Wesley was aware of a trademark claim, the designations have been printed with initial capital letters or in all capitals.

The author and publisher have taken care in the preparation of this book, but make no expressed or implied warranty of any kind and assume no responsibility for errors or omissions. No liability is assumed for incidental or consequential damages in connection with or arising out of the use of the information or programs contained herein.

The publisher offers discounts on this book when ordered in quantity for bulk purchases and special sales. For more information, please contact:

U.S. Corporate and Government Sales
(800) 382-3419
corpsales@pearsontechgroup.com

For sales outside of the U.S., please contact:

International Sales
(317) 581-3793
international@pearsontechgroup.com

Visit Addison-Wesley on the Web: www.awprofessional.com

Library of Congress Cataloging-in-Publication Data

Hillegass, Aaron.
  Cocoa : programming for Mac OS X / Aaron Hillegass.—2nd ed.
    p. cm.
  Includes bibliographical references and index.
  ISBN 0-321-21314-9 (pbk. : alk. paper)
  1. Cocoa (Application development environment) 2. Mac OS. 3. Operating systems
(Computers) 4. Macintosh (Computer)—Programming. I. Title.
  QA76.76.063H57145 2004
  005.26'8—dc22   2004003054

ISBN 0-321-21314-9
Text printed on recycled paper
1 2 3 4 5 6 7 8 9 10—CRS—0807060504
First printing, May 2004

For my son, Walden Carter Hillegass

CONTENTS

PREFACE TO THE SECOND EDITION

I once studied with a wise mathematician named Soo Bong Chae. Dr. Chae had written a few really good books, and one day he told me his secret: "After I write a book, I put it away for two years. After avoiding the book for two years, I read it and rewrite the parts that need work. Then I publish it." The idea was a good one: By ignoring the book for two years, he could revise it with fresh eyes.

But that's not what happened in my case.

It has, indeed, been two years since I wrote the first edition of *Cocoa® Programming for Mac® OS X*. In that time, however, I have taught 20 classes using the book as a text. Overall, the first edition was a good book, but it was far from perfect. Where the book was weak, I have suffered. It was with great relish I eliminated these sore spots from this edition.

During these two years, Apple has continued innovating upon the strong base that Mac OS X created. Hundreds of tiny improvements were made, and two large changes occurred: Project Builder was replaced by Xcode, and Cocoa bindings were added to Cocoa. Throughout this book, you will use Xcode, and Cocoa bindings are covered in Chapter 6.

Also, during these years, I continued my work as a programmer. As my clients asked for certain features to be added to their products, I came to realize that several topics needed to be addressed in a new edition the book. Besides many new "For the More Curious" sections, the second edition has five entirely new chapters:

- Chapter 7 describes how to add undo capabilities to an application using NSUndoManager.
- Chapter 28 demonstrates how to make an application AppleScript-able.
- Chapter 29 shows how you can use OpenGL calls within a Cocoa application.

- Chapter 30 gives the necessary steps to create a reusable framework.
- Chapter 31 will get you started creating Cocoa applications on Linux using GNUstep.

The final improvement is a physical one: The second edition has a lay-flat binding so that it can sit at your elbow as you work through the book. Although a subtle change, I think it will make your experience with the book and its ideas a little bit more pleasant.

I don't get to ignore this book after it has been published—the quality of the book has a direct influence on the quality of the courses I teach. Is it a good book? Let me put it this way: I am looking forward to going through it with my students a dozen times this year. I guess that says something.

Preface to the First Edition

Cocoa is a powerful collection of tools and libraries that enable developers to write applications for Mac OS X. iPhoto, iChat, iCal, iSync and Safari were all written using Cocoa. Why Cocoa? Because it allows programmers to develop full-featured applications faster than ever before.

The increased speed does not, however, come for free. The new technologies have a steep learning curve. This book will guide you through the ideas and techniques that separate the great Cocoa programmers from the wanna-be's.

This book is written for programmers who already know some C programming and something about objects. The reader is not expected to have any experience with Mac programming. It is a hands-on book and assumes that the reader has access to Mac OS X and the developer tools. The developer tools are free. If you bought a shrink-wrapped copy of Mac OS X, the developer tools CD was in the box. The tools can also be downloaded from the Apple Developer Connection Web site (http://connect.apple.com/).

—Aaron Hillegass

ACKNOWLEDGMENTS

Creating this book required the efforts of many people. I want to thank them for their help. Their contributions have made this a better book than I could have ever written alone.

First, I want to thank the students who took the Cocoa programming course at the Big Nerd Ranch. They helped me work the kinks out of the exercises and explanations that appear here. Their curiosity inspired me to make the book more comprehensive, and their patience made it possible.

By helping me teach and develop materials at the Ranch, Chris Campbell played a very important role in the revisions for the second edition. He made great additions and caught many of my most egregious errors. He also took all the screenshots.

Many people read the drafts of this edition and gave me corrections and suggestions. They include Mike Ferris, Kris Jensen at Stone Design, Bill Bumgarner, Brandon Kirby, Adam Fedor, and Don Briggs. Each reader added something to what is here.

I had the great honor of working for several years with Kai Christiansen. He taught me many things about Cocoa and about teaching. Together, we wrote several courses on OpenStep and WebObjects. For me, writing this book was a natural continuation of our work. Although my hands were on the keyboard, Kai's voice was frequently what came out on the page.

The great people at Addison-Wesley took my manuscript and made it into a book. They put the book on trucks and convinced bookstores to put it on the shelves. Without their help, it would still be just a stack of papers in my office.

The final thank-you goes to my family. Some of the attention that would normally be given to my wife, Michele, was diverted into the creation of this book. My son, Walden, was in the womb while I wrote the first edition. While I did the revisions for the second edition, he was at the bottom of the stairs yelling, "Daddy, come DOWN!" He also deserves thanks for his patience and understanding.

Chapter 1

COCOA: WHAT IS IT?

A Little History

The story of Cocoa starts with a delightful bit of history. Once upon a time, two guys named Steve started a company called Apple Computer in their garage. The company grew rapidly, so they hired an experienced executive named John Sculley to be its CEO. After a few conflicts, John Sculley moved Steve Jobs to a position where he had no control over the company at all. Steve Jobs left to form another computer company, called NeXT Computer.

NeXT hired a small team of brilliant engineers. This small team developed a computer, an operating system, a printer, a factory, and a set of development tools. Each piece was years ahead of competing technologies, and the masses were excited and amazed. Unfortunately, the excited masses did not buy either the computer or the printer. In 1993, the factory was closed, and NeXT Computer, Inc., became NeXT Software, Inc.

The operating system and the development tools continued to sell under the name NeXTSTEP. While the average computer user had never heard of NeXTSTEP, it was very popular with several groups: scientists, investment banks, and intelligence agencies. These were people who developed new applications every week, and they found that NeXTSTEP enabled them to implement their ideas faster than any other technology.

What was this operating system? NeXT decided to use Unix as the core of NeXTSTEP. It relied on the source code for BSD Unix from the University of California at Berkeley. Why Unix? Unix crashed much less frequently than Microsoft Windows or Mac OS, and it came with powerful, reliable networking capabilities.

NeXT put the BSD Unix on top of a microkernel called *Mach*, which had been developed at Carnegie-Mellon University. The microkernel approach was a good way to sell Unix to the masses: Because everything that is not absolutely necessary is kept out of the kernel, no one should ever have to recompile it. OSF/1 Unix and the GNU HURD are also based on the Mach microkernel.

Apple has made the source code to the Mach/Unix part of Mac OS X available under the name Darwin. A community of developers cotinues to work to improve Darwin. You can learn more about Darwin at http://www.opendarwin.org/ or http://developer.apple.com/darwin.

NeXT then wrote a *window server* for the operating system. A window server takes events from the user and forwards them to the applications. The application then sends drawing commands back to the window server to update what the user sees. One of the nifty things about the NeXT window server is that the drawing code that goes to the window server is the exact same drawing code that would be sent to the printer. Thus a programmer has to write the drawing code only once, and it can then be used for display on the screen or printing. In the NeXTSTEP days, programmers were writing code that generated PostScript. With Mac OS X, programmers are writing code that uses the CoreGraphics framework (also known as Quartz). Quartz can composite those graphics onto the screen, send them to the printer printer, or generate PDF data. The Portable Document Format is an open standard for vector graphics created by the Adobe Corporation.

If you have used Unix machines before, you are probably familiar with the X window server. The window server for Mac OS X is completely different, but fulfills the same function as the X window server: It gets events from the user, forwards them to the applications, and puts data from the applications onto the screen. At the moment, the X protocol has poor support for things like anti-aliased fonts and transparency. This is one of the reasons that the Mac OS X window server looks so much better than an X window server.

NeXTSTEP came with a set of libraries and tools to enable programmers to deal with the window manager in an elegant manner. The libraries were called frameworks. In 1993, the frameworks and tools were revised and renamed OpenStep, which was itself later renamed Cocoa.

As shown in Figure 1.1, the window server and your application are Unix processes. Cocoa enables your application to receive events from the window server and draw to the screen.

Programming with the frameworks is done in a language called *Objective-C*. Like C++, Objective-C is an extension to the C programming language that made it object-oriented. Unlike C++, Objective-C is weakly typed and extremely powerful. With power comes responsibility: Objective-C also allows programmers to make ridiculous errors. Objective-C is a very simple addition to C, and you will find it very easy to learn.

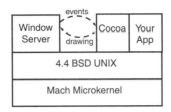

Figure 1.1   Classes Create Instances

Programmers loved OpenStep. It enabled them to experiment more easily with new ideas. In fact, Tim Berners-Lee developed the first Web browser and the first Web server on NeXTSTEP. Securities analysts could code and test new financial models much more quickly. Colleges could readily develop the applications that made their research possible. I don't know what the intelligence community was using it for, but they bought thousands of copies of OpenStep. Because they were so useful, the OpenStep development tools were ported to Solaris and Windows NT, and the NeXTSTEP operating system was ported to most of the popular CPUs of the day: Intel, Motorola, Hewlett+Packard's PA-RISC, and SPARC. (Oddly enough, OpenStep didn't run on a Mac until the first version of Mac OS X Server, known as Rhapsody, shipped in 1999.)

For many years, Apple Computer had been working to develop an operating system with many of the features of NeXTSTEP. This effort was known as Copland. Project Copland gradually spun out of control, and Apple finally decided to pull the plug and buy the next version of Mac OS from another company. After surveying the existing operating systems, it selected NeXTSTEP. Because NeXT was small, Apple simply bought the whole company in December 1996.

Where do I fit into this story? I was writing code for NeXT computers on Wall Street until NeXT hired me to teach OpenStep programming to other developers. I was an employee at NeXT when it merged with Apple, and I taught many of the Apple engineers how to write applications for Mac OS X. No longer an Apple employee, I now teach Cocoa programming for Big Nerd Ranch, Inc.

NeXTSTEP became Mac OS X. It is Unix underneath, and you can get all the standard Unix programs (like the Apache Web server) on Mac OS X. It is more stable than Windows and Mac OS 9, and the user interface is spectacular. You, the developer, are going to love Mac OS X, because Cocoa will enable you to write full-featured applications in a radically more efficient and elegant manner.

Tools

You *will* love Cocoa, but perhaps not immediately. First, you will learn the basics. Let's start with the tools that you will use.

All the tools for Cocoa development come as part of the Mac OS X Developer Tools, and you get them for free with Mac OS X. Although the developer tools will add about a dozen handy applications to your system, you will use primarily two applications: Xcode and Interface Builder. Behind the scenes, the GNU C compiler (gcc) will be used to compile your code and the GNU debugger (gdb) will help you find your errors.

Xcode tracks all the resources that will go into an application: code, images, sounds, and so on. You will edit your code in Xcode, and Xcode can compile and launch your application. Xcode can also be used to invoke and control the debugger.

Interface Builder is a GUI builder. It allows you to lay out windows and add widgets to those windows. It is, however, much more. Interface Builder allows the developer to create objects and edit their attributes. Most of those objects are UI elements like buttons and text fields, but some will be instances of classes that you create.

Language

This book uses Objective-C for all of the examples. Objective-C is a simple and elegant extension to C, and mastering it will take about two hours if you already know C and an object-oriented language like Java or C++.

You *can* write Cocoa applications with Java, but I don't recommend it. After all, the major benefit to Java is portability. If you use Cocoa, you lose that portability. The tools and the frameworks were written in Objective-C for Objective-C, and you will find that your Cocoa applications have better performance and fewer bugs if you write them in Objective-C rather than Java. Almost no one is developing Cocoa applications with Java.

This is not to say that I dislike Java. In fact, I rather like Java. If you are writing an application in Java, I'd suggest that you use Swing for your GUI layer. Swing is not nearly as elegant as Cocoa, but it was developed in Java for Java and it is portable between platforms.

The Objective-C code will be compiled by the GNU C compiler, gcc. The compiler allows you to freely mix C, C++, and Objective C code in a single file.

The GNU debugger, gdb, will be used to set breakpoints and browse variables at runtime. Objective-C gives you a lot of freedom to do dumb things; you will be glad to have a decent debugger.

Objects, Classes, Methods, and Messages

All Cocoa programming is done using object-oriented concepts. This section very briefly reviews terms used in object-oriented programming. If you have not done any object-oriented programming before, I recommend that you read *The Objective-C Language*. The PDF file for the book is in the documentation that came with the developer tools; it is called `/Developer/Documentation/Cocoa/Conceptual/ObjectiveC/ObjC.pdf`.

What is an object? An *object* is like a C struct: It takes up memory and has variables inside it. The variables in an object are called *instance variables*. So when dealing with objects, the first questions we typically ask are "How do you allocate space for one?", "What instance variables does the object have?", and "How do you destroy the object when you are done with it?"

Some of the instance variables of an object will be pointers to other objects. These pointers enable one object to "know about" another.

Classes are structures that can create objects. Classes specify the variables that the object has, and they are responsible for allocating memory for the object. We say that the object is an *instance* of the class that created it (Figure 1.2).

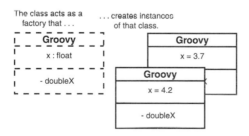

Figure 1.2 Classes Create Instances

An object is better than a struct, because an object can have functions associated with it. We call the functions *methods*. To call a method, you send the object a *message* (Figure 1.3).

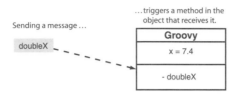

Figure 1.3   Messages Trigger Methods

Frameworks

A *framework* is a collection of classes that are intended to be used together. That is, the classes are compiled together into a reusable library of code. Any related resources are put into a directory with the library. The directory is renamed with the extension `.framework`. You can find the built-in frameworks for your machine in `/System/Library/Frameworks`. All Cocoa applications use two of these frameworks: Foundation and AppKit.

> *Foundation*: Every object-oriented programming language needs the standard value, collection, and utility classes. Things like strings, dates, lists, threads, and timers are in the Foundation framework.
>
> *AppKit*: All things related to the user interface are in the AppKit framework. These include windows, buttons, text fields, events, and drawing classes. You will also see this framework called the *ApplicationKit*.

There are numerous other frameworks that handle duties like encryption, QuickTime, and CD burning, but we will focus on Foundation and AppKit because they are used by all Cocoa applications. Once you have mastered these two, the other frameworks will be easier to understand.

You can also create your own frameworks from the classes that you create. Typically, if a set of classes is used in several applications, you will want to turn them into a framework.

How to Read This Book

When I sat down to write this book, I imagined that I was guiding a friend through activities that would help him understand Cocoa programming. This book acts as the guide through these activities. Often, I will ask you to do something and explain the details or theory afterward. If you are confused, read a little more. Usually the help you seek will be only a paragraph or two away.

If you are still stumped, you can get help on the Web site for this book. (http://www.bignerdranch.com/products/). Errata, hints, and examples are listed there as well. Also, all the solutions for the exercises can be downloaded from there.

Each chapter will guide you through the process of adding features to an application. This is not, however, a cookbook. This book teaches ideas, and the exercises show these ideas in action. Don't be afraid to experiment.

There are about 140 classes in AppKit and about 100 classes in Foundation. All are documented in the online reference (/Developer/Documentation/Cocoa/Reference/). Cocoa programmers spend a lot of time browsing through these pages. But until you understand a lot about Cocoa, it is hard to find the right starting place in your search for answers. As this book introduces you to a new class, look it up in the reference. You may not understand everything you find there, but browsing through the reference will give you some appreciation for the richness of the frameworks. When you reach the end of this book, the reference will become your guide.

Most of the time, Cocoa fulfills the promise: Common things are easy and uncommon things are possible. If you find yourself writing many lines of code to do something rather ordinary, you are probably on the wrong track.

Typographical Conventions

To make the book easier to comprehend, I've used several typographical conventions.

In Objective-C, class names are always capitalized. In this book, I've also made them appear in a monospaced bold font. In Objective-C, method names start with a lowercase letter. Method names will also appear in a monospaced bold font. For example, you might see "The class **NSObject** has the method **dealloc**."

Other literals that you would see in code (including instance variable names) will appear in a regular monospaced font. Also, filenames will appear in this same font. Thus, you might see "In `MyClass.m`, set the variable `favoriteColor` to `nil`."

Common Mistakes

Having watched many, many people work through this material, I've seen the same mistakes made hundreds of times. I see two mistakes particularly often: capitalization mistakes and forgotten connections.

Capitalization mistakes happen because C and Objective-C are case-sensitive languages—the compiler does not consider `Foo` and `foo` to be the same thing. If you are having trouble making something compile, check to make sure that you have typed all the letters in the correct case.

When creating an application, you will use Interface Builder to connect objects together. Forgotten connections usually allow your application to build and run, but result in aberrant behavior. If your application is misbehaving, go back to Interface Builder and check your connections.

It is easy to miss some warnings the first time a file is compiled. Because Xcode does incremental compiles, you may not see those warnings again unless you clean and rebuild the project. If you are stuck, cleaning and rebuilding is certainly worth a try.

How to Learn

I have all sorts of people come to my class: the bright and the not-so-bright, the motivated and the lazy, the experienced and the novice. Inevitably, the people who get the most from the class share one characteristic: They remain focused on the topic at hand.

The first trick to maintaining focus is to get enough sleep. I suggest 10 hours of sleep each night while you are studying new ideas. Before dismissing this idea, try it. You will wake up refreshed and ready to learn. *Caffeine is not a substitute for sleep.*

The second trick is to stop thinking about yourself. While learning something new, many students will think, "Damn, this is hard for me. I wonder if I am stupid." Because stupidity is such an unthinkably terrible thing in our culture, the students will then spend hours constructing arguments that explain why they are intelligent yet are having difficulties. The moment you start down this path, you have lost your focus.

I used to have a boss named Rock. Rock had earned a degree in astrophysics from Cal Tech and had never had a job where he used his knowledge of the heavens. Once I asked him if he regretted getting the degree. "Actually, my degree in astrophysics has proved to be very valuable," he said. "Some things in this world are just hard. When I am struggling with something, I sometimes think 'Damn, this is hard for me. I wonder if I am stupid,' and then I remember that I have a degree in astrophysics from Cal Tech, I must not be stupid."

Before going any further, assure yourself that you are not stupid and that some things are just hard. Armed with this silly affirmation and a well-rested mind, you are ready to conquer Cocoa.

Chapter 2
LET'S GET STARTED

Many books would start off by giving you a lot of philosophy. This would be a waste of precious paper at this point. Instead, I am going to guide you through writing your first Cocoa application. Upon finishing, you will be excited and confused...and ready for the philosophy.

Our first project will be a random number generator application. It will have two buttons labeled Seed random number generator with time and Generate random number. There will be a text field that will display the generated number. This is a simple example that involves taking user input and generating output. At times, the description of what you are doing and why will seem, well, terse. Don't worry—we will explore all of this in more detail throughout this book. For now, just play along.

Figure 2.1 shows what the completed application will look like.

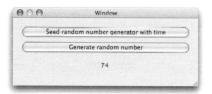

Figure 2.1   Completed Application

In Xcode

Assuming you have installed the developer tools, you will find Xcode in /Developer/Applications/. Drag the application to the dock at the bottom of your screen; you will be using it a lot. Launch Xcode.

As mentioned earlier, Xcode will keep track of all the resources that go into your application. All these resources will be kept in a directory called the *project directory*. The first step in developing a new application is to create a new project directory with the default skeleton of an application.

Create a New Project

Under the File menu, choose New Project.... When the panel appears (see Figure 2.2), choose the type of project you would like to create: Cocoa Application. Notice that there are many other types of projects available as well.

Figure 2.2   Choose Project Type

In this book, we will discuss the following major types of projects:

Application: A program that creates windows.

Tool: A program that does not have a graphical user interface. Typically, a tool is a command-line utility or a daemon that runs in the background.

Bundle or Framework: A directory of resources that can be used in an application or tool. A bundle is dynamically loaded at runtime. An application typically links against a framework at compile time.

For the project name, type in RandomApp, as in Figure 2.3. Application names are typically capitalized. You can also pick the directory into which your project directory will be created. By default, your project directory will be created inside your home directory. Click the Finish button.

Figure 2.3   Name Project

A project directory will be created for you, with the skeleton of an application inside it. You will extend this skeleton into the source for a complete application and then compile the source into a working application.

Looking at the new project in Xcode, you will see an outline view on the left side of the window. Each item in the outline view represents one type of information that might be useful to a programmer. Some items are files, others are messages like compiler errors or find results. For now, you will be dealing with editing files, so open the item that says RandomApp to see folders that contain the files that will be compiled into an application.

The skeleton of a project that was created for you will actually compile and run. It has a menu and a window. Click on the toolbar item with the hammer and green circle to build and run the project as shown in Figure 2.4.

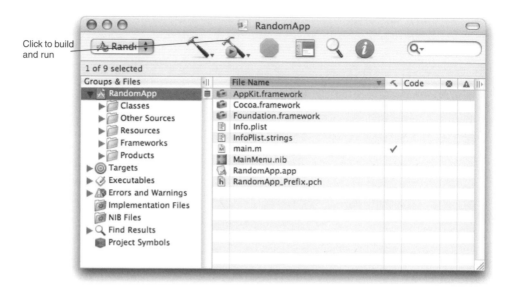

Click to build
and run

Figure 2.4   Skeleton of a Project

While the application is launching, you will see a bouncing icon in the dock. The name of your application will then appear in the menu. This means that your application is now active. The window for your application may be hidden by another window. If you do not see your window, choose Hide Others from the RandomApp menu. You should see an empty window as shown in Figure 2.5.

Figure 2.5   Running the Project

It doesn't do much, but notice that it is already a fully functional application. Printing even works. Quit RandomApp and return to Xcode.

The main Function

Select main.m by single-clicking on it. If you double-click on the filename, it will open in a new window. Because I deal with many files in a day, this tends to overwhelm me rather quickly, so I use the single-window style. Click on the Editor toolbar item to split the window and create an editor view. The code will appear in the editor view (Figure 2.6).

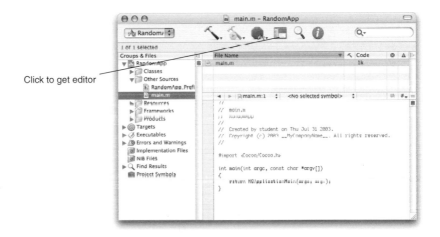

Figure 2.6   main() Function

You will almost never modify main.m in an application project. The default **main()** simply calls **NSApplicationMain()**, which in turn loads the user interface objects from a *nib file*. Nib files are created with Interface Builder. (Trivia: "NIB" stands for "NeXT Interface Builder"; "NS" stands for "NeXTSTEP.") Once your application has loaded the nib file, it simply waits for the user to do something. When the user clicks or types, your code will be called automatically. If you have never written an application with a graphical user interface before, this change will be startling to you: The user is in control, and your code simply reacts to what the user does.

In Interface Builder

In the outline view under Resources, you will find a nib file called
MainMenu.nib. Double-click on it to open the nib in Interface Builder. Lots of
windows will appear, so this is a good time to hide your other applications. In the
Interface Builder menu, you will find Hide Others.

Interface Builder allows you to create and edit user interface objects (like
windows and buttons) and save those objects into a file. You can also create
instances of your custom classes and make connections between those instances
and the standard user interface objects. When users interact with the user
interface objects, the connections you have made between them and your custom
classes will cause your code to be executed.

The Standard Palettes

The palette window (Figure 2.7) is where you will find user interface widgets
that can be dragged into your interface. For example, if you want a button, you
can drag it from the palette window. Notice the row of buttons at the top of the
palette window. As you click the buttons, the various palettes will appear. In
Chapter 27, you will learn to create your own palettes.

Figure 2.7   Palette Window

The Blank Window

The blank window (Figure 2.8) represents an instance of the **NSWindow** class that is inside your nib file.

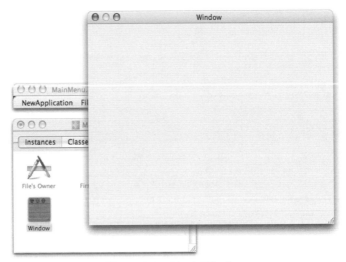

Figure 2.8   Blank Window

As you drop objects from the palettes onto the window, they will be added to the nib file. After you have created instances of these objects and edited their attributes, saving the nib file is like "freeze-drying" the objects into the file. When the application is run, the nib file will be read and the objects will be revived. The cool kids say, "The objects are *archived* into the nib file by Interface Builder and *unarchived* when the application is run."

Lay Out the Interface

I am going to walk you through it, but keep in mind that your goal is to create a user interface that looks like Figure 2.9.

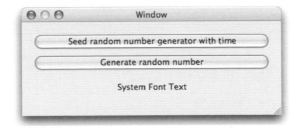

Figure 2.9   Completed Interface

Drag a button from the palette window (as shown in Figure 2.10) and drop it onto the blank window.

Figure 2.10   Dragging a Button

Double-click on the button to change its title to Seed random number generator with time.

Drag another button out, and relabel it Generate random number. Drag out the text field that says System Font Text (as shown in Figure 2.11) and drop it on the window.

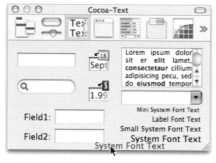

Figure 2.11   Dragging a Text Field

Make the window smaller.

The text field should be as wide as possible. Drag the left and right sides of the text field toward the sides of the window. Notice that blue lines appear when you are close to the edge of the window. These guides are intended to help you conform to Apple's GUI guidelines (Figure 2.12).

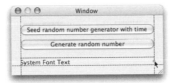

Figure 2.12   Resize Text Field

To make the text field center its contents, you will need to use the Info Panel (also known as the "Inspector"). Select the text field, and choose Show Info from the Tools menu. Click on the center justify button (Figure 2.13).

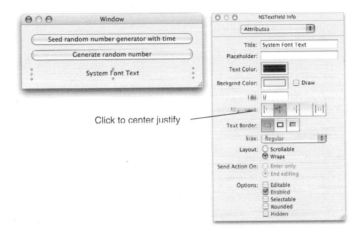

Click to center justify

Figure 2.13   Center Justify Text Field

The Doc Window

In your nib file, some objects (like buttons) are visible, and others (like your custom controller objects) are invisible. The icons that represent the invisible objects appear in the *doc window* (Figure 2.14).

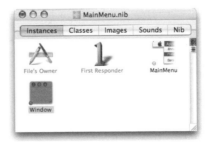

Figure 2.14   The Doc Window

In the doc window (the one entitled MainMenu.nib), you will see icons representing the main menu and the window. First Responder is a fictional object, but it is a very useful fiction. It will be fully explained in Chapter 18. File's Owner in this nib is the **NSApplication** object for your application. The **NSApplication** object takes events from the event queue and forwards them to the appropriate window. We will discuss File's Owner in depth in Chapter 9.

Create a Class

The doc window also has a simple class browser that you can use to create a skeleton of your custom class. Click on the Classes tab and select **NSObject** (Figure 2.15). In the Classes menu, choose Subclass NSObject. Rename the new class **Foo**. Interface Builder now knows that you intend to create a subclass of **NSObject** called **Foo**. **NSObject** is the root class for the entire Objective-C class hierarchy. That is, all objects in the framework are descendants of **NSObject**.

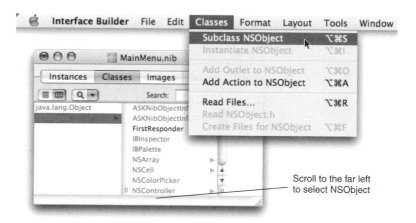

Figure 2.15   Foo Is a Subclass of NSObject

Class names, by convention, are capitalized.

Next, you will add instance variables and methods to your class. Instance variables that are pointers to other objects are called *outlets*. Methods that can be triggered by user interface objects are called *actions*. If you select the **Foo** class and bring up the inspector (use the Show Info menu item to activate the inspector), you will see that your class doesn't have any outlets or actions yet (Figure 2.16).

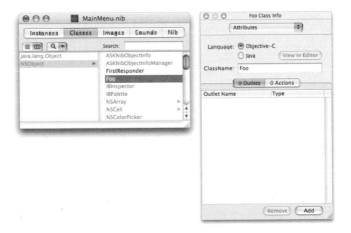

Figure 2.16   View Outlets and Actions

To add an outlet, select the Outlets tab and click **Add**. Rename the new outlet textField. You can set the type of the pointer in a pop-up. Here textField will be a pointer to an **NSTextField** object. Set its type using the pop-up as shown in Figure 2.17.

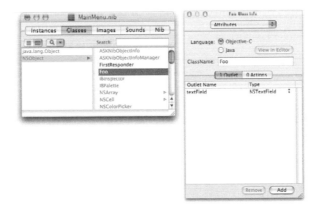

Figure 2.17   Create an Outlet

To add an action, select the Actions tab and click **Add**. Rename the new action seed. (When you press Enter, it will add a colon to the end of the action name. Thus **seed:** is the actual name of the method that will be created.) Add a second action, and name it generate: (Figure 2.18).

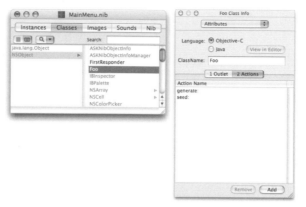

Figure 2.18   Create Two Actions

By convention, the names of methods and instance variables start with lowercase letters. If the name would be multiple words in English, each new word is capitalized—for example, favoriteColor.

Now you will create the files for the class **Foo**. In Objective-C, every class is defined by two files: a header file and an implementation file. The header file, also known as the interface file, declares the instance variables and methods your class will have. The implementation file actually defines what those methods do.

Under the Classes menu, choose Create files for Foo... (Figure 2.19).

Figure 2.19   Create Files

A save panel will appear. The default location (your project directory) is perfect. Save Foo.h (the header file) and Foo.m (the implementation file) there. Note that the files are being added to your RandomApp project (Figure 2.20).

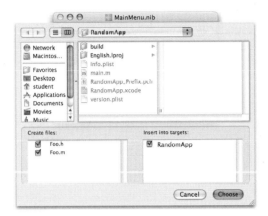

Figure 2.20   Choose a Location for the Files

Create an Instance

Next, you will create an instance of the class **Foo** in your nib file. Select **Foo** in the class browser and choose Instantiate Foo from the Classes menu (Figure 2.21).

Interface Builder will take you back to the Instances tab, where you will see a symbol representing your instance of **Foo** (Figure 2.22).

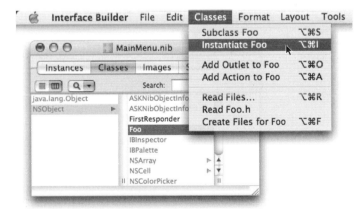

Figure 2.21   Create an Instance of Foo

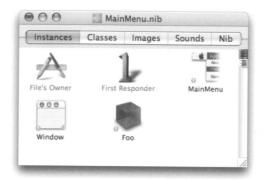

Figure 2.22   An Instance of Foo

Make Connections

A lot of object-oriented programming has to do with which objects need to know about which other objects. Now you are going to introduce some objects to each other. Cocoa programmers would say, "We are now going to set the outlets of our objects." To introduce one object to another, you will control-drag from *the object that needs to know* to the *object it needs to know about*. The object diagram in Figure 2.23 shows which objects need to be connected in your example.

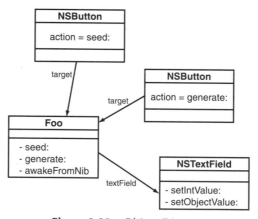

Figure 2.23   Object Diagram

You will set **Foo**'s textField instance variable to point to the **NSTextField** object on the window that currently says System Font Text. Control-drag from the symbol that represents your instance of **Foo** to the text field. The inspector panel will then appear. Choose textField in the view on the left, and click Connect. You should see a dot appear next to textField (Figure 2.24).

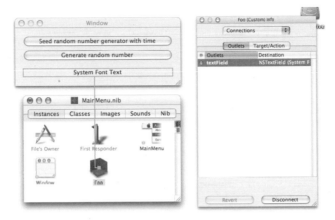

Figure 2.24 Set the textField Outlet

This step is all about pointers: You have just set the pointer textField in your **Foo** object to point to the text field.

Now you will set the Seed button's target outlet to point to your instance of **Foo**. Furthermore, you want the button to trigger **Foo**'s seed: method. Control-drag from the button to your instance of **Foo**. Choose the Target/Action tab in the inspector and select **seed:**. Click the Connect button to complete the connection (or double-click the word **seed:**). You should see a dot appear next to **seed:** (Figure 2.25).

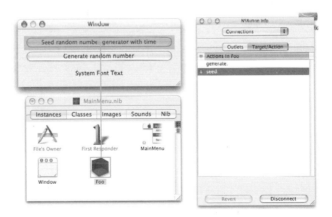

Figure 2.25 Set the Target and Action of the Seed Button

Similarly, you will set the Generate button's `target` instance variable to point to your instance of **Foo** and set its action to the **generate:** method. Control-drag from the button to **Foo**. Choose **generate:** in the Target/Action view. Double-click on the action name (**generate:**) to complete the connection. Note the appearance of the dot (Figure 2.26).

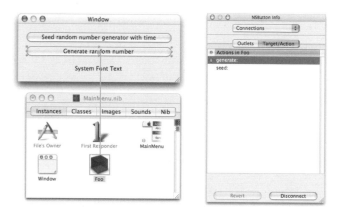

Figure 2.26   Set the Target and Action of the Generate Button

You are done with Interface Builder, so save the file and hide the application. Click on the Xcode icon in the dock to bring Xcode to the front.

Back in Xcode

In Xcode, you will see that `Foo.h` and `Foo.m` have been added to the project. Most programmers would put these files under the Classes group (Figure 2.27). Drag the files into the Classes group if they aren't there already.

Figure 2.27   The New Class In Xcode

If this is the first time that you are seeing Objective-C code, you may be alarmed to discover that it looks quite different from C++ or Java code. The syntax may be different, but the underlying concepts are the same. For example, in Java a class would be declared like this:

```
import com.megacorp.Bar;
import com.megacorp.Baz;

public class Rex extends Bar implements Baz {
...methods and instance variables...
}
```

This says, "The class **Rex** inherits from the class **Bar** and implements the methods declared in the **Baz** interface."

The analogous class in Objective-C would be declared like this:

```
#import <megacorp/Bar.h>
#import <megacorp/Baz.h>

@interface Rex : Bar <Baz> {
...instance variables...
}
...methods...
@end
```

If you know Java, Objective-C really isn't so strange. Note that like Java, Objective-C allows only single inheritance; that is, a class has only one superclass.

Types and Constants in Objective-C

Objective-C programmers use a few types that are not found in the rest of the C world.

- id is a pointer to any type of object.
- BOOL is the same as char, but is used as a Boolean value.
  YES is 1.
  NO is 0.
- IBOutlet is a macro that evaluates to nothing. Ignore it. (IBOutlet is a hint to Interface Builder when it reads the declaration of a class from a .h file.)
- IBAction is the same as void. It also acts as a hint to Interface Builder.
- nil is the same as NULL. We use nil instead of NULL for pointers to objects.

Look at the Header File

Click on Foo.h. Study it for a moment. You should see that it declares **Foo** to be a subclass of **NSObject**. Instance variables are declared inside the curly braces.

```
#import <Cocoa/Cocoa.h>

@interface Foo : NSObject
{
    IBOutlet NSTextField *textField;
}
- (IBAction)generate:(id)sender;
- (IBAction)seed:(id)sender;
@end
```

#import is similar to the C preprocessor's #include. However, #import ensures that the file is included only once.

Notice that the declaration of the class starts with @interface. The @ symbol is not used in the C programming language. To minimize conflicts between C code and Objective-C code, Objective-C keywords are prefixed by @. Here are a few other Objective-C keywords: @end, @implementation, @class, @selector, and @encode.

In general, you will find entering code easier if you turn on syntax-aware indention. In Xcode's Preferences, select the Indentation pane. Check the box labeled Syntax-aware indenting, as shown in Figure 2.28.

Figure 2.28   The New Class in Xcode

Edit the Implementation File

Now look at Foo.m. It contains the implementations of the methods. In C++ or Java, you might implement a method something like this:

```
public void increment(Object sender) {
    count++;
    textField.setIntValue(count);
}
```

In English, you would say, "**increment** is a public instance method that takes one argument that is an object. The method doesn't return anything. The method increments the count instance variable and then sends the message **setIntValue()** to the textField object with count as an argument."

In Objective-C, the analogous method would look like this:

```
- (void)increment:(id)sender
{
    count++;
    [textField setIntValue:count];
}
```

Objective-C is a very simple language. It has no visibility specifiers: All methods are public, and all instance variables are protected. (Actually, there are visibility specifiers for instance variables, but they are rarely used. The default is protected, and that works nicely.)

In Chapter 3, we will explore Objective-C in all its beauty. For now, just copy the methods:

```
#import "Foo.h"

@implementation Foo

- (IBAction)generate:(id)sender
{
    // Generate a number between 1 and 100 inclusive
    int generated;
    generated = (random() % 100) + 1;

    // Ask the text field to change what it is displaying
    [textField setIntValue:generated];
}

- (IBAction)seed:(id)sender
{
    // Seed the random number generator with the time
    srandom(time(NULL));
    [textField setStringValue:@"Generator seeded"];
}

@end
```

(Remember that IBAction is the same as void. Neither method returns anything.)

Because Objective-C is C with a few extensions, you can call functions (such as **random()** and **srandom()**) from the standard C and Unix libraries.

Build and Run

Your application is now finished. To build and run the application, click on the hammer/green circle toolbar item (Figure 2.29). If your app is already running, the toolbar item will be disabled; quit your app before trying to run it again.

If your code has an error, the compiler's message indicating a problem will appear at the view in the upper-right corner. If you click on the message, the erroneous line of code will be selected in the view on the lower right. In Figure 2.29, the programmer has forgotten a semicolon.

Click to build and run

Figure 2.29 Compiling

Launch your application. Click the buttons and see the generated random numbers. Congratulations—you have a working Cocoa application.

awakeFromNib

Notice that your application is flawed: When the application first starts, instead of anything interesting, the words System Font Text appear in the text field. Let's fix that problem. You will make the text field display the time and date that the application started.

The nib file is a collection of objects that have been archived. When the program is launched, the objects are brought back to life before the application handles any events from the user. Notice that this mechanism is a bit unusual—most GUI builders generate source code that lays out the user interface. Instead, Interface Builder allows the developer to edit the state of the objects in the interface and save that state to a file.

After being brought to life but before any events are handled, all objects are automatically sent the message **awakeFromNib**. You will add an **awakeFromNib** method that will initialize the text field's value.

Add the **awakeFromNib** method to Foo.m. For now, just type it in. You will understand it later on. Briefly, you are creating an instance of **NSCalendarDate** that represents the current time. Then you are telling the text field to set its value to the new calendar date object:

```
- (void)awakeFromNib
{
    NSCalendarDate *now;
    now = [NSCalendarDate calendarDate];
    [textField setObjectValue:now];
}
```

The order in which the methods appear in the file is not important. Just make sure that you add them after @implementation and before @end.

You will never have to call **awakeFromNib**; it gets called automatically. Simply build and run your application again. You should now see the date and time when the app runs (Figure 2.30).

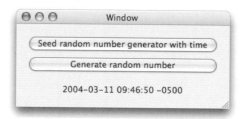

Figure 2.30 Completed Application

In Cocoa, a lot of things (like **awakeFromNib**) get called automatically. Some of the confusion that you may experience as you read this book will come from trying to figure out which methods you have to call and which will get called for you automatically. I'll try to make the distinction clear.

Documentation

Before this chapter wraps up, you should know where to find the documentation, as it may prove handy if you get stuck while doing an exercise later in the book. The online developer documentation is kept in the directory /Developer/ Documentation/. The easiest way to get to it is by choosing Show Documentation Window from Xcode's Help menu (Figure 2.31).

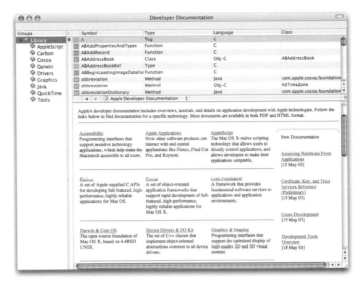

Figure 2.31 The Documentation

What Have You Done?

You have now gone through the steps involved in creating a simple Cocoa application:

- Create a new project.
- Lay out an interface.
- Create custom classes.
- Connect the interface to your custom class or classes.
- Add code to the custom classes.
- Compile.
- Test.

Let's briefly discuss the chronology of an application: When the process is started, it runs the **NSApplicationMain** function. The **NSApplicationMain** function creates an instance of **NSApplication**. A global variable called NSApp points to that instance of **NSApplication**. NSApp reads the main nib file and unarchives the objects inside. The objects are all sent the message **awakeFromNib**. Then NSApp checks for events. The timeline for these events appears in Figure 2.32.

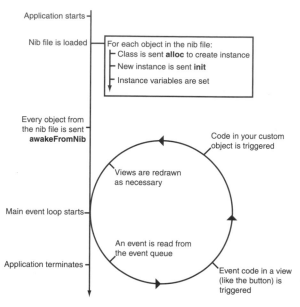

Figure 2.32   A Timeline

When the window server receives an event from the keyboard and mouse, it puts the event data into the event queue for the appropriate application, as shown in Figure 2.33. NSApp reads the event data from its queue and forwards it to a user interface object (like a button), and your code gets triggered. If your code changes the data in a view, the view is redisplayed. Then NSApp checks its event queue for another event. This process of checking for events and reacting to them constitutes the *main event loop*.

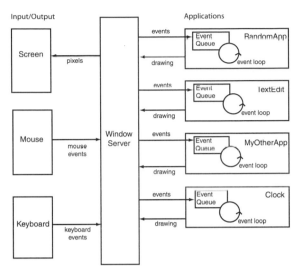

Figure 2.33 The Role of the Window Server

When the user chooses Quit from the menu, NSApp is sent the **terminate:** message. This ends the process, and all your objects are destroyed.

Puzzled? Excited? Move on to the next chapter so we can fill in some blanks.

Chapter 3
OBJECTIVE-C

Once upon a time a man named Brad Cox decided that it was time for the world to move toward a more modular programming style. C was a popular and powerful language. Smalltalk was an elegant untyped object-oriented language. Starting with C, Brad Cox added Smalltalk-like classes and message-sending mechanisms. He called the result *Objective-C*. Objective-C is a very simple extension of the C language. In fact, it was originally just a C preprocessor and a library.

Objective-C is not a proprietary language. Rather, it is an open standard that has been included in the Free Software Foundation's GNU C compiler (gcc) for many years. Cocoa was developed using Objective-C, and most Cocoa programming is done in Objective-C.

Teaching C and basic object-oriented concepts could consume an entire book. Instead of writing that book, this chapter assumes that you already know a little C and something about objects and introduces you to the basics of Objective-C. If you fit the profile, you will find learning Objective-C to be easy. If you do not, Apple's *The Objective-C Language* is a more gentle introduction.

Creating and Using Instances

Chapter 1 mentioned that classes are used to create objects, that the objects have methods, and that you can send messages to the objects to trigger these methods. In this section, you will learn how to create an object, send messages to it, and destroy it when you no longer need it.

As an example, we will use the class **NSMutableArray**. You can create a new instance of **NSMutableArray** by sending the message **alloc** to the **NSMutableArray** class like this:

```
[NSMutableArray alloc];
```

This method returns a pointer to the space that was allocated for the object. You could hold onto that pointer in a variable like this:

```
NSMutableArray *foo;
foo = [NSMutableArray alloc];
```

While working with Objective-C, it is important to remember that foo is just a pointer. In this case, it points to an object.

Before using the object that foo points to, you would need to make sure that it is fully initialized. The **init** method will handle this task, so you might write code like this:

```
NSMutableArray *foo;
foo = [NSMutableArray alloc];
[foo init];
```

Take a long look at the last line; it sends the message **init** to the object that foo points to. We would say, "foo is the receiver of the message **init**." Notice that a message send consists of a receiver (the object foo points to) and a message (**init**) wrapped in square brackets. Note that you can also send messages to *classes*, as demonstrated by sending the message **alloc** to the class **NSMutableArray**.

The method **init** actually returns the newly initialized object. As a consequence, you will always nest the message sends like this:

```
NSMutableArray *foo;
foo = [[NSMutableArray alloc] init];
```

What about destroying the object when we no longer need it?

```
[foo release];
```

We will discuss **release** and what it really means later in this chapter.

Some methods take arguments. If a method takes an argument, the method name (called a *selector*) will end with a colon. For example, to add objects to the end of the array, you use the **addObject:** method (assume bar is a pointer to another object):

```
[foo addObject:bar];
```

If you have multiple arguments, the selector will have multiple parts. For example, to add an object at a particular index, you could use the following:

```
[foo insertObject:bar atIndex:5];
```

Note that **insertObject:atIndex:** is one selector, not two. It will trigger one method with two arguments. This outcomes seems strange to most C and Java programmers, but should be familiar to Smalltalk programmers. The syntax also makes your code easier to read. For example, it is not uncommon to see a C++ method call like this:

```
if (x.intersectsArc(35.0, 19.0, 23.0, 90.0, 120.0))
```

It is much easier to guess the meaning of the following code:

```
if ([x intersectsArcWithRadius:35.0
                 centeredAtX:19.0
                           Y:23.0
                   fromAngle:90.0
                     toAngle:120.0])
```

If it seems odd right now, just use it for a while. Most programmers grow to really appreciate the Objective-C messaging syntax.

You are now at a point where you can read simple Objective-C code, so it is time to write a program that will create an instance of **NSMutableArray** and fill it with 10 instances of **NSNumber**.

Using Existing Classes

If it isn't running, start Xcode. Close any projects that you were working on. Under the Project menu, choose New Project…. When the panel pops up, choose to create a Foundation Tool (Figure 3.1).

Name the project lottery (Figure 3.2). Unlike the names of applications, most tool names are lowercase.

Figure 3.1   Choose Project Type

Figure 3.2   Name Project

A *Foundation tool* has no graphical user interface and typically runs on the command line or in the background as a daemon. Unlike in an application project, you will always alter the main.m file of a Foundation tool.

When the new project appears, select main.m under Source. It should look like Figure 3.3.

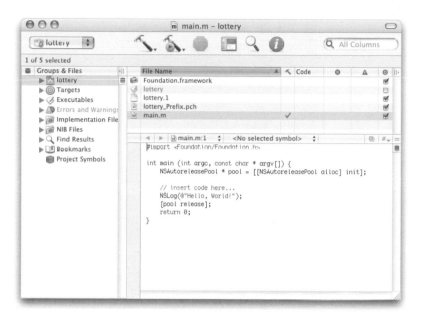

Figure 3.3 main.m

Edit main.m to look like this:

```
#import <Foundation/Foundation.h>

int main (int argc, const char * argv[])
{
    NSMutableArray *array;
    int i;
    NSNumber *newNumber;
    NSNumber *numberToPrint;

    NSAutoreleasePool *pool = [[NSAutoreleasePool alloc] init];

    array = [[NSMutableArray alloc] init];
    for ( i = 0; i < 10; i++) {
        newNumber = [[NSNumber alloc] initWithInt:(i * 3)];
        [array addObject:newNumber];
        // If you already know some Cocoa, you might notice that
        // I have a memory leak here.  We will fix it soon.
    }

    for ( i = 0; i < 10; i++) {
        numberToPrint = [array objectAtIndex:i];
        NSLog(@"The number at index %d is %@",  i, numberToPrint);
    }

    [array release];
    [pool release];
    return 0;
}
```

Here is the play-by-play for the code:

```
#import <Foundation/Foundation.h>
```

You are including the headers for all the classes in the Foundation framework. The headers are precompiled, so this approach is not as computationally intensive as it sounds.

```
int main (int argc, const char *argv[])
```

The **main** function is declared just as it would be in any Unix C program.

```
NSMutableArray *array;
int i;
NSNumber *newNumber;
NSNumber *numberToPrint;
```

Four variables are declared here: array is a pointer to an instance of **NSMutableArray**, i is an int, and the pointers newNumber and numberToPrint each point to an instance of **NSNumber**. Note that no objects actually exist yet. You have simply declared pointers that will refer to the objects once they are created.

```
NSAutoreleasePool *pool = [[NSAutoreleasePool alloc] init];
```

This code declares a variable and points it to a new instance of **NSAutoreleasePool**. We will discuss the importance of autorelease pools later in the chapter.

```
for (i = 0; i < 10; i++) {
        newNumber = [[NSNumber alloc] initWithInt:(i*3)];
        [array addObject:newNumber];
}
```

Inside the for loop you have created an instance of **NSNumber** and made the variable newNumber point to it. Then you have added that object to the array. This case offers a perfect example of the difference between the pointer and the object it points to. Here you have one variable of type NSNumber *, but you have 10 instances of **NSNumber** (Figure 3.4).

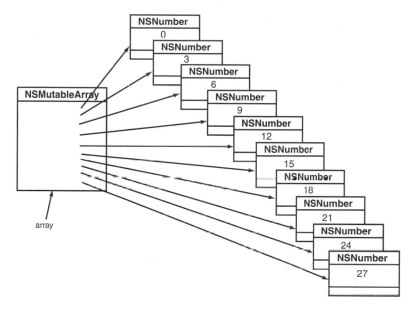

Figure 3.4 The Array of Number Objects

The array does not make copies of the **NSNumber** objects. Instead, it simply keeps a list of pointers to the **NSNumber** objects. Objective-C programmers make very few copies of objects, because it is seldom necessary.

```
for ( i = 0; i < 10; i++) {
    numberToPrint = [array objectAtIndex:i];
    NSLog(@"The number at index %d is %@", i, numberToPrint);
}
```

Here you are printing the contents of the array to the console. **NSLog** is a function much like **printf()**; it takes a format string and a comma-separated list of variables to be substituted into the format string. When displaying the string, **NSLog** prefixes the generated string with the name of the application and a time stamp.

In **printf**, for example, you would use %x to display an integer in hexadecimal form. With **NSLog**, we have all the tokens from **printf** and the token %@ to display an object. The object gets sent the message **description**, and the string it returns replaces %@ in the string. We will discuss the **description** method in detail soon.

All the tokens recognized by **NSLog()** are listed in Table 3.1.

Table 3.1   Possible Tokens in Objective-C Format Strings

Symbol	Displays
%@	id
%d, %D, %i	long
%u, %U	unsigned long
%hi	short
%hu	unsigned short
%qi	long long
%qu	unsigned long long
%x, %X	unsigned long printed as hexadecimal
%o, %O	unsigned long printed as octal
%f, %e, %E, %g, %G	double
%c	unsigned char as ASCII character
%C	unichar as Unicode character
%s	char * (a null-terminated C string of ASCII characters)
%S	unichar * (a null-terminated C string of Unicode characters)
%p	void * (an address printed in hexadecimal with a leading 0x)
%%	A % character

Note: If the @ symbol before the quotes in @"The number at index %d is %@" looks a little strange, remember that Objective-C is the C language with a couple of extensions. One of the extensions is that strings are instances of the class **NSString**. In C, strings are just pointers to a buffer of characters that ends in the null character. Both C strings and instances of **NSString** can be used in the same file. To differentiate between constant C strings and constant **NSString**s, you must put @ before the opening quote of a constant **NSString**.

```
// C string
char *foo;
// NSString
NSString *bar;
foo = "this is a C string";
bar = @"this is an NSString";
```

You will use mostly **NSString** in Cocoa programming. Wherever a string is needed, the classes in the frameworks expect an **NSString**. However, if you already have a bunch of C functions that expect C strings, you will find yourself using char * frequently.

You can convert between C strings and **NSString**s:

```
const char *foo = "Blah blah";
NSString *bar;
// Create an NSString from a C string
bar = [NSString stringWithUTF8String:foo];

// Create a C string from an NSString
foo = [bar UTF8String];
```

Because **NSString** can hold Unicode strings, you will need to deal with the multibyte characters correctly in your C strings, and this can be quite difficult and time-consuming. (Besides the multibyte problem, you will have to wrestle with the fact that some languages read from right to left.) Whenever possible, you should use **NSString** instead of C strings.

Continuing with the code in **main()**, you have the following:

```
    [array release];
    [pool release];
    return(0);
}
```

Now that you no longer need the array or the autorelease pool, you send them the **release** message so that they will be deallocated.

Build the program. The log (which will contain the output) should appear automatically.

Build and run the program (Figure 3.5).

Memory Management: Retain Count, Releasing, and Retaining

Let's discuss the **release** method. Every object has a retain count. The retain count is an integer. When an object is created by the **alloc** method, the retain count is set to 1. When the retain count becomes zero, the object is deallocated. You increment the retain count by sending the message **retain** to the object. You decrement the retain count by sending the message **release** to the object.

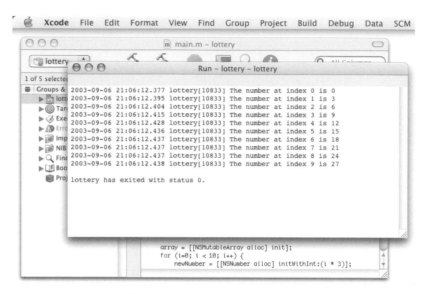

Figure 3.5   Completed Execution

Why is there a retain count at all? In C, after all, you would simply **malloc** memory and then **free** the memory when it is no longer needed. Imagine for a moment that you are an object that would be useful to several other objects. They are willing to share you, but how will you get deallocated when none of the other objects need you any more? When an object gets a reference to you, it will send you a **retain** message. When an object no longer needs you, it will send you a **release** message. Thus, your retain count represents how many other objects have references to you. When the retain count becomes zero, this indicates that no one cares about you any more. You are deallocated so that the memory you were occupying can be freed.

A commonly used analogy is that of the dog and the leash. Each person who wants to ensure that the dog will stay around retains the dog by attaching a leash to its collar. Many people can retain the dog, and as long as at least one person is retaining the dog, the dog will not go free. When zero people are retaining the dog, it will be freed. The retain count of an object, then, is the number of "leashes" on that object (Figure 3.6).

Whereas Java has a garbage collector, Objective-C offers its retain count mechanism. It gives the developer lots of control over how and when objects are freed, but it requires that you meticulously retain and release objects. You will spend some time every day walking through code and thinking about the retain count of the objects involved. If you release an object too much, it will be freed prematurely and your program will crash. If you retain an object too much, it will never get freed and you will waste memory.

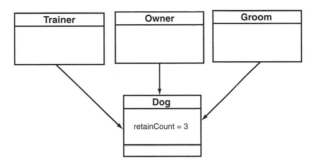

Figure 3.6 Objects Retain Each Other

When you ran your program a moment ago, it worked, didn't it? You would like to think that all the **NSNumber** objects neatly deallocated themselves when the array was released. If you believed that, you would be fooling yourself.

An array does not make a copy of an object when it is added. Instead, the array stores a pointer to the object and sends it the message **retain**. When the array is deallocated, the objects in the array are sent the message **release**. (Also, if an object is removed from an array, it is sent **release**.)

Back to the lottery project: We have a memory leak. Let's quickly go over the life of the **NSNumber** in your application:

- When the number object is created, it has a retain count of 1.
- When the number object is added to the array, its retain count is incremented to 2.
- When the array is deallocated, it releases the number. This decrements the retain count to 1.

The number object is not deallocated. In this example, the process ends an instant later, and the operating system reclaims all the memory. Thus the lack of deallocation is not a big deal. However, in a program that ran a long time, such a memory leak would be a bad thing. To practice being a tidy Objective-C programmer, fix the code.

After inserting the number into the array, release it. The revised loop should look like this:

```
for (i = 0; i < 10; i++) {
    newNumber = [[NSNumber alloc] initWithInt:(i*3)];
    [array addObject:newNumber];
    [newNumber release];
}
```

Sending Messages to nil

In most object-oriented languages, your program will crash if you send a message to `nil`. In applications written in those languages, you will see many checks for `nil` before sending a message. In Java, for example, you frequently see the following:

```
if (foo != null) {
    foo.doThatThingYouDo();
}
```

In Objective-C, it is okay to send a message to `nil`. The message is simply discarded, which eliminates the need for these sorts of checks. For example, this code will build and run without an error:

```
id foo;
foo = nil;
[foo count];
```

This approach is different from how most languages work, but you will get used to it.

Although you may send a message to `nil`, sending a message to a freed object will crash your program. For example, this code would not work:

```
id foo = [[NSMutableArray alloc] init];
[foo release];
[foo count];
```

To prevent this possibility, many developers set the pointer to `nil` after releasing an object:

```
[foo release];
foo = nil;
```

If you find yourself asking over and over "Why isn't this gosh-darned method getting called?", chances are that the pointer you are using, assuming it is not `nil`, is actually `nil`.

NSObject, NSArray, NSMutableArray, and NSString

You now have a fine program that uses a couple of the classes that came with Cocoa: **NSObject**, **NSMutableArray**, and **NSString**. (All classes that come with Cocoa have names with the "NS" prefix. Classes that you will create will *not* start with "NS".) These classes are all part of the Foundation framework. Figure 3.7 shows an inheritance diagram for these classes.

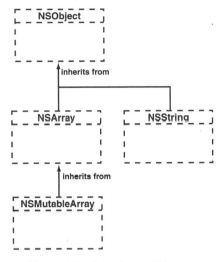

Figure 3.7   Inheritance Diagram

Let's go through a few of the commonly used methods on these classes. For a complete listing, you can access the online documentation in `/Developer/ Documentation/Cocoa/Reference/Foundation/ObjC_classic/`

NSObject

NSObject is the root of the entire Objective-C class hierarchy. Some commonly used methods on **NSObject** are described next.

```
- (id)init
```

Initializes the receiver after memory for it has been allocated. An **init** message is generally coupled with an **alloc** message in the same line of code:

```
TheClass *newObject = [[TheClass alloc] init];
```

```
+(id)new
```

Calls **alloc** to create a new instance and sends **init** to that new instance. For example, you can create a new instance of **NSMutableArray** like this:

```
myArray = [[NSMutableArray alloc] init];
```

or like this:

```
myArray = [NSMutableArray new];
```

Both are equivalent.

- (NSString *)**description**

Returns an **NSString** that describes the receiver. The debugger's print object command ("po") invokes this method. A good **description** method will often make debugging easier. Also, if you use %@ in a format string, the object that should be substituted in is sent the message **description**. The value returned by the **description** method is put into the log string. For example, the line in your main function

```
NSLog(@"The number at index %d is %@", i, numberToPrint);
```

is equivalent to

```
NSLog(@"The number at index %d is %@", i,
                       [numberToPrint description]);
```

- (id)**retain**

Increments the receiver's retain count.

- (void)**release**

Decrements the receiver's retain count and sends it a **dealloc** message if its retain count becomes zero.

- (void)**dealloc**

Deallocates the object's memory. It is similar to a destructor in C++. This method is called automatically when the retain count becomes zero; you should not call it directly.

- (BOOL)**isEqual:**(id)anObject

Returns YES if the receiver and anObject are equal and NO otherwise. You might use it like this:

```
if ([myObject isEqual:anotherObject]) {
    NSLog(@"They are equal.");
}
```

But what does "equal" really mean? In **NSObject**, this method is defined to return YES if and only if the receiver and anObject are the same object—that is, if both are pointers to the same memory location.

Clearly, this is not always the "equal" that you would hope for, so this method is overridden by many classes to implement a more appropriate idea of equality. For example, **NSString** overrides the method to compare the characters in the receiver and anObject. If the two strings have the same characters in the same order, they are considered equal.

Thus, if x and y are **NSStrings**, there is a big difference between these two expressions:

```
x == y
```

and

```
[x isEqual:y]
```

The first expression compares the two pointers. The second expression compares the characters in the strings. Note, however, that if x and y are instances of a class that has not overridden **NSObject**'s **isEqual:** method, the two expressions are equivalent.

NSArray

An **NSArray** is a list of pointers to other objects. It is indexed by integers: Thus, if there are *n* objects in the array, the objects are indexed by the integers 0 through *n* − 1. You cannot put a nil in an **NSArray**. (This means that there are no "holes" in an **NSArray**, which may confuse some programmers who are used to Java's Object[].) **NSArray** inherits from **NSObject**.

An **NSArray** is created with all the objects that will ever be in it. You can neither add nor remove objects from an instance of **NSArray**. We say that **NSArray** is *immutable*. (Its mutable subclass, **NSMutableArray**, will be discussed next.) Immutability is nice in some cases. Because it is immutable, a horde of objects can share one **NSArray** without worrying that one object in the horde might change it. **NSString** and **NSNumber** are also immutable. Instead of changing a string or number, you will simply create another one with the new value. (In the case of **NSString**, there is also the class **NSMutableString** that allows its instances to be altered.)

Here are some commonly used methods implemented by **NSArray**:

- (unsigned)**count**

Returns the number of objects currently in the array.

- (id)**objectAtIndex:**(unsigned)i

Returns the object located at index i. If i is beyond the end of the array, you will get an error at runtime.

- (id)**lastObject**

Returns the object in the array with the highest index value. If the array is empty, nil is returned.

- (BOOL)**containsObject:**(id)anObject

Returns YES if anObject is present in the array. This method determines whether an object is present in the array by sending an **isEqual:** message to each of the array's objects and passing anObject as the parameter.

- (unsigned)**indexOfObject:**(id)anObject

Searches the receiver for anObject and returns the lowest index whose corresponding array value is equal to anObject. Objects are considered equal if **isEqual:** returns YES. If none of the objects in the array are equal to anObject, **indexOfObject:** returns NSNotFound.

NSMutableArray

NSMutableArray inherits from **NSArray** but extends it with the ability to add and remove objects. Objects are retained when added and are released when removed. To create a mutable array from an immutable one, use **NSArray**'s **mutableCopy** method.

Here are some commonly used methods implemented by **NSMutableArray**:

- (void)**addObject:**(id)anObject

Inserts anObject at the end of the receiver. You are not allowed to add nil to the array.

- (void)**addObjectsFromArray:**(NSArray *)otherArray

Adds the objects contained in otherArray to the end of the receiver's array of objects.

- (void)**insertObject:**(id)anObject **atIndex:**(unsigned)index

Inserts anObject into the receiver at index. If index is already occupied, the objects at index and beyond are shifted up one slot to make room. index cannot be greater than the number of elements in the array. You will get an error if anObject is nil or if index is greater than the number of elements in the array.

- (void)**removeAllObjects**

Empties the receiver of all its elements.

- (void)**removeObject:**(id)anObject

Removes all occurrences of anObject in the array. Matches are determined on the basis of anObject's response to the **isEqual:** message.

- (void)**removeObjectAtIndex:**(unsigned)index

Removes the object at index and moves all elements beyond index down one slot to fill the gap. You will get an error if index is beyond the end of the array.

As mentioned earlier, you cannot add nil to an array. Sometimes you will want to put an object into an array to represent nothingness. The **NSNull** class exists for exactly this purpose. There is exactly one instance of **NSNull**, so if you want to put a placeholder for nothing into an array, use **NSNull** like this:

```
[myArray addObject:[NSNull null]];
```

NSString

An **NSString** is a buffer of Unicode characters. In Cocoa, all manipulations involving character strings are done with **NSString**. As a convenience, the Objective-C language also supports the @"..." construct to create a string object constant from a 7-bit ASCII encoding:

```
NSString *temp = @"this is a constant string";
```

NSString inherits from **NSObject**. Here are some commonly used methods implemented by **NSString**:

```
- (id)initWithFormat:(NSString *)format, ...
```

Works like **sprintf**. Here format is a string containing tokens like %d. The additional arguments are substituted for the tokens:

```
int x = 5;
char *y = "abc";
id z = @"123";
NSString *aString = [[NSString alloc] initWithFormat:
    @"Here's the int %d, the C String %s, and the NSString
    %@", x, y, z];
```

```
- (unsigned int)length
```

Returns the number of characters in the receiver.

```
- (NSString *)stringByAppendingString:(NSString *)aString
```

Returns a string object made by appending aString to the receiver. The following code snippet, for example, would produce the string "Error: unable to read file."

```
NSString *errorTag = @"Error: ";
NSString *errorString = @"unable to read file.";
NSString *errorMessage;
errorMessage = [errorTag stringByAppendingString:errorString];
```

"Inherits from" Versus "Uses" or "Knows About"

Beginning Cocoa programmers are often eager to create subclasses of **NSString** and **NSMutableArray**. Don't. Stylish Objective-C programmers almost never do. Instead, they use **NSString** and **NSMutableArray** as parts of larger objects, a technique known as composition. For example, a **BankAccount** class *could* be a subclass of **NSMutableArray**. After all, isn't a bank account simply a collection of transactions? The beginner would follow this path. In contrast, the old hand would create a class **BankAccount** that inherited from **NSObject** and has an instance variable called transactions that would point to an **NSMutableArray**.

It is important to keep track of the difference between "uses" and "is a subclass of." The beginner would say, "**BankAccount** inherits from **NSMutableArray**." The old hand would say, "**BankAccount** uses **NSMutableArray**." In the common idioms of Objective-C, "uses" is much more common than "is a subclass of."

You will find it is much easier to use a class than it is to subclass one. Subclassing involves more code and requires a deeper understanding of the superclass. By using composition instead of inheritance, Cocoa developers can take advantage of very powerful classes without really understanding how they work.

In a strongly typed language like C++, inheritance is crucial. In an untyped language like Objective-C, inheritance is just a hack that saves the developer some typing. There are only two inheritance diagrams in this entire book. All the other diagrams are object diagrams that indicate which objects know about which other objects. This is much more important information to a Cocoa programmer.

Creating Your Own Classes

Where I live, the state government has decided that the uneducated have entirely too much money: You can play the lottery every week here. Let's imagine that a lottery entry has two numbers between 1 and 100, inclusive. You will write a program that will make up lottery entries for the next 10 weeks. Each **LotteryEntry** object will have a date and two random integers (Figure 3.9). Besides learning how to create classes, you will build a tool that will certainly make you fabulously wealthy.

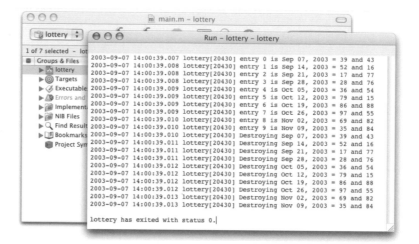

Figure 3.8   Completed Program

Creating the LotteryEntry Class

First you will create files for the **LotteryEntry** class. In the File menu, choose New file…. Select Objective-C class as the type (Figure 3.10).

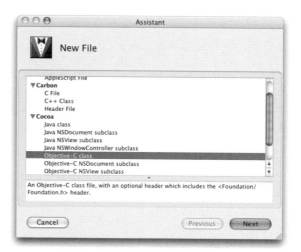

Figure 3.9   Choose Type of File

Name the file LotteryEntry.m (Figure 3.11). Note that you are also causing LotteryEntry.h to be created.

Figure 3.10 Name File

LotteryEntry.h

Edit the LotteryEntry.h file to look like this:

```
#import <Foundation/Foundation.h>

@interface LotteryEntry : NSObject {
    NSCalendarDate *entryDate;
    int firstNumber;
    int secondNumber;
}
- (void)prepareRandomNumbers;
- (void)setEntryDate:(NSCalendarDate *)date;
- (NSCalendarDate *)entryDate;
- (int)firstNumber;
- (int)secondNumber;
@end
```

You have created a header file for a new class called **LotteryEntry** that inherits from **NSObject**. It has three instance variables:

- entryDate is an **NSCalendarDate**.
- firstNumber and secondNumber are both ints.

You have declared five methods in the new class:

- **prepareRandomNumbers** will set firstNumber and secondNumber to random values between 1 and 100. It takes no arguments and returns nothing.
- **entryDate** and **setEntryDate:** will allow other objects to read and set the variable entryDate. The method **entryDate** will return the value stored in the entryDate variable. The method **setEntryDate:** will allow the value of the entryDate variable to be set. Methods that allow variables to be read and set are called *accessor methods*.
- You have also declared accessor methods for reading firstNumber and secondNumber. (You have not declared accessors for setting these variables; you are going to set them directly in **prepareRandomNumbers**.)

LotteryEntry.m

Edit LotteryEntry.m to look like this:

```
#import "LotteryEntry.h"

@implementation LotteryEntry

- (void)prepareRandomNumbers
{
    firstNumber = random() % 100 + 1;
    secondNumber = random() % 100 + 1;
}

- (void)setEntryDate:(NSCalendarDate *)date
{
    [date retain];
    [entryDate release];
    [date setCalendarFormat:@"%b %d, %Y"];
    entryDate = date;
}

- (NSCalendarDate *)entryDate
{
    return entryDate;
}

- (int)firstNumber
{
    return firstNumber;
}

- (int)secondNumber
{
    return secondNumber;
}
```

```
- (void)dealloc
{
    NSLog(@"Destroying %@", self);
    [entryDate release];
    [super dealloc];
}
@end
```

Here is the play-by-play for each method:

prepareRandomNumbers uses the standard **random** function to generate a pseudo-random number. You use the mod operator (%) and add 1 to get the number in the range 1–100.

setEntryDate: releases the old date and retains the new one. You then set the format on the date object so that it will display itself like this: "Feb 14, 1934." Next, you set the entryDate variable to point to the new value.

entryDate, **firstNumber**, and **secondNumber** return the values of variables.

dealloc

So far, the most interesting part of this class is the **dealloc** method. It will be called automatically when the retain count becomes zero. The first thing in the method is the line

```
NSLog(@"Destroying %@", self);
```

Printing this message indicates that the **dealloc** method got called.

Notice the use of self. Every method has an implicit local variable called self, which is a pointer to the object that is executing the method. You will often use self to have an object send a message to itself like this:

```
[self setNeedsDisplay:YES];
```

Continuing with the **dealloc** method, you come to the line

```
[entryDate release];
```

Here entryDate is a pointer to an **NSCalendarDate** object. This line informs the object that you are no longer interested in it and decrements the retain count. If the retain count goes to zero, the **NSCalendarDate** object will also be deallocated.

Notice that you do not have to release the ints. Because they are not objects, they actually reside inside the **LotteryEntry** object. When it is deallocated, the space will be freed. By contrast, entryDate is a pointer to an object that is outside the **LotteryEntry** object, so you must release it.

The last line,

```
[super dealloc];
```

shows how we can call a superclass's implementation of a method. Here we are calling the **dealloc** method of the superclass (**NSObject**, in this example). **NSObject**'s **dealloc** method actually frees the memory of the object, so make sure that it is always the last line of the **dealloc** method.

Changing main.m

Now let's look at main.m. Many of the lines have stayed the same, but several have changed. The most important change is that we are using **LotteryEntry** objects instead of **NSNumber** objects.

Here is the heavily commented code. (You don't have to type in the comments.)

```
#import <Foundation/Foundation.h>
#import "LotteryEntry.h"

int main (int argc, const char *argv[]) {
    NSMutableArray *array;
    int i;
    LotteryEntry *newEntry;
    LotteryEntry *entryToPrint;

    NSCalendarDate *now;
    NSAutoreleasePool *pool = [[NSAutoreleasePool alloc] init];

    // Create the date object
    now = [[NSCalendarDate alloc] init];

    // Initialize the random number generator
    srandom(time(NULL));
    array = [[NSMutableArray alloc] init];

    for (i = 0; i < 10; i++){
        // Create a new instance of LotteryEntry
        newEntry = [[LotteryEntry alloc] init];
        [newEntry prepareRandomNumbers];

        // Create a date/time object that is i weeks from now
```

```
[newEntry setEntryDate:[now dateByAddingYears:0
                                       months:0
                                         days:(i * 7)
                                        hours:0
                                      minutes:0
                                      seconds:0]];

    // Add the LotteryEntry object to the array
    [array addObject:newEntry];

    // Decrement the retain count of the lottery entry
    [newEntry release];
}

for (i = 0; i < 10; i++){

    // Get an instance of LotteryEntry
    entryToPrint = [array objectAtIndex:i];

    // Display its contents
    NSLog(@"entry %d is %@", i, entryToPrint);
}

[array release];

// Release the current time
[now release];
[pool release];
return 0;
}
```

This program will create an array of LotteryEntry objects, as shown in Figure 3.11.

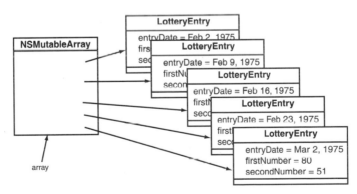

Figure 3.11 Object Diagram

Implementing a description Method

Build and run your application. You should see something like Figure 3.12.

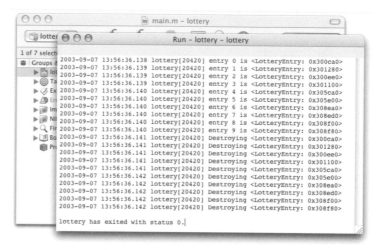

Figure 3.12   Completed Execution

Hmm. Not quite what we hoped for. After all, the program is supposed to reveal the dates and the numbers you should play on those dates, and you can't see either. Next you will make the **LotteryEntry** objects display themselves in a more meaningful manner.

Creating Autoreleased Objects

As we saw in the **NSObject** summary, every object has a **description** method that returns a string. The default method returns the name of the class and the hexadecimal address of the object. It would look like this: <LotteryEntry: 0x3da23>. You will now override the **description** method so that it returns a more meaningful string.

A first attempt might look something like this:

```
- (NSString *)description
{
    NSString *result;
    result = [[NSString alloc] initWithFormat:@"%@ = %d and %d",
        entryDate, firstNumber, secondNumber];
    return result;
}
```

This code would work perfectly well, but would result in an annoying memory leak. The **alloc** operation always yields an object with a retain count of 1; thus the string being returned has a retain count of 1. Any object asking for the string would retain it. The string would then have a retain count of 2. When the object was no longer interested in the string, it would release it. The retain count would become 1. As you see, the string would never be deallocated.

Our next attempt might look something like this:

```
- (NSString *)description
{
    NSString *result;
    result = [[NSString alloc] initWithFormat:@"%@ = %d and %d",
                           entryDate, firstNumber, secondNumber];
    [result release];
    return result;
}
```

This code would not work at all. When sent the message **release**, the string's retain count would go to zero, and the string would be deallocated. The object asking for the string would get a pointer to a freed object.

The problem, then, is that you need to return a string, but you do not want to retain it. This is a common problem throughout the frameworks, which leads us to **NSAutoreleasePool**.

Objects are added to the current autorelease pool when they are sent the message **autorelease**. When the autorelease pool is deallocated, it sends the message **release** to all objects in the pool.

In other words, when an object is autoreleased, it is marked to be sent **release** sometime in the future. In particular, in a Cocoa application, an autorelease pool is created before every event is handled and deallocated after the event has been handled. Thus, unless the objects in the autorelease pools are being retained, they will be destroyed as soon as the event has been handled.

A correct solution then is

```
- (NSString *)description
{
    NSString *result;
    result = [[NSString alloc] initWithFormat:@"%@ = %d and %d",
                           entryDate, firstNumber, secondNumber];
    [result autorelease];
    return result;
}
```

Rules Concerning Release

- Objects created by **alloc**, **new**, **copy**, or **mutableCopy** have a retain count of 1 and are not in the autorelease pool.
- If you get an object by *any* other method, assume that it has a retain count of 1 and is in the autorelease pool. If you do not wish it to be deallocated with the current autorelease pool, you must retain it.

Because you will frequently need objects that you are not retaining, many classes have class methods that return autoreleased objects. **NSString**, for example, has **stringWithFormat:**. The simplest correct solution then would be

```
- (NSString *)description
{
    return [NSString stringWithFormat:@"%@ = %d and %d",
        entryDate, firstNumber, secondNumber];
}
```

Note that this is equivalent to the code from the previous version. Add this code to your LotteryEntry.m file, and then build and run your application (Figure 3.13).

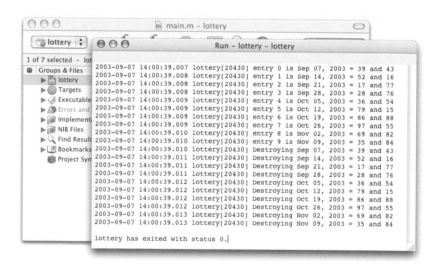

Figure 3.13   Completed Execution

Temporary Objects

Notice that the autoreleased object won't be released until the event loop ends. This behavior makes it perfect for providing an intermediate result. For example, if you had an array of **NSString** objects, you could create a string with all the elements in uppercase and concatenated together, like this:

```
- (NSString *)concatenatedAndAllCaps
{
    int i;
    NSString *sum = @"";
    NSString *upper;

    for (i=0; i < [myArray count]; i++) {
      upper = [[myArray objectAtIndex:i] uppercaseString];
      sum = [NSString stringWithFormat:@"%@%@", sum, upper];
    }
    return sum;
}
```

With this method, if you have 13 strings in the array, 26 autoreleased strings will be created (13 by **uppercaseString** and 13 by **stringWithFormat:**; the initial constant string is a special case and doesn't count). One of the resulting strings is returned and may be retained by the object that asked for it. The other 25 strings are deallocated automatically at the end of the event loop. (Note that you would probably get better performance in this example by appending the uppercased string to an **NSMutableString** instead of creating a brand-new string and adding it to the autorelease pool each time through the loop.)

Accessor Methods

An object has instance variables. Other objects cannot access these variables directly. To enable other objects to read and set an instance variable, an object will usually have a pair of accessor methods.

For example, if a class **Rex** has an instance variable named fido, the class will probably have at least two other methods: **fido** and **setFido:**. The **fido** method enables other objects to read the fido variable; the **setFido:** method enables other objects to set the fido variable.

If you have a nonpointer type, the accessor methods are quite simple. For example, if your class has an instance variable called foo of type int, you would create the following accessor methods:

```
- (int)foo
{
    return foo;
```

```
}

- (void)setFoo:(int)x
{
    foo = x;
}
```

These methods will allow other objects to get and set the value of foo.

Matters become more complicated if foo is a pointer to an object. In the "setter" method, you need to make sure that the new value is retained and the old value is released, as shown in Figure 3.14. If you assume that foo is a pointer to an **NSCalendarDate**, there are three common idioms in setter methods. All three work correctly, and you can probably find some experienced Cocoa programmers who will argue the superiority of any one of them. I'll list the tradeoffs after each one.

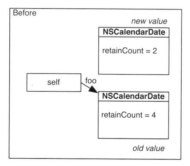

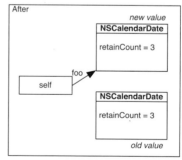

Figure 3.14   Before and After setFoo:

The first idiom is "Retain, Then Release":

```
- (void)setFoo:(NSCalendarDate *)x
{
    [x retain];
```

```
    [foo release];
    foo = x;
}
```

Here it is important to retain before releasing. Suppose that you reverse the order. If x and foo are both pointers to the same object, the release would cause the object to be deallocated before it was retained. Tradeoff: If they are the same value, this method performs an unnecessary retain and release.

The second idiom is "Check Before Change":

```
- (void)setFoo:(NSCalendarDate *)x
{
    if (foo != x) {
      [foo release];
      foo = [x retain];
    }
}
```

Here you are not setting the variable unless a different value is passed in. Tradeoff: An extra if statement is necessary.

The final idiom is "Autorelease Old Value":

```
- (void)setFoo:(NSCalendarDate *)x
{
    [foo autorelease];
    foo = [x retain];
}
```

Here, you autorelease the old value. Tradeoff: An error in retain counts will result in a crash one event loop after the error. This behavior makes the bug harder to track down. In the first two idioms, your crash will happen closer to your error. Also, **autorelease** carries some performance overhead.

You have read the tradeoffs and you can make your own decision on which to use. In this book, I will use "Retain, Then Release."

The "getter" method for an object is the same as that for a nonpointer type:

```
- (NSCalendarDate *)foo
{
    return foo;
}
```

Most Java programmers would name this method **getFoo**. Don't. Objective-C programmers call this method **foo**. In the common idioms of Objective-C, a method prefixed with "get" takes an address where data can be copied. For example, if you have an **NSColor** object and you want its red, green, blue, and alpha components, you would call **getRed:green:blue:alpha:** as follows:

```
float r, g, b, a;

[myFavoriteColor getRed:&r green:&g blue:&b alpha:&a];
```

(For readers who might be a bit rusty with their C, "&" returns the address where the variable holds its data.)

If you used your accessor methods to read the variables, your **description** method would look like this:

```
- (NSString *)description
{
    return [NSString stringWithFormat:@"%@ = %d and %d",
        [self entryDate], [self firstNumber], [self secondNumber]];
}
```

This would be considered the "most correct" implementation of the **description** method.

NSCalendarDate

Before moving on to any new ideas, let's examine **NSCalendarDate** in some depth. Instances of **NSCalendarDate** have a date and time, a time zone, and a format string. **NSCalendarDate** inherits from **NSDate**.

Instances of **NSCalendarDate** are basically immutable: You can't change the day or time of a calendar date once it is created (although you can change its format string and its time zone). Because it is basically immutable, many objects often share a single calendar date object. There is seldom any need to create a copy of an **NSCalendarDate** object.

Here are some of the commonly used methods implemented by **NSCalendarDate**:

> **+ (id)calendarDate**
>
> This method creates and returns a calendar date initialized to the current date and time in the default format for the locale. The time zone will be the time zone to which the machine is set. Remember that the returned object is autoreleased.

This is a *class method*. A class method is triggered by sending a message to the class instead of an instance. This one, for example, could be used as follows:

```
NSCalendarDate *now;
now = [NSCalendarDate calendarDate];
```

In the interface file, implementation file, and documentation, class methods are recognizable because they start with "+" instead of "-".

```
+ (id)dateWithYear:(int)year
           month:(unsigned)month
             day:(unsigned)day
            hour:(unsigned)hour
          minute:(unsigned)minute
          second:(unsigned)second
        timeZone:(NSTimeZone *)aTimeZone
```

This class method returns an autoreleased object. Specifically, it creates and returns a calendar date initialized with the specified values. The year value must include the century (for example, 2001 instead of 1). The other values are the standard ones: 1 through 12 for months, 1 through 31 for days, 0 through 23 for hours, and 0 through 59 for both minutes and seconds. The following code fragment shows a calendar date created with a date on 3 August 2000, 4 P.M., Pacific Standard Time (**timeZoneWithName:** returns the **NSTimeZone** object that represents the time zone with the specified name):

```
NSTimeZone *pacific = [NSTimeZone timeZoneWithName:@"PST"]

NSCalendarDate *hotTime = [NSCalendarDate dateWithYear:2000
                                                month:8
                                                  day:3
                                                 hour:16
                                               minute:0
                                               second:0
                                             timeZone:pacific];
```

```
- (NSCalendarDate *)dateByAddingYears:(int)year
                               months:(int)month
                                 days:(int)day
                                hours:(int)hour
                              minutes:(int)minute
                              seconds:(int)second
```

This method returns a calendar date with the year, month, day, hour, minute, and second offsets specified as arguments. A positive offset is the future, and a negative offset represents the past. You used this method in `main.m`. Here, we are creating a day six months after `hotTime`:

```
NSCalendarDate *coldTime = [hotTime dateByAddingYears:0
                                               months:6
                                                 days:0
                                                hours:0
                                              minutes:0
                                              seconds:0];
```

- (int)**dayOfCommonEra**

This method returns the number of days since the beginning of 1 A.D.

- (int)**dayOfMonth**

This method returns a number that indicates the day of the month (1 through 31) of the receiver.

- (int)**dayOfWeek**

This method returns a number that indicates the day of the week (0 through 6) of the receiver, where 0 indicates Sunday.

- (int)**dayOfYear**

This method returns a number that indicates the day of the year (1 through 366) of the receiver.

- (int)**hourOfDay**

This method returns the hour value (0 through 23) of the receiver.

- (int)**minuteOfHour**

This method returns the minutes value (0 through 59) of the receiver.

- (int)**monthOfYear**

This method returns a number that indicates the month of the year (1 through 12) of the receiver.

- (void)**setCalendarFormat:**(NSString *)format

Table 3.2   Possible Tokens in the Calendar Format String

Symbol	Meaning
%y	Year without century (00–99)
%Y	Year with century ("1990")
%b	Abbreviated month name ("Jan")
%B	Full month name ("January")
%m	Month as a decimal number (01–12)
%a	Abbreviated weekday name ("Fri")
%A	Full weekday name ("Friday")
%w	Weekday as a decimal number (0–6), where Sunday is 0
%d	Day of the month as a decimal number (01–31)
%e	Same as %d but does not print the leading 0
%j	Day of the year as a decimal number (001–366)
%H	Hour based on a 24-hour clock as a decimal number (00–23)
%I	Hour based on a 12-hour clock as a decimal number (01–12)
%p	A.M./P.M. designation for the locale
%M	Minute as a decimal number (00–59)
%S	Second as a decimal number (00–59)
%F	Milliseconds as a decimal number (000–999)
%x	Date using the date representation for the locale
%X	Time using the time representation for the locale
%c	Shorthand for %X %x, the locale format for date and time
%Z	Time zone name ("EST")
%z	Time zone offset in hours and minutes from GMT (HHMM)
%%	A "%" character

This method sets the default calendar format for the receiver. A calendar format is a string formatted with date-conversion specifiers, as given in Table 3.2.

- (NSDate *)**laterDate:**(NSDate *)anotherDate

This method is inherited from **NSDate**. It compares the receiver to anotherDate and returns the later of the two.

- (NSTimeInterval)**timeIntervalSinceDate:**(NSDate *)anotherDate

This method returns the interval in seconds between the receiver and anotherDate. If the receiver is earlier than anotherDate, the return value is negative. **NSTimeInterval** is the same as double.

Writing Initializers

Notice the following lines in your **main** function:

```
newEntry = [[LotteryEntry alloc] init];
[newEntry prepareRandomNumbers];
```

You are creating a new instance and then immediately calling **prepareRandom-Numbers** to initialize firstNumber and secondNumber. This is something that should really be handled by the initializer, so you are going to override the **init** method in your **LotteryEntry** class.

In the LotteryEntry.m file, change the method **prepareRandomNumbers** into an **init** method:

```
- (id)init
{
    [super init];
    firstNumber = random() % 100 + 1;
    secondNumber = random() % 100 + 1;
    return self;
}
```

The **init** method calls the superclass's initializer at the beginning, initializes its own variables, and then returns self.

Now delete the following line in main.m:

```
[newEntry prepareRandomNumbers];
```

In LotteryEntry.h, delete the following declaration:

```
- (void)prepareRandomNumbers;
```

Build and run your program to reassure yourself that it still works.

A few of the initializers in Cocoa will return nil if initialization was impossible. Also, some initializers in Cocoa return an object that is not the receiver. If a programmer is worried that the superclass's initializer may be one of these cases, he will create an initializer that is something like this:

```
- (id)init
{
    self = [super init];
    if (self != nil) {
        [self setFirstNumber:random() % 100 + 1];
        [self setSecondNumber:random() % 100 + 1];
    }
    return self;
}
```

This version will always work and is considered the most correct form; however, none of the classes that you will subclass in this book require these checks. For simplicity, this book will sometimes leave out the checks.

Initializers with Arguments

Look at the same place in main.m. It should now look like this:

```
newEntry = [[LotteryEntry alloc] init];
[newEntry setEntryDate:[now dateByAddingYears:0
                                       months:0
                                         days:(i * 7)
                                        hours:0
                                      minutes:0
                                      seconds:0]];
```

It might be nicer if you could supply the date as an argument to the initializer. Change those lines to look like this:

```
newEntry = [[LotteryEntry alloc] initWithEntryDate:
                                  [now dateByAddingYears:0
                                                  months:0
                                                    days:(i * 7)
                                                   hours:0
                                                 minutes:0
                                                 seconds:0]];
```

First, declare the method in LotteryEntry.h:

```
- (id)initWithEntryDate:(NSCalendarDate *)theDate;
```

Now, change the initializer:

```
- (id)initWithEntryDate:(NSCalendarDate *)theDate
{
    [super init];
    [self setEntryDate:theDate];
    firstNumber = random() % 100 + 1;
    secondNumber = random() % 100 + 1;
    return self;
}
```

Build and run your program. It should work correctly.

However, your class **LotteryEntry** has a problem. You are going to e-mail the class to your friend Rex. Rex plans to use the class **LotteryEntry** in his program but might not realize that you have written **initWithEntryDate:**. If he made this mistake, he might write the following lines of code:

```
NSCalendarDate *today = [NSCalendarDate calendarDate];
LotteryEntry *bigWin = [[LotteryEntry alloc] init];
[bigWin setEntryDate:today];
```

This code will not create an error. Instead, it will simply go up the inheritance tree until it finds **NSObject**'s **init** method. The problem is that firstNumber and secondNumber will not get initialized properly—both will be zero.

To protect Rex from his own ignorance, you will override **init** to call your initializer with a default date:

```
- (id)init
{
    return [self initWithEntryDate:[NSCalendarDate calendarDate]];
}
```

Add this method to your LotteryEntry.m file.

Notice that **initWithEntryDate:** still does all the work. Because a class can have multiple initializers, we call the one that does the work the *designated initializer*. If a class has several initializers, the designated initializer typically takes the most arguments. You should clearly document which of your initializers is the designated initializer. Note that the designated initializer for **NSObject** is **init**.

> ### Conventions for Creating Initializers (rules that Cocoa programmers try to follow regarding initializers):
>
> - You do not have to create any initializer in your class if the superclass's initializers are sufficient.
> - If you decide to create an initializer, you must override the superclass's designated initializer.
> - If you create multiple initializers, only one does the work—the designated initializer. All other initializers call the designated initializer.
> - The designated initializer of your class will call its superclass's designated initializer.

The Debugger

The Free Software Foundation developed the compiler (gcc) and the debugger (gdb) that come with Apple's developer tools. NeXT and Apple have made significant improvements to both over the years. This section discusses the processes of setting breakpoints, invoking the debugger, and browsing the values of variables.

While browsing code, you may have noticed a gray margin to the left of your code. If you click in that margin, a breakpoint will be added at the corresponding line. Add a breakpoint in `main.m` at the following line (Figure 3.15):

```
[array addObject:newEntry];
```

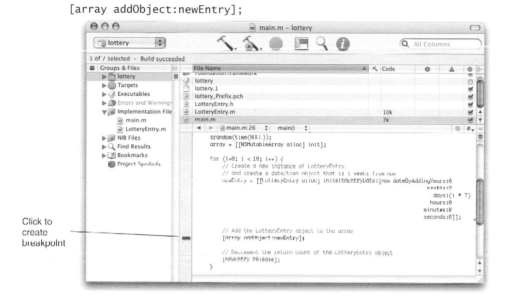

Figure 3.15 Creating a Breakpoint

If your program is compiled, you can invoke the debugger by clicking on the button that looks like a can of bug spray in Xcode. The debugger will take a few seconds to get started, and then it will run your program until it hits the breakpoint (Figure 3.16).

In the list on the left, you can see the frames on the stack. Because our breakpoint is in **main()**, the stack is not very deep. In the outline view on the right, you can see the variables and their values. Note that the variable i is currently 0.

The buttons above the stack information are for pausing, continuing, and stepping over, into, and out of functions. Click the continue button to execute another iteration of the loop. Click the step-over button to walk through the code line by line.

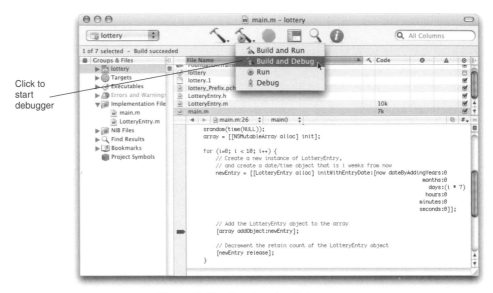

Click to
start
debugger

Figure 3.16   Starting the Debugger

The gdb debugger, being a Unix thing, is usually run from a terminal. To see the terminal-like view of the gdb process, click on the tab labeled Console (Figure 3.17).

In the console, you have full access to all of gdb's capabilities. One very handy feature is "print-object" ("po"). If a variable is a pointer to an object, when you "po" it, the object is sent the message **description** and the result is printed in the console. Try printing the newEntry variable.

```
po newEntry
```

You should see the result of your **description** method (Figure 3.18). (If you get a warning message from the debugger, ignore it.)

One amazing and nifty feature of Xcode is "fix and continue." As an example, imagine for a moment that the lottery in your town is run every two weeks instead of every week. While the application is running in the debugger, you can change code and see the new behavior without restarting the app. Try it. Change the line to say

```
newEntry = [[LotteryEntry alloc] initWithEntryDate:
                         [now dateByAddingYears:0
                                 months:0
                                   days:(i * 14)
                                  hours:0
```

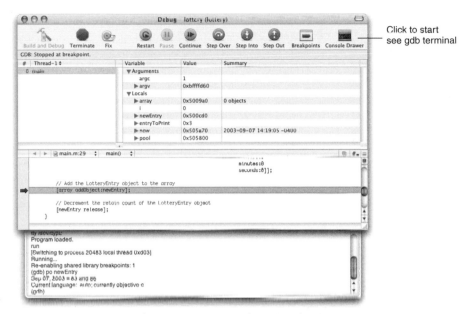

Click to start
see gdb terminal

Figure 3.17   Stopped at a Breakpoint

```
                                    minutes:0
                                    seconds:0]];
```

Click the Fix toolbar item. When that is complete, click the Continue toolbar item several times. The new entries should be two weeks apart.

To remove the breakpoint, just drag it out of the margin. Remove your breakpoint and put another one in **LotteryEntry**'s **dealloc** method next to the line that reads

```
NSLog(@"Destroying %@", self);
```

Click the continue button to run the application until the first **LotteryEntry** object executes its **dealloc** method. Notice that the stack is deeper this time. You can choose a frame in the stack in the list. The variables for that frame will appear in the outline view on the right.

Many things that go wrong create an instance of **NSException** and send it the message **raise**. For this reason, is a good idea to always have a breakpoint on **NSException**'s **raise** method. The easiest way to do this for all your projects is to create a .gdbinit file in your home directory (/Users/YourName-

Here/.gdbinit). This file is read by gdb every time it launches. Using TextEdit, create a file containing this line:

```
fb -[NSException raise]
```

You can test this breakpoint by changing the second loop to overrun the limits of the array in **main()**:

```
for (i = 0; i < 11; i++) {
    entryToPrint = [array objectAtIndex:i];
```

Remove your other breakpoints and restart the debugger. Your program should stop when the exception is raised.

You can also add such a breakpoint in Xcode. Bring up the Breakpoints window, and then click the New Breakpoint button. In the new line, type

```
-[NSException raise]
```

as shown in Figure 3.18.

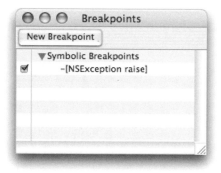

Figure 3.18   Adding a Breakpoint

That's enough to get you started with the debugger. For more in-depth information, refer to the documentation from the Free Software Foundation (http://www.gnu.org/).

What Have You Done?

You have written a simple program in Objective-C, including a **main()** function that created several objects. Some of these objects were instances of **LotteryEntry**, a class that you created. The program logged some information to the console.

At this point, you have a fairly complete understanding of Objective-C. Objective-C is not a complex language. The rest of the book is concerned with the frameworks that make up Cocoa. From now on, you will be creating event-driven applications, not command-line tools.

For the More Curious: How Does Messaging Work?

As mentioned earlier, an object is like a C struct. **NSObject** declares an instance variable called isa. Because **NSObject** is the root of the entire class inheritance tree, every object has an isa pointer to the class structure that created the object (Figure 3.19). The class structure includes the names and types of the instance variables for the class. It also has the implementation of the class's methods. The class structure has a pointer to the class structure for its superclass.

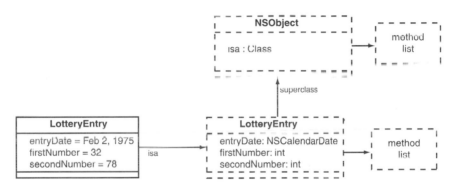

Figure 3.19   Each Object Has a Pointer to Its Class

The methods are indexed by the selector. The selector is of type SEL. Although, SEL is actually defined to be char *, it is most useful to think of it as an int. Each method name is mapped to a unique int. For example, the method name **addObject:** might map to the number 12. When you look up methods, you will use the selector, not the string @"addObject:".

As part of the Objective-C data structures, a table maps the names of methods to their selectors. Figure 3.20 shows an example.

At compile time, the compiler looks up the selectors wherever it sees a message send. Thus,

```
[myObject addObject:yourObject];
```

becomes (assuming the selector for **addObject:** is 12)

Figure 3.20   The Selector Table

```
objc_msgSend(myObject, 12, yourObject);
```

Here objc_msgSend() looks at myObject's isa pointer to get to its class structure and looks for the method associated with 12. If it does not find the method, it follows the pointer to the superclass. If the superclass does not have a method for 12, it continues searching up the tree. If it reaches the top of the tree without finding a method, the function throws an exception.

Clearly, this is a very dynamic way of handling messages. These class structures can be changed at runtime. In particular, using the **NSBundle** class, it is relatively easy to add classes and methods to your program while it is running. This very powerful technique has been used to create applications that can be extended by other developers.

Challenge

Change the format string on the calendar date objects in your **LotteryEntry** class.

Create another loop in **main()** that removes the **LotteryEntry** objects from the array one-by-one. Notice that the objects are deallocated as they are removed.

Chapter 4
CONTROLS

Once upon a time, there was a company called Taligent. Taligent was created by IBM and Apple to develop a set of tools and libraries like Cocoa. About the time Taligent reached the peak of its mindshare, I met one of its engineers at a trade show. I asked him to create a simple application for me: A window would appear with a button, and when the button was clicked, the words "Hello, World!" would appear in a text field. The engineer created a project and started subclassing madly: subclassing the window and the button and the event handler. Then he started generating code: dozens of lines to get the button and the text field onto the window. After 45 minutes, I had to leave. The app still did not work. That day, I knew that the company was doomed. A couple of years later, Taligent quietly closed its doors forever.

Most C++ and Java tools work on the same principles as the Taligent tools. The developer subclasses many of the standard classes and generates many lines of code to get controls to appear on windows. Most of these tools actually work.

While writing an application that uses the AppKit framework, you will seldom subclass the classes that represent windows, buttons, or events. Instead, you will create objects that will work with the existing classes. Also, you will not create code to get controls on windows. Instead, the nib file will contain all of this information. The resulting application will have significantly fewer lines of code. At first, this outcome may be alarming. In the long run, most programmers find it delightfully elegant.

To understand the AppKit framework, a good place to start is with the class **NSControl**. **NSButton**, **NSSlider**, **NSTextView**, and **NSColorWell** are all subclasses of **NSControl**. A control has a *target* and an *action*. The `target` is simply a pointer to another object. The `action` is a message (a selector) to send to the `target`. Recall that you set the `target` and `action` for two buttons in Chapter 2. There you set your **Foo** object to be the `target` of both buttons, and you set the `action` on one to **seed:** (Figure 4.1) and the `action` on the other to **generate:**.

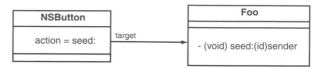

Figure 4.1   A Button Has a Target and an Action

When the user interacts with the control, it sends the `action` message to its `target`. For example, when the button is clicked, the button sends the `target` its `action` message (Figure 4.2).

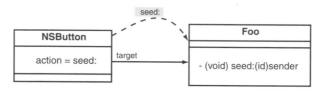

Figure 4.2   The Button Sends a Message

The action methods take one argument: the sender. This enables the receiver to know which control sent the message. Often, you will call back to the sender to get more information. For example, a check box will send its action message when it is turned on and when it is turned off. After getting the action message, the receiver might call back to the button to find out whether it is currently on or off:

```
- (IBAction)toggleFoo:(id)sender
{
    foo = [sender state];
}
```

To better understand **NSControl**, you should become acquainted with its ancestors: **NSControl** inherits from **NSView**, which inherits from **NSResponder**, which inherits from **NSObject**. Each member of the family tree adds some capabilities (Figure 4.3).

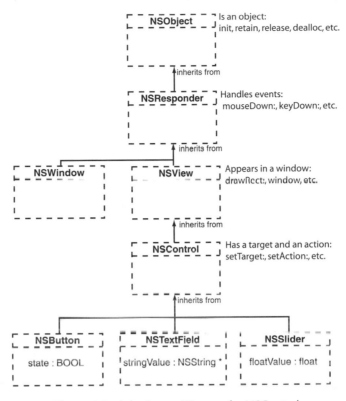

Figure 4.3   Inheritance Diagram for NSControl

At the top of the class hierachy is **NSObject**. All classes inherit from **NSObject**, and this is where they get the basic methods like **retain**, **release**, **dealloc**, and **init**. **NSResponder** is a subclass of **NSObject**. Responders have the ability to handle events with methods like **mouseDown:** and **keyDown:**. **NSView** is a subclass of **NSResponder**. **NSView** has a place on a window, where it draws itself. You can create subclasses of **NSView** to do things like display graphs and allow the user to drag and drop data. **NSControl** inherits from **NSView** and adds the target and the action.

Some Commonly Used Subclasses of NSControl

Before using some controls, let's take a brief look at the three most commonly used controls: **NSButton**, **NSSlider**, and **NSTextField**.

NSButton

Instances of **NSButton** can have several different appearances: oval, square, check box. They can also have different behavior when clicked: toggle (like a check box) or momentarily on (like most other buttons). Buttons can have icons and sounds associated with them. Figure 4.4 shows the Attributes information panel for an **NSButton** in Interface Builder.

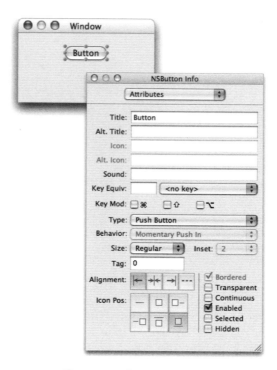

Figure 4.4   Button Inspector

Here are three methods that you will frequently send to buttons.

- (void)**setEnabled:**(BOOL)yn

The user can click on an enabled button. Disabled buttons are grayed out.

- (int)**state**

This method returns NSOnState (which is 1) if the button is on, or NSOffState (which is 0) if the button is off. It allows you to see whether a checkbox is checked or unchecked.

- (void)**setState:**(int)aState

This method turns the button on or off. It allows you to check or uncheck a check box programmatically. Set the state to NSOnState to check the check box and to NSOffState to uncheck it.

NSSlider

Instances of **NSSlider** can be vertical or horizontal. They can send the action to the target continuously while being changed, or they can wait to send the action until the user releases the mouse button. A slider can have markers, and it can prevent users from choosing values between the markers (Figure 4.5). Circular sliders are also possible.

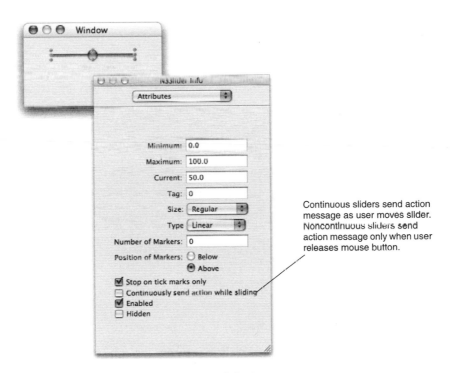

Figure 4.5   Slider Inspector

Here are two methods of **NSSlider** that you will use frequently:

- (void)**setFloatValue:**(float)x

Moves the slider to x.

- (float)**floatValue**

Returns the current value of the slider.

NSTextField

An instance of **NSTextField** can allow a user to type a single line of text. Text fields may or may not be editable. Uneditable text fields are commonly used as labels on a window. Compared to buttons and sliders, text fields are relatively complex. We will plumb the depths of the mysteries surrounding text fields in later chapters. Figure 4.6 shows the Attributes information panel for an **NSTextField** in Interface Builder.

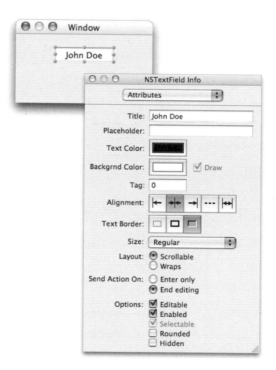

Figure 4.6   Text Field Inspector

Notice the Scrollable radio button. It permits scrolling from left to right, and vice versa, but not up and down. If you want to have multiple rows of text, use an **NSTextView**, not an **NSTextField**.

Text fields have a placeholder string. When the text field is empty, the placeholder string is displayed in gray.

NSSecureTextField is a subclass of **NSTextField** that is used for things like passwords. As the user types, bullets appear instead of the typed characters. You cannot copy or cut from an **NSSecureTextField**.

Here are a few of the most commonly used **NSTextField** methods:

- (NSString *)**stringValue**

- (void)**setStringValue:**(NSString *)aString

These methods allow you to get and set the string data being displayed in the text field.

- (NSObject *)**objectValue**

- (void)**setObjectValue:**(NSObject *)

These methods allow you to get and set the data being displayed in the text field as an arbitrary object type. This behavior is helpful if you are using a formatter. **NSFormatter**s are responsible for converting a string into another type, and vice versa. If no formatter is present, these methods use the **description** method.

For example, you might use a text field to allow the user to type in a date. As the programmer, you don't want the string that the user typed in; you really want an instance of **NSCalendarDate**. By attaching an **NSDateFormatter**, you ensure that the text field's **objectValue** method will return an **NSCalendarDate**. Also, when you call **setObjectValue:** with an **NSCalendarDate**, the **NSDateFormatter** will format it as a string for the user.

You will create a custom formatter class in Chapter 23.

Start the SpeakLine Example

As a simple example of using controls, you will build an application that enables users to type in a line of text and hear it spoken by the Mac OS X speech synthesizer. The app will look like Figure 4.7 when you are done with this chapter.

Figure 4.7   Completed Application

Figure 4.8 presents a diagram of the objects that you will create and their pointers to one another. Note that all of the classes that start with "NS" are part of the Cocoa frameworks and thus already exist. Your code will be in the **AppController** class.

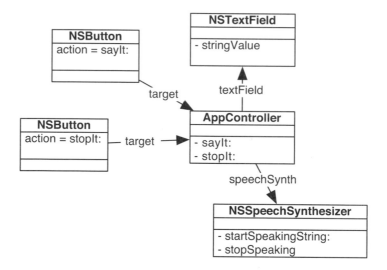

Figure 4.8   Object Diagram

In Xcode, create a new project of type Cocoa Application (Figure 4.9). Name the project SpeakLine. A new project will appear.

Figure 4.9   Choose Project Type

Lay Out the Nib File

Double-click on MainMenu.nib to open it in Interface Builder. From the palette window, drag out a text field and two buttons. Change the text in the text field to read "Peter Piper picked a peck of pickled peppers." (or some other text that will amuse you when it is spoken by the machine). Change the labels on the buttons to read Say It and Stop. The result should look like Figure 4.10.

Figure 4.10   Window with Text Field and Buttons

In the classes browser, create a subclass of **NSObject**. Name it **AppController**, as shown in Figure 4.11.

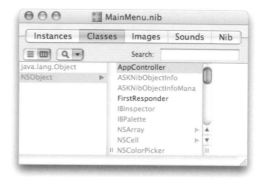

Figure 4.11   Create a Subclass of NSObject

AppController will be the target of the two buttons. Each control will trigger a different action method. Add two actions to the class **AppController**, **sayIt:** and **stopIt:**, as shown in Figure 4.12.

Figure 4.12   Create Actions

AppController will also need a pointer to the text field so that it can send messages to it. Add an outlet to the class **AppController** called **textField** (an **NSTextField**) as shown in Figure 4.13.

Figure 4.13   Create Outlet

To generate AppController.h and AppController.m, click on **AppController** in the Classes browser and select the Create Files for AppController menu item. When the save sheet appears, click Choose to save these files into the project directory.

To create one instance of **AppController** in the nib file, select the Instantiate AppController menu item from the Classes menu. You should see a blue cube appear in the doc window (the one entitled MainMenu.nib).

Making Connections in Interface Builder

Making a connection is analogous to introducing people. You say, "Mrs. Robinson, this is Dr. Pepper." If it is important that Dr. Pepper also know Mrs. Robinson, you would continue, "Dr. Pepper, this is Mrs. Robinson." With objects in Interface Builder, you will control-drag from *the object that needs to know* to the object that *it needs to know about*. You might also control-drag the other way to create a connection in the opposite direction, if necessary.

That last paragraph is so important that I am going to make you read it again: Making a connection is analogous to introducing people. You say, "Mrs. Robinson, this is Dr. Pepper." If it is important that Dr. Pepper also know Mrs. Robinson, you would continue, "Dr. Pepper, this is Mrs. Robinson." With objects in Interface Builder, you will control-drag from *the object that needs to know* to the object that *it needs to know about*. You might also control-drag the other way to create a connection in the opposite direction, if necessary.

For example, when a user clicks the Say It button, the button needs to send a message to your **AppController**, so the button needs to know about the **AppController**. For this reason, you will control-drag from the button to the **AppController**. When the inspector appears, you will indicate that you are setting the Target/Action and that the action will be **sayIt:** as shown in Figure 4.14.

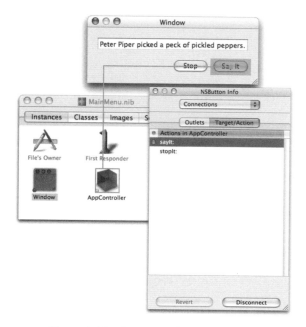

Figure 4.14   Set Action for Say It Button

Also, control-drag from the Stop button to the **AppController** and set its action to be **stopIt:**.

For the **AppController** to synthesize the speech for the line of text, it will need to ask the text field for the line of text. Thus, the **AppController** needs to have a pointer to the text field. Control-drag from the **AppController** to the text field. Set the outlet named textField, as shown in Figure 4.15.

At this point, you have set all but one of the connections shown in the object diagram in Figure 4.8. The missing connection, speechSynth, will be done pro-grammatically—not in Interface Builder.

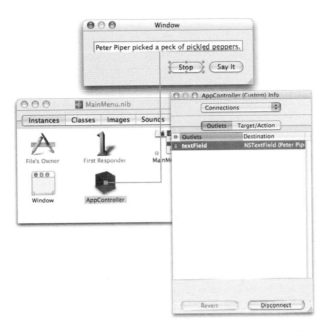

Figure 4.15   Connect AppController to the Text Field

NSWindow's initialFirstResponder Outlet

When your application runs and the new window appears, users should not have to click on a text field before they type. You can tell the window which view should be receiving keyboard events when the window appears. Control-drag from the window icon to the text field where the user will type the text to be spoken. Choose initialFirstResponder in the connection info panel (Figure 4.16).

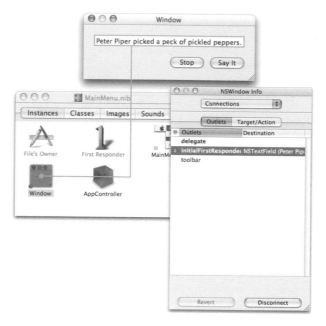

Figure 4.16   Set Window's Initial FirstResponder

Implementing the AppController Class

Now you need to write some code, so return to Xcode and select the AppController.h file. Add an instance variable named speechSynth of type **NSSpeechSynthesizer**.:

```
#import <Cocoa/Cocoa.h>

@interface AppController : NSObject
{
    IBOutlet NSTextField *textField;
    NSSpeechSynthesizer *speechSynth;
}
- (IBAction)sayIt:(id)sender;
- (IBAction)stopIt:(id)sender;

@end
```

Open the AppController.m file. This is where you will make the methods actually do something:

```objc
#import "AppController.h"

@implementation AppController

- (id)init
{
    [super init];

    // Logs can help the beginner understand what
    // is happening and hunt down bugs.
    NSLog(@"init");

    // Create a new instance of NSSpeechSynthesizer
    // with the default voice.
    speechSynth = [[NSSpeechSynthesizer alloc] initWithVoice:nil];
    return self;
}

- (IBAction)sayIt:(id)sender
{
    NSString *string = [textField stringValue];

    // Is the string zero-length?
    if ([string length] == 0) {
        return;
    }
    [speechSynth startSpeakingString:string];
    NSLog(@"Have started to say: %@", string);
}

- (IBAction)stopIt:(id)sender
{
    NSLog(@"stopping");
    [speechSynth stopSpeaking];
}

- (void)dealloc
{
    NSLog(@"dealloc");
    [speechSynth release];
    [super dealloc];
}
@end
```

Your application is done. Build it and run it. To see your log messages, use the
Show Run Log menu item in the Debug menu of Xcode. You should be able to
start the recitation of the text in the text field and stop it in mid-sentence.

Extending an Existing User Interface

Next, you will add a color well to the window so that the user can choose a preferred text color, as shown in Figure 4.17. **NSColorWell** is a subclass of **NSControl**. You will need to add an action and an outlet to your **AppController** class. The new object diagram is shown in Figure 4.18.

Figure 4.17   Completed Application

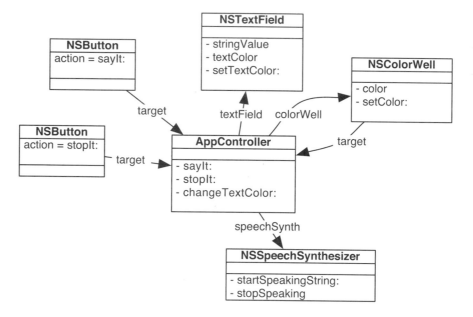

Figure 4.18   Object Diagram

Adding actions and outlets to existing classes sometimes causes confusion for new Cocoa programmers. The first round of actions and outlets were created using the inspector in Interface Builder. However, after the .h and .m files have been created, the easiest way to create new actions and outlets is to simply type them into the header file. Interface Builder can then parse the file to learn about the changes. You can also delete actions and outlets this way.

Note that you can add outlets and actions in Interface Builder, but when you regenerate the interface and implementation files, they might (if you are not careful) overwrite the files that you have been carefully editing for a few weeks. That's why I create the files from Interface Builder only once.

Open AppController.h and add an outlet named colorWell and an action named **changeTextColor:**.

```
#import <Cocoa/Cocoa.h>

@interface AppController : NSObject
{
    IBOutlet NSTextField *textField;
    IBOutlet NSColorWell *colorWell;
    NSSpeechSynthesizer *speechSynth;
}
- (IBAction)sayIt:(id)sender;
- (IBAction)stopIt:(id)sender;
- (IBAction)changeTextColor:(id)sender;

@end
```

Save the file and drag its icon into the doc window in Interface Builder, as shown in Figure 4.19.

Drop a color well onto the window, as shown in Figure 4.20. Control-drag from the color well to the **AppController**. Set the action to be **changeTextColor:**.

Control-drag from the **AppController** to the color well and set the outlet named colorWell.

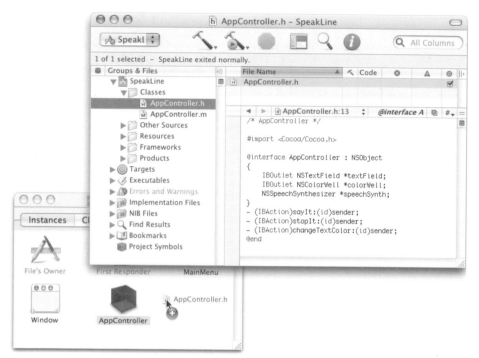

Figure 4.19   Drag AppController.h into the Doc Window

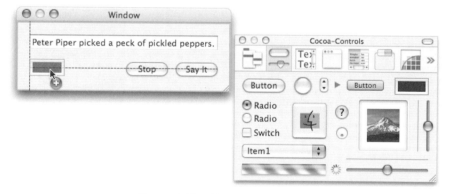

Figure 4.20   Choose Project Type

In this case, you have created connections in both directions: The color well has a pointer to the **AppController**, and the **AppController** has a pointer to the color well. This relationship is shown in the updated object diagram in Figure 4.18.

Add two methods to AppController.m:

```
// Make sure that the text field and the color well
// start off on the same color
- (void)awakeFromNib
{
    NSColor *initialColor = [textField textColor];
    NSLog(@"setting initial color for color well");
    [colorWell setColor:initialColor];
}

- (void)changeTextColor:(id)sender
{
    NSColor *newColor = [sender color];
    NSLog(@"changing the color");
    [textField setTextColor:newColor];
}
```

Build and run your application.

For the More Curious: Setting the Target Programmatically

Notice that the action of a control is a selector. **NSControl** includes the following method:

```
- (void)setAction:(SEL)aSelector
```

But how would you get a selector? The Objective-C compiler directive @selector will tell the compiler to look up the selector for you. For example, to set the action of a button to the method **drawMickey:**, you could do the following:

```
SEL mySelector;
mySelector = @selector(drawMickey:);
[myButton setAction:mySelector];
```

At compile time, @selector(drawMickey:) will be replaced by the selector for **drawMickey:**.

If you needed to find a selector for an **NSString** at runtime, you could use the function **NSSelectorFromString()**:

```
SEL mySelector;
mySelector = NSSelectorFromString(@"drawMickey:");
[myButton setAction:mySelector];
```

Challenge

This exercise is an important challenge. You should actually do it before moving on. Although it is easy to follow my instructions, eventually you will want to create your own applications. Here is where you can start to develop some independence. Feel free to refer back to the earlier examples for guidance.

Create another application that will present the user with the window shown in Figure 4.21. This application can have only one window open, so it is not a document-based application.

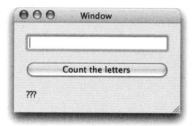

Figure 4.21   Before Input

When the user types in a string and clicks the button, change the message text to display the input string and the number of characters it has (Figure 4.22).

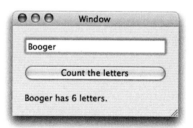

Figure 4.22   After Input

It is important to know how to use the Cocoa classes in your application. For this exercise, you should recognize that the **NSTextField** class has the following methods:

```
-  (NSString *)stringValue;
-  (void)setStringValue:(NSString *)aString;
```

You will also find it useful to know about the following methods of the class **NSStrings**:

```
-  (int)length;
+  (NSString *)stringWithFormat:(NSString *),...;
```

You will create a controller object with two outlets and one action. (This is hard, and you are not stupid. Good luck!)

Chapter 5
HELPER OBJECTS

Once upon a time (before *Baywatch*), there was a man with no name. Knight Industries decided that if this man were given guns and wheels and booster rockets, he would be the perfect crime-fighting tool. First they thought, "Let's subclass him and override everything we need to add the guns and wheels and booster rockets." The problem was that to subclass Michael Knight, you would need to know an awful lot about his guts so that you could wire them to guns and booster rockets. So instead, they created a helper object, the Knight Industries 2000 Super Car, or "Kitt."

Notice how this is different from the RoboCop approach. RoboCop was a man subclassed and extended. The whole RoboCop project involved dozens of surgeons who extended the man's brain into a fighting machine. This is the approach taken with many object-oriented frameworks.

While approaching the perimeter of an arms dealer's compound, Michael Knight would speak to Kitt over his watch-radio. "Kitt," he would say, "I need to get to the other side of that wall." Kitt would then blast a big hole in the wall with a small rocket. After destroying the wall, Kitt would return control to Michael, who would stroll through the rubble.

Many objects in the Cocoa framework are extended in much the same way. That is, there is an existing object that needs to be extended for your purpose. Instead of subclassing the table view, you simply supply it with a helper object. For example, when a table view is about to display itself, it will turn to the helper object to ask things like "How many rows of data am I displaying?" and "What should be displayed in the first column, second row?"

Thus, to extend an existing Cocoa class, you will frequently write a helper object. This chapter focuses on creating helper objects and connecting them to the standard Cocoa objects.

Delegates

In the SpeakLine application, the use of your interface would be more obvious if the Stop button remained disabled unless the speech synthesizer were speaking. Thus, the **AppController** should enable the button when it starts the speech synthesizer and then disable the button when the speech synthesizer stops.

Many classes in the Cocoa framework have an instance variable called delegate. You can set the delegate outlet to point to a helper object. In the documentation for the class, the delegate methods are clearly described. For example, the **NSSpeechSynthesizer** class has the following delegate methods:

```
- (void)speechSynthesizer:(NSSpeechSynthesizer *)sender
        didFinishSpeaking:(BOOL)finishedSpeaking;

- (void)speechSynthesizer:(NSSpeechSynthesizer *)sender
             willSpeakWord:(NSRange)characterRange
                  ofString:(NSString *)string;

- (void)speechSynthesizer:(NSSpeechSynthesizer *)sender
          willSpeakPhoneme:(short)phonemeOpcode;
```

Of the three messages that the speech synthesizer sends to its delegate, you care about only the first one: **speechSynthesizer:didFinishSpeaking:**.

In your application, you will make the **AppController** the delegate of the speech synthesizer and implement **speechSynthesizer:didFinishSpeaking:**. The method will be called automatically when the utterance is complete. The new object diagram is shown in Figure 5.1.

Note that you do not have to implement any of the other delegate methods. The implemented methods will be called; the unimplemented ones will be ignored. Also notice that the first argument is always the object that is sending the message—in this case, the speech synthesizer.

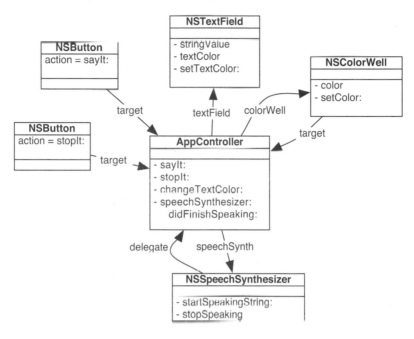

Figure 5.1 Drop a Table View on the Window

In AppController.m, set the delegate outlet of the speech synthesizer:

```
- (id)init
{
    [super init];
    NSLog(@"init");
    speechSynth = [[NSSpeechSynthesizer alloc] initWithVoice:nil];
    [speechSynth setDelegate:self];
    return self;
}
```

Next, add the delegate method. For now, just log a message:

```
- (void)speechSynthesizer:(NSSpeechSynthesizer *)sender
        didFinishSpeaking:(BOOL)finishedSpeaking
{
    NSLog(@"didFinish = %d", finishedSpeaking);
}
```

Build and run the application. Note that the delegate method is called if you click the Stop button or if the utterance plays all the way to the end.

To enable and disable the Stop button, you will need an outlet for it. Add an instance variable to AppController.h:

```
IBOutlet NSButton *stopButton;
```

Also in AppController.h, declare the delegate method that you are going to implement:

```
// Speech Synthesizer delegate methods
- (void)speechSynthesizer:(NSSpeechSynthesizer *)sender
        didFinishSpeaking:(BOOL)finishedSpeaking;
```

Declaring methods in the header file is completely optional, but such declarations act as nice documentation for programmers who have to read your code. If you call a method that has not been declared in the header file, you will get a warning from the compiler but everything will work correctly at runtime. Notice, however, that you will never call this delegate method; thus, if you left out this declaration, you would not receive a warning from compiler.

Save the file and drag AppController.h into the nib file.

Control-drag from the **AppController** to the Stop button and set the outlet stopButton as shown in Figure 5.2.

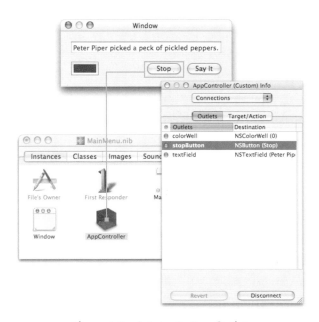

Figure 5.2   Set stopButton Outlet

The button should be disabled when it first appears on screen, so select the button and disable it in the Attributes inspector as shown in Figure 5.3. Save the nib file.

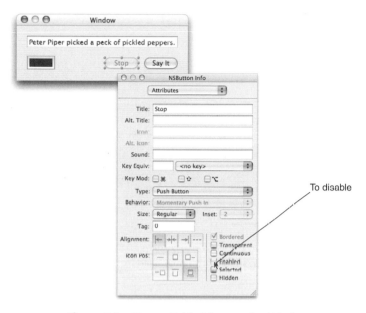

Figure 5.3 Drop a Table View on the Window

In Xcode, edit the AppController.m file to properly enable and disable the button. In **sayIt:**, enable the button:

```
- (IBAction)sayIt:(id)sender
{
    NSString *string = [textField stringValue];
    if ([string length] == 0) {
        return;
    }

    [speechSynth startSpeakingString:string];
    NSLog(@"Have started to say: %@", string);
    [stopButton setEnabled:YES];
}
```

In **speechSynthesizer:didFinishSpeaking:**, disable the button:

```
- (void)speechSynthesizer:(NSSpeechSynthesizer *)sender
        didFinishSpeaking:(BOOL)finishedSpeaking
{
    NSLog(@"didFinish = %d", finishedSpeaking);
    [stopButton setEnabled:NO];
}
```

Build and run the application. You should see that the button is enabled only when the synthesizer is generating speech.

The NSTableView and Its dataSource

A table view is used for displaying columns of data. An **NSTableView** has a helper object called a dataSource (as shown in Figure 5.4) that must implement two methods:

```
- (int)numberOfRowsInTableView:(NSTableView *)aTableView;
```

The dataSource will reply with the number of rows that will be displayed.

```
- (id)tableView:(NSTableView *)aTableView
    objectValueForTableColumn:(NSTableColumn *)aTableColumn
                          row:(int)rowIndex;
```

The dataSource will reply with the object that should be displayed in the row rowIndex of the column aTableColumn.

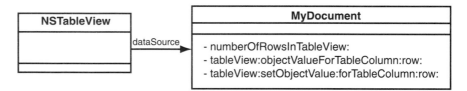

Figure 5.4   NSTableView's dataSource

If you have editable cells in your table view, you will need to implement one more method:

```
- (void)tableView:(NSTableView *)aTableView
    setObjectValue:(id)anObject
    forTableColumn:(NSTableColumn *)aTableColumn
               row:(int)rowIndex;
```

The dataSource takes the input that the user put into row rowIndex of aTableColumn. You do not have to implement this method if your table view is not editable.

Notice that you are taking a very passive position in getting data to appear. Your data source will wait until the table view asks for the data. When they first work with **NSTableView** (or **NSBrowser**, which works in a very similar manner), most programmers want to boss the table view around and tell it, "You will display 7 in the third row in the fifth column." It doesn't work that way. When the table view is ready to display the third row and the fifth column, it will ask its dataSource for the object to display.

How, then, will you get the table view to fetch updated information? You will tell the table view to **reloadData**. It will then reload all the cells that the user can see.

Next, you will add a table view that will enable the user to change the voice, as shown in Figure 5.5.

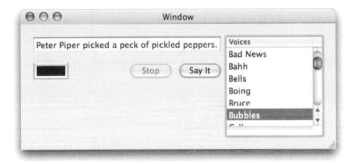

Figure 5.5 Completed Application

AppController Interface File

You are going to make your instance of **AppController** become the dataSource of the table view. This involves two steps: implementing the two methods listed above and setting the table view's dataSource outlet to the instance of **AppController**.

First, you will add the declaration of a few methods and instance variables to AppController.h:

```
#import <Cocoa/Cocoa.h>

@interface AppController : NSObject
{
    IBOutlet NSTextField *textField;
    IBOutlet NSColorWell *colorWell;
    IBOutlet NSButton *stopButton;
    IBOutlet NSTableView *tableView;
    NSSpeechSynthesizer *speechSynth;
}
```

```
// Action methods
- (IBAction)sayIt:(id)sender;
- (IBAction)stopIt:(id)sender;
- (IBAction)changeTextColor:(id)sender;

// Speech synthesizer delegate methods
- (void)speechSynthesizer:(NSSpeechSynthesizer *)sender
        didFinishSpeaking:(BOOL)finishedSpeaking;

// Table view data source methods
- (int)numberOfRowsInTableView:(NSTableView *)aTableView;
- (id)tableView:(NSTableView *)aTableView
objectValueForTableColumn:(NSTableColumn *)aTableColumn
                    row:(int)row;

@end
```

After editing it, save the file.

Lay Out the User Interface

Open `MainMenu.nib`. You will edit the window to look like Figure 5.6.

Figure 5.6   Completed Interface

Drag an **NSTableView** onto the window (Figure 5.7). In the inspector, make the table view have only one column. Also, disable column selection.

Double-click on the header of the column to change the title to Voices.

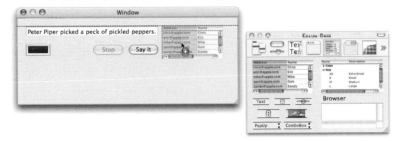

Figure 5.7   Drop a Table View on the Window

Interface Builder needs to be informed of the new outlet (`tableView`) that you added to `AppController.h`. Drag `AppController.h` from Xcode into your nib's document window (Figure 5.8).

Figure 5.8   Parse AppController.h

If you inspect the **AppController** class under the Classes tab, you should see the outlets and actions from your `AppController.h` file in the `Attributes` page of the inspector. Notice that the delegate and data source methods don't appear; only methods that are actions are visible. An action is a method that takes one argument (usually called `sender`) of type `id` and returns nothing.

Make Connections

Now make the connections. Figure 5.9 shows the object diagram.

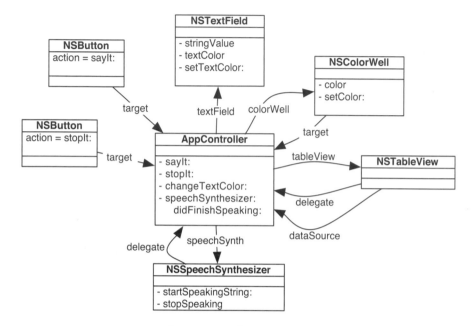

Figure 5.9   Object Diagram

First, you will set the dataSource outlet of the **NSTableView** to be your instance of **AppController**. Select the **NSTableView**. Control-drag from the table view to the **AppController**. In the Connections page of the info panel, choose dataSource and click the Connect button (Figure 5.10).

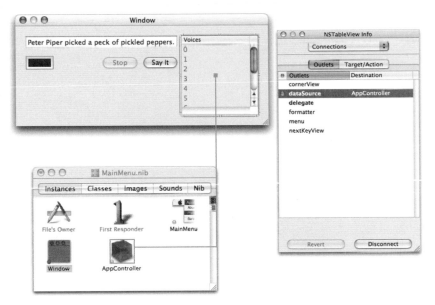

Figure 5.10   Set the tableView's dataSource Outlet

If you do not see dataSource in the Inspector, you have selected **NSScrollView**, not **NSTableView** inside it. The scroll view is the object that takes care of scrolling and the scroll bars. You will learn more about scroll views in Chapter 12. For now, just double-click in the interior of the table view until the title of the inspector window says **NSTableView**.

Next, you will connect your **AppController** object's tableView outlet to the table view. Control-drag from the **AppController** to the middle of the table view. In the info panel, connect to the tableView outlet (Figure 5.11).

Save the nib file and close it.

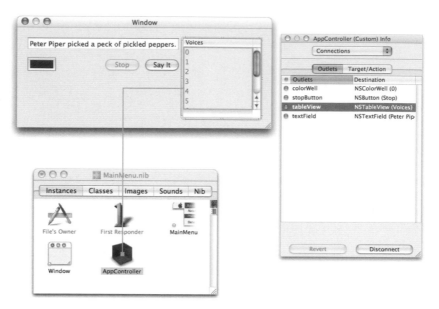

Figure 5.11   Set the AppController's Object's tableView Outlet

Edit AppController.m

Now you have to implement the methods that you declared in `AppControl-ler.h`. Implement the data source methods:

```
- (int)numberOfRowsInTableView:(NSTableView *)tableView
{
    return [[NSSpeechSynthesizer availableVoices] count];
}

- (id)tableView:(NSTableView *)tableView
        objectValueForTableColumn:(NSTableColumn *)tableColumn
                            row:(int)row
{
    return [[NSSpeechSynthesizer availableVoices] objectAtIndex:row];
}
```

The identifer for a voice is actually a long string like `com.apple.speech.syn-thesis.voice.Fred`. If you want just the name `Fred`, replace the last method with this one:

```
- (id)tableView:(NSTableView *)tableView
    objectValueForTableColumn:(NSTableColumn *)tableColumn
                            row:(int)row
{
    NSString *voice = [[NSSpeechSynthesizer availableVoices]
                                            objectAtIndex:row];
    return [[NSSpeechSynthesizer attributesForVoice:voice]
                                valueForKey:NSVoiceName];
}
```

(The screenshots in this chapter assume that you've done the pretty version.)

Next, build and run the application. Notice that now you get a list of the possible voices, but selecting a voice doesn't actually do anything yet.

Besides having a dataSource outlet, a table view has a delegate outlet. The delegate is informed whenever the selection changes. In AppController.m, implement **tableViewSelectionDidChange:**. (The class **NSNotification** will be introduced later in this book. For now, just note that you are passed a notification object as an argument to this delegate method.)

```
- (void)tableViewSelectionDidChange:(NSNotification *)notification
{
    NSArray *availableVoices = [NSSpeechSynthesizer availableVoices];
    int row = [tableView selectedRow];
    NSString *selectedVoice = [availableVoices objectAtIndex:row];
    [speechSynth setVoice:selectedVoice];
    NSLog(@"new voice = %@", selectedVoice);
}
```

The speech synthesizer will not allow you to change the voice while it is speaking, so you should prevent the user from changing the selected row. By implementing a delegate method, you can explicitly accept or deny all changes of the selection:

```
- (BOOL)selectionShouldChangeInTableView:(NSTableView *)aTableView
{
    if ([speechSynth isSpeaking]) {
        NSBeep();
        return NO;
    } else {
        return YES;
    }
}
```

Your users will want to see that the default voice is selected in table view when the application starts. In **awakeFromNib**, select the appropriate row and scroll to it if necessary:

```
- (void)awakeFromNib
{
    NSColor *initialColor = [textField textColor];
    NSLog(@"setting initial color for color well");
    [colorWell setColor:initialColor];

    // When the table view appears on screen, the default voice
    // should be selected
    NSString *defaultVoice = [NSSpeechSynthesizer defaultVoice];
    NSArray *voices = [NSSpeechSynthesizer availableVoices];
    int defaultRow = [voices indexOfObject:defaultVoice];
    [tableView selectRow:defaultRow byExtendingSelection:NO];
    [tableView scrollRowToVisible:defaultRow];
}
```

Back in Interface Builder, control-drag from the table view to the **AppController** and set the delegate outlet.

Build and run the application. If the speech synthesizer is speaking, you should get a system beep when you try to change the voice. If it is not speaking, you should be able to change the voice.

Common Errors in Implementing a Delegate

There are two very common errors that people make when implementing a delegate:

- *Misspelling the name of the method.* The method will not be called and you will not get any error or warning from the compiler. The best way to avoid this problem is to copy and paste the declaration of the method from the documentation or the header file.
- *Forgetting to set the delegate outlet.* You will not get any error or warning from the compiler if you make this error.

Many Objects Have Delegates

Delegation is a design pattern that you will see used many places in Cocoa. The following classes in the AppKit framework have delegate outlets:

```
NSAlert
NSApplication
NSBrowser
NSDrawer
NSFontManager
NSImage
NSLayoutManager
NSMatrix
NSMenu
NSSavePanel
NSSound
NSSpeechRecognizer
NSSpeechSynthesizer
NSSplitView
NSTabView
NSTableView
NSText
NSTextField
NSTextStorage
NSTextView
NSToolbar
NSWindow
```

Retain Cycles

Notice the problem with retain counts: If object X retains object Y, and Y retains X, the objects will never be deallocated. This situation is known as a *retain cycle*. A retain cycle can allow large islands of garbage to accumulate in your application's memory space.

To prevent retain cycles, the standard Cocoa objects do not retain their delegates, data sources, or targets.

For the More Curious: How Delegates Work

The delegate doesn't have to implement all of the methods, but if the object does implement a delegate method it will get called. In many languages, this sort of thing would be impossible. How is it achieved in Objective-C?

NSObject has the the following method:

```
- (BOOL)respondsToSelector:(SEL)aSelector
```

Because every object inherits (directly or indirectly) from **NSObject**, every object has this method. It returns YES if the object has a method called aSelector. Notice that aSelector is a SEL, not an **NSString**.

Imagine for a moment that you are the engineer who has to write **NSTableView**. You are writing the code that will change the selection from one row to another. You think to yourself, "I should check with the delegate." To do so, you add a snippet of code that looks like this:

```
// About to change to row "rowIndex"

// Set the default behavior
BOOL ok = YES;

// Check whether the delegate implements the method
if ([delegate respondsToSelector:
                          @selector(tableView:shouldSelectRow:)])
{
    // Execute the method
    ok = [delegate tableView:self shouldSelectRow:rowIndex];
}

// Use the return value
if (ok)
{
    ...actually change the selection...
}
```

Notice that the delegate is sent the message only if it has implemented the method. If the delegate doesn't implement the message, the default behavior happens. (In reality, the result from **respondsToSelector:** is usually cached by the object with the delegate outlet. This makes performance considerably faster than would be implied by the code above.)

After writing this method, you would carefully make note of its existence in the documentation for your class.

If you wanted to see the checks for the existence of the delegate methods, you could override **respondsToSelector:** in your delegate object:

```
- (BOOL)respondsToSelector:(SEL)aSelector
{
    NSString *methodName = NSStringFromSelector(aSelector);
    NSLog(@"respondsToSelector:%@", methodName);
    return [super respondsToSelector:aSelector];
}
```

You might want try adding this method to AppController.m now.

Challenge

Create a new application with one window. Make an object that is a delegate of the window. As the user resizes the window, make sure that the window always remains twice as tall as it is wide.

Here is the signature of the delegate method you will implement:

```
- (NSSize)windowWillResize:(NSWindow *)sender
                    toSize:(NSSize)frameSize;
```

The first argument is the window being resized. The second argument is a C struct that contains the size that the user has asked for:

```
typedef struct _NSSize {
    float width;
    float height;
} NSSize;
```

Return an NSSize structure containing the size that you would like the window to become.

Chapter 6
BINDINGS AND NSCONTROLLER

In the object-oriented programming community, there is a very common design pattern known as *Model-View-Controller*. The Model-View-Controller design pattern says that each class you write should fall into exactly one of the following groups:

- Model: Model classes describe your data. For example, if you write banking systems, you would probably create a model class called **SavingsAccount** that would have a list of transactions and a current balance. The best model classes include nothing about the user interface and can be used in several applications.

- View: A view class is part of the GUI. For example, **NSSlider** is a view class. The best views are general-purpose classes and can be used in several applications.

- Controller: Controller classes are usually application-specific. They are responsible for controlling the flow of the application. The user needs to see the data, so a controller object reads the model from a file or a database and then displays the model using view classes. When the user makes changes, the view objects inform the controller, which subsequently updates the model objects. The controller also saves the data to the filesystem or database.

Until Mac OS X 10.3, Cocoa programmers wrote a lot of code in their controller objects that simply moved data from the model objects into the view objects and back again. To make common sorts of controller classes easier to write, Apple introduced **NSController** and bindings.

NSController is actually an abstract class (Figure 6.1). **NSObjectController** is a subclass of **NSController** that displays the information for an object (known as its *content*). **NSArrayController** is a controller that has an array of data objects as its content. In this exercise, we will use an **NSArrayController**.

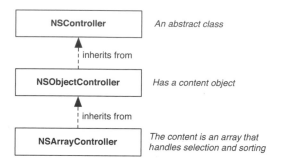

Figure 6.1   Controller classes

The **NSArrayController** holds onto an array of model objects. When the user selects an object in the array, the **NSArrayController** updates all the views to reflect the new selection. When the user edits the views, the **NSArrayController** updates the model objects. The **NSArrayController** also allows the user to create new model objects and to delete existing model objects.

Of course, it would be awful if the **NSController** had to handle the logic of every possible view class. For this reason, some of the smarts are moved out to the views themselves. Each view has *bindings* that hold the information necessary to update that view.

Starting the RaiseMan Application

Over the next few chapters, you will create a full-featured application for keeping track of employees and the raise that each person will receive this year. As this book progresses, you will add file saving, undo, user preferences, and printing capabilities. After this chapter, the application will look like Figure 6.2.

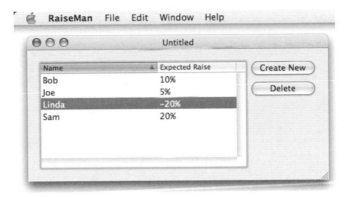

Figure 6.2   Completed Application

Create a new project in Xcode. Choose the Cocoa Document-based Application for the type and name the application RaiseMan.

What is a document-based application? An application where several documents can be open simultaneously. TextEdit, for example, is a document-based application. Conversely, System Preferences is not a document-based application. You will learn more about document architecture in the next chapter.

The object diagram for this application is shown in Figure 6.3. The table columns are connected to the **NSArrayController** by bindings, rather than by outlets.

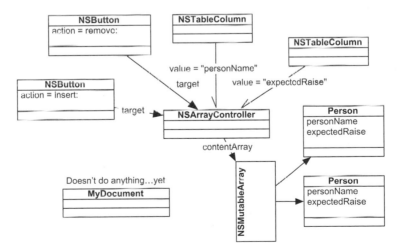

Figure 6.3   Object diagram

Notice that the class **MyDocument** has already been created for you. **MyDocument** is a subclass of **NSDocument**. The document object is responsible for reading and writing files. In this exercise, we will use an **NSArrayController** and bindings to construct our simple interface, so we won't be adding any code to **MyDocument** just yet.

To create a new **Person** class, choose the File -> New File... menu item. When presented with the possibilities, choose Objective-C Class. Name the new file Person.m and make sure that it is going to create a Person.h file, as shown in Figure 6.4.

Figure 6.4   Creating a Person Class

Edit the Person.h file to declare two instance variables and accessors for them:

```
#import <Foundation/Foundation.h>

@interface Person : NSObject {
    NSString *personName;
    float expectedRaise;
}

- (float)expectedRaise;
- (void)setExpectedRaise:(float)x;
- (NSString *)personName;
- (void)setPersonName:(NSString *)aName;

@end
```

Now edit Person.m to implement these methods and to override **init** and **dealloc**:

```objc
#import "Person.h"

@implementation Person

- (id)init
{
    [super init];
    [self setExpectedRaise:5.0];
    [self setPersonName:@"New Person"];
    return self;
}

- (float)expectedRaise
{
    return expectedRaise;
}

- (void)setExpectedRaise:(float)x
{
    expectedRaise = x;
}

- (NSString *)personName
{
    return personName;
}

- (void)setPersonName:(NSString *)aName
{
    aName = [aName copy];
    [personName release];
    personName = aName;
}

- (void)dealloc
{
    [personName release];
    [super dealloc];
}

@end
```

Notice the method **setPersonName:**. When it is passed a string, the input could be an **NSString** or an **NSMutableString**. If it is a mutable string, you want to make an immutable copy of it. If it is an immutable string, you just want to retain it. This is exactly what **NSString**'s **copy** method does. If the object is immutable, it is retained and returns itself. A mutable object makes an immutable copy of itself and returns that copy.

Notice that **Person** is a model class—it has no information about the user interface.

Key-Value Coding

NSObject defines two incredibly useful methods for every object—a method for reading and a method for setting variables by name:

```
- (id)valueForKey:(NSString *)attrName;
- (void)setValue:(id)newValue forKey:(NSString *)attrName;
```

The valueForKey: method allows you to read the value of a variable by name. Of course, there may be an accessor method for the variable. You will want the accessor used if it exists. If there is no accessor method, you will want the variable read directly.

Suppose that **valueForKey:** is passed a string like @"foo". If the object has a method **foo**, it is executed and the result is returned. If there is no method **foo**, the method looks for an instance variable called **foo**. If the variable exists, the value of **foo** is returned. If there is neither a method nor a variable, you get an error. Thus, if you have an instance of **Person**, the following code will get the person's name:

```
NSString *theName = [aPerson valueForKey:@"personName"];
```

It works by calling the **personName** method.

The setValue:forKey: method allows you to set the value of a variable by name. Once again, the accessor method (**setFoo:**, for instance) is used if it exists. Otherwise, the method sets the variable directly. If there is neither a method nor a variable, you get an error. Thus, you can set a person's name this way:

```
[aPerson setValue:@"Grant Balfour" forKey:@"personName"];
```

This works by calling the **setPersonName:** method.

This mechanism is called *key-value coding*. Key-value coding enables Cocoa classes to look at and edit the attributes of your objects. Thanks to this technique, it is easy to make your application AppleScript-able. Key-value coding also makes **NSController** and the bindings mechanism possible.

It is very important, then, that you make your classes amenable to key-value coding. For example, if you have an instance variable **foo**, you should name your accessors **setFoo:** and **foo**, because that is what the key-value coding methods expect—it is more than just a convention.

In Interface Builder

In Xcode, double-click on MyDocument.nib to open it in Interface Builder.

Delete the text field that says Your document contents here. Drop a table view and two buttons on the window. Relabel and arrange them as shown in Figure 6.5.

Figure 6.5   Document Window

Drag out an **NSArrayController** and drop it in the doc window. (To find the Controllers palette, you will need to use the pop-up as shown in Figure 6.6.)

Figure 6.6   Getting to the Controllers Palette

In the inspector, set its Object Class Name to **Person**. Add the keys for personName and expectedRaise as shown in Figure 6.7. Also, uncheck the box that says Preserves selection.

Figure 6.7   Controller Classes

The first column of the table view displays each employee's name. Change the title of the column to Name. Click and double-click the column to select it (the header on the column should turn blue). In the bindings page of the inspector, set the value to display the personName of the arrangedObjects of the **NSArrayController**, as shown in Figure 6.8.

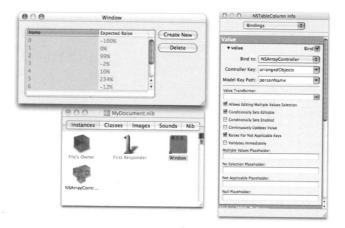

Figure 6.8   Binding the Name Column

The second column of the table view displays each employee's expected raise. Drop a number formatter on the column, as shown in Figure 6.9. In the inspector, set the formatter to display the number as a percentage, as shown in Figure 6.10.

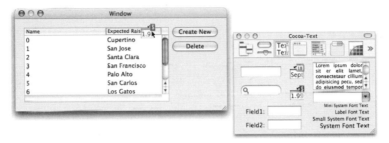

Figure 6.9   Adding a Number Formatter

Figure 6.10   Display Number as Percentage

In the bindings page of the inspector, set the value to display the expectedRaise of the arrangedObjects of the **NSArrayController**, as shown in Figure 6.11.

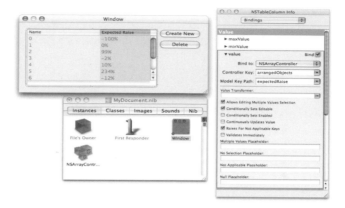

Figure 6.11   Bind Second Column to expectedRaise of arrangedObjects

Control-drag to make the array controller become the target of the Create New button. Set the action to **insert:**.

Control-drag to make the array controller become the target of the Delete button. Set the action to **remove:**. Also, in the bindings inspector, bind the button's enabled binding to the canRemove attribute of the **NSArrayController**, as shown in Figure 6.12.

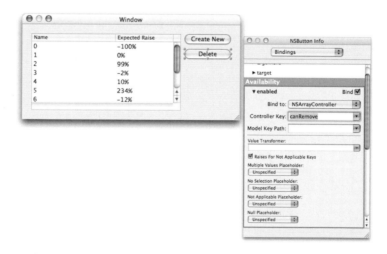

Figure 6.12   Binding the enabled Attribute of the Delete Button

Build and run your application. You should be able to create and delete **Person** objects. You should also be able to edit the attributes of the **Person** objects using the table view. Finally, you should be able to open multiple untitled documents. (No, you can't save those documents to a file. Soon, Grasshopper.)

Key-Value Coding and nil

Notice that our example contains very little code. You described what should be displayed in each of the columns in Interface Builder, but there is no code that actually calls the accessor methods of your **Person** class. How does this work? Key-value coding. Key-value coding makes generic, reusable classes like **NSArrayController** possible.

Notice that the key-value coding methods will automatically coerce the type for you. For example, when the user types in a new expected raise, the formatter creates an instance of **NSDecimalNumber**. The key-value coding method **setValue:forKey:** automatically converts that into a float before calling **setExpectedRaise:**. This behavior is extremely convenient.

There is, however, a problem with converting an NSDecimalNumber * into a float: Pointers can be nil, but floats cannot. If **setValue:forKey:** is passed a nil value that needs to be converted into a nonpointer type, it will call its own

```
- (void)setNilValueForKey:(NSString *)s
```

method. This method, as defined in **NSObject**, throws an exception. Thus, if the user left the Expected Raise field empty, your object would throw an exception. You should override this method in your **Person** class. Add the following method to Person.m:

```
- (void)setNilValueForKey:(NSString *)key
{
    if ([key isEqual:@"expectedRaise"]) {
        [self setExpectedRaise:0.0];
    } else {
        [super setNilValueForKey:key];
    }
}
```

NSObject's implementation of **setNilValueForKey:** throws an exception. Typically, you will override **setNilValueForKey:** so that it sets the instance variable to some default value. (In this case, expectedRaise is set to 0.0.)

Add Sorting

Adding sorting to your application is surprisingly easy. Open MyDocument.nib. You can set the sorting criteria in the inspector for each column. Users will be able to choose on which attribue the data will be sorted by clicking on the header of the column containing that attribute.

Select the column that displays personName. In the inspector, set the sort key to be personName and the selector to be **caseInsensitiveCompare:**, as shown in Figure 6.13. The **caseInsensitiveCompare:** method is part of **NSString**. For example, you might do this:

```
NSString *x = @"Piaggio";
NSString *y = @"Italjet"
NSComparisonResult result = [x caseInsensitiveCompare:y];

// Would x come first in the dictionary?
if (result == NSOrderedAscending)  {
     ...
}
```

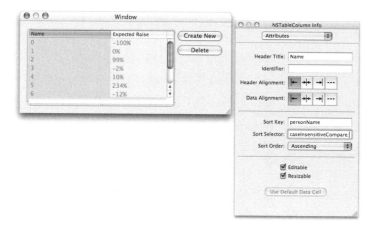

Figure 6.13   Sorting on personName

NSComparisonResult is just an integer. NSOrderedAscending is -1. NSOrderedSame is 0. NSOrderedDescending is 1.

Select the column that displays expectedRaise. In the inspector, set the sort key to be expectedRaise and the selector to be **compare:**, as shown in Figure 6.14.

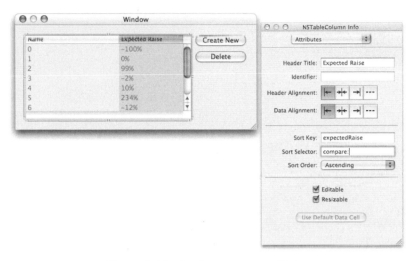

Figure 6.14 Sorting on expectedRaise

Build and run your application. Click on the header of the column to sort the data. Click again to see the data in reverse order.

For the More Curious: Sorting Without NSArrayController

In Chapter 5, you created a table view by implementing the dataSource methods explicitly. You might have wondered then how you could implement this sorting behavior in your own application.

The information that you added to the columns of the table is packed into an array of **NSSortDescriptor** objects. A sort descriptor includes the key, a selector, and an indicator of whether data should be sorted into ascending or descending order. If you have an **NSMutableArray** of objects, to sort it you can use the following method:

```
- (void)sortUsingDescriptors:(NSArray *)sortDescriptors
```

An optional table view dataSource method is triggered when the user clicks on the header of a column with a sort descriptor:

```
- (void)tableView:(NSTableView *)tableView
  sortDescriptorsDidChange:(NSArray *)oldDescriptors
```

Thus, if you have a mutable array that holds the information for a table view, you can implement the method like this:

```
- (void)tableView:(NSTableView *)tableView
          sortDescriptorsDidChange:(NSArray *)oldDescriptors
{
    NSArray *newDescriptors = [tableView sortDescriptors];
    [myArray sortUsingDescriptors:newDescriptors];
    [tableView reloadData];
}
```

And voila!, sorting in your application.

For the More Curious: Key Paths

Objects are often arranged in a network. For example, a person might have a spouse who has a scooter that has a model name. To get the selected person's spouse's scooter's model name, you can use a key path:

```
NSString *mn;
mn = [selectedPerson valueForKeyPath:@"spouse.scooter.modelName"]
```

We'd say that spouse and scooter are relationships of the **Person** class and that modelName is an attribute of the **Scooter** class.

There are also operators that you can include in key paths. For example, if you have an array of **Person** objects, you could get their average expectedRaise by using key paths:

```
NSNumber *theAverage;
theAverage = [employees valueForKeyPath:@"@avg.expectedRaise"];
```

Here are some commonly used operators:

```
@avg
@count
@max
@min
@sum
```

Now that you know about key paths, we can discuss how to create bindings programmatically. If you had a text field in which you wanted to show the average expected raise, you could create a binding like this:

```
[textField bind:@"value"
        toObject:personController
    withKeyPath:@"arrangedObjects.@avg.expectedRaise"
        options:nil];
```

Of course, it is usually easier to create a binding in Interface Builder.

Challenge 1

Make the application sort people based on the number of characters in their name. You can complete this challenge using only Interface Builder—the trick is to use a key path. (*Hint:* Strings have a **length** method.)

Challenge 2

In the first edition of this book, readers created the RaiseMan application without using **NSController** or the bindings mechanism. (These features were added in Mac OS X 10.3.) To do so, readers used the ideas from previous chapters. The challenge, then, is to rewrite the RaiseMan application without using **NSArrayController** or the bindings mechanism. Bindings often seem rather magical, and it is good to know how to do things without resorting to magic.

Be sure to start afresh with a new project—in the next chapter, we will build on your existing project.

The **Person** class will stay exactly the same. In MyDocument.nib, you will set the identifier of each column to be the name of the variable that you would like displayed. Then, the **MyDocument** class will be the dataSource of the table view and the target of the Create New and Delete buttons. **MyDocument** will have an array of **Person** objects that it displays. To get you started, here is MyDocument.h:

```
#import <Cocoa/Cocoa.h>

@interface MyDocument : NSDocument
{
    NSMutableArray *employees;
    IBOutlet NSTableView *tableView;
}
- (IBAction)createEmployee:(id)sender;
- (IBAction)deleteSelectedEmployees:(id)sender;
@end
```

Here are the interesting parts of MyDocument.m:

```
- (id)init
{
    [super init];
    employees = [[NSMutableArray alloc] init];
    return self;
}

// Action methods

- (IBAction)deleteSelectedEmployees:(id)sender
{
    // Which row is selected?
    NSIndexSet *rows = [tableView selectedRowIndexes];

    // Is there a selected row?
    if ([rows count] > 0) {
        unsigned int row =  [rows lastIndex];

        // Remove the selected people
        while (row != NSNotFound) {
            [employees removeObjectAtIndex:row];
            row = [rows indexLessThanIndex:row];
        }
        [tableView reloadData];
    } else {
        NSBeep();
    }
}

- (IBAction)createEmployee:(id)sender;
{
    Person *newEmployee = [[Person alloc] init];
    [employees addObject:newEmployee];
    [newEmployee release];
    [tableView reloadData];
}

// Table view dataSource methods

- (int)numberOfRowsInTableView:(NSTableView *)aTableView
{
    return [employees count];
}

- (id)tableView:(NSTableView *)aTableView
        objectValueForTableColumn:(NSTableColumn *)aTableColumn
                            row:(int)rowIndex
{
    // What is the identifier for the column?
    NSString *identifier = [aTableColumn identifier];
```

```
    // What person?
    Person *person = [employees objectAtIndex:rowIndex];

    // What is the value of the attribute named identifier?
    return [person valueForKey:identifier];
}

- (void)tableView:(NSTableView *)aTableView
    setObjectValue:(id)anObject
    forTableColumn:(NSTableColumn *)aTableColumn
             row:(int)rowIndex
{
    NSString *identifier = [aTableColumn identifier];
    Person *person = [employees objectAtIndex:rowIndex];

    // Set the value for the attribute named identifier
    [person setValue:anObject forKey:identifier];
}
```

Once you have it working, be sure to add sorting!

Chapter 7
NSU<small>NDO</small>M<small>ANAGER</small>

Using **NSUndoManager**, you can add undo capabilities to your applications in a very elegant manner. As objects are added, deleted, and edited, the undo manager keeps track of all messages that must be sent to undo these changes. As you invoke the undo mechanism, the undo manager keeps track of all messages that must be sent to redo *those* changes. This mechanism works by utilizing two stacks of **NSInvocation** objects.

This is a pretty heavy topic to cover so early in a book. (Sometimes when I think about undo, my head starts to swim a bit.) However, undo interacts with the document architecture. If we tackle this work now, you will see in the next chapter how the document architecture is supposed to work.

NSInvocation

As you might imagine, it is handy to be able to package up a message (including the selector, the receiver, and all arguments) as an object that can be invoked at your leisure. Such an object is an instance of **NSInvocation**.

One exceedingly convenient use for invocations is in message forwarding. When an object is sent a message that it does not understand, before raising an exception, the message-sending system checks whether the object has implemented:

```
- (void)forwardInvocation:(NSInvocation *)x
```

If the object has such a method, the message sent is packed up as an **NSInvocation** and **forwardInvocation:** is called.

One common use of **forwardInvocation:** is to pass the message on to another object that might be able to handle it (hence the name).

In the process of packing the message into an **NSInvocation**, the system needs to know the signature for that message. To get the signature, it calls

```
- (NSMethodSignature *)methodSignatureForSelector:(SEL)aSel
```

Thus, if you were an object that had a helper object, you could forward all messages that you were unable to understand to the helper by adding these three methods to your class:

```
- (void)forwardInvocation:(NSInvocation *)invocation
{
    SEL aSelector = [invocation selector];
    if ([helper respondsToSelector:aSelector])
        [invocation invokeWithTarget:helper];
    else
        [self doesNotRecognizeSelector:aSelector];
}

- (BOOL)respondsToSelector:(SEL)aSelector
{
    BOOL result = [super respondsToSelector:aSelector];
    if (result == NO) {
        result = [helper respondsToSelector:aSelector];
    }
    return result;
}

// This gets run before forwardInvocation:
- (NSMethodSignature *)methodSignatureForSelector:(SEL)aSelector
{
    NSMethodSignature *result;
    result = [super methodSignatureForSelector:aSelector];
    if (!result){
        result = [helper methodSignatureForSelector:aSelector];
    }
    return result;
}
```

The other nifty use for invocations is the undo manager.

How the NSUndoManager Works

Suppose that the user opens a new RaiseMan document and makes three edits:

- Inserts a new record

- Changes the name from "New Employee" to "Rex Fido"

- Changes the raise from zero to 20

As each edit is performed, your controller will add an invocation that would undo that edit to the undo stack. For the sake of simplifying the prose, let's say, "The *inverse* of the edit gets added to the undo stack."

Figure 7.1 shows what the undo stack would look like after these three edits.

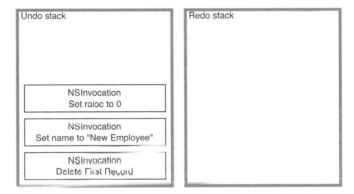

Figure 7.1   The Undo Stack

If the user now chooses the Undo menu item, the first invocation is taken off the stack and invoked. This would change the person's raise back to zero. If the user chooses the Undo menu item again, it would change the person's name back to "New Employee."

Each time an item is popped off the undo stack and invoked, the inverse of the undo operation must be added to the redo stack. Thus, after undoing the two operations as described above, the undo and redo stacks should look like Figure 7.2.

The undo manager is actually quite clever: When the user is doing edits, the undo invocations go onto the undo stack. When the user is undoing edits, the undo invocations go onto the redo stack. When the user is redoing edits, the undo invocations go onto the undo stack. These tasks are handled automatically for you; your only job is to give the undo manager the inverse invocations that need to be added.

Now suppose that you are writing a method called **makeItHotter** and that the inverse of this method is called **makeItColder**. Here is how you would enable the undo:

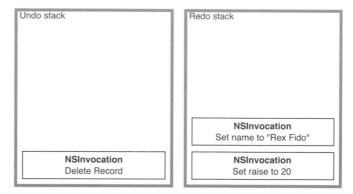

Figure 7.2   The Revised Undo Stack

```
- (void)makeItHotter
{
    temperature = temperature + 10;
    [[undoManager prepareWithInvocationTarget:self] makeItColder];
    [self showTheChangesToTheTemperature];
}
```

As you might guess, the **prepareWithInvocationTarget:** method notes the target and returns the undo manager itself. Then, the undo manager cleverly overrides **forwardInvocation:** such that it adds the invocation for **makeItColder:** to the undo stack.

To complete the example, you would implement **makeItColder**:

```
- (void)makeItColder
{
    temperature = temperature - 10;
    [[undoManager prepareWithInvocationTarget:self] makeItHotter];
    [self showTheChangesToTheTemperature];
}
```

Note that we have again registered the inverse with the undo manager. If **makeItColder** is invoked as a result of an undo, this inverse will go onto the redo stack.

The invocations on either stack are grouped. By default, all invocations added to a stack during a single event are grouped together. Thus, if one user action causes changes in several objects, all the changes are undone by a single click of the Undo menu item.

The undo manager can also change the label on the undo and redo menu items. For example, "Undo Insert" is more descriptive than just "Undo." To set the label, use the following code:

```
[undoManager setActionName:"Insert"];
```

How do you get an undo manager? You can create one explicitly, but note that each instance of **NSDocument** already has its own undo manager.

Adding Undo to RaiseMan

Let's give the user the ability to undo the effects of clicking the Create New and Delete buttons, as well as the ability to undo the changes they make to **Person** objects in the table. The necessary code will go into your **MyDocument** class.

Currently, the **NSArrayController** object keeps its own array of **Person** objects. To give the user the ability to undo insertions and deletions, **MyDocument** must be the object that manages the array of employees. You plan to store the array inside **MyDocument** and to set the **NSArrayController**'s contentArray binding so as to tell it to use **MyDocument**'s array as its content. You will also write two methods that will be called when **NSArrayController** wishes to insert or remove a **Person** object.

Open MyDocument.h and add two instance variables and two actions:

```
@interface MyDocument : NSDocument
{
    IBOutlet NSArrayController *personController;
    NSMutableArray *employees;
}
- (void)insertObject:(Person *)p inEmployeesAtIndex:(int)index;
- (void)removeObjectFromEmployeesAtIndex:(int)index;
- (void)setEmployees:(NSMutableArray *)array
@end
```

Because these declarations include the class **Person**, you will need to add the following line to MyDocument.h after #import <Cocoa/Cocoa.h>:

```
@class Person;
```

Drag the MyDocument.h file from the Xcode project into the MyDocument.nib window.

Control-drag from the file's owner to the array controller. Set the outlet personController as shown in Figure 7.3.

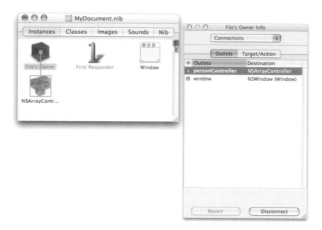

Figure 7.3   Setting the personController Outlet

In the bindings inspector for the array controller, expand the settings for the contentArray binding. Choose File's Owner (MyDocument) from the Bind to: pop-up menu. Enter employees for the Model Key Path, as shown in Figure 7.4.

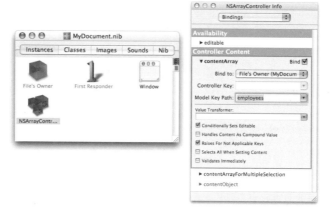

Figure 7.4   Setting the contentArray Binding

Back in Xcode, edit the MyDocument.m file. First, import the Person.h file:

```
#import "Person.h"
```

Next, edit the **init** and **dealloc** methods to create and destroy the employees array:

```
- (id)init
{
    self = [super init];
    if (self) {
        employees = [[NSMutableArray alloc] init];
    }
    return self;
}

- (void)setEmployees:(NSMutableArray *)array
{
    if (array == employees)
        return;

    [employees release];
    [array retain];
    employees = array;
}

- (void)dealloc
{
    [self setEmployees:nil];
    [super dealloc];
}
```

Finally, implement the two methods in **MyDocument** that will be called automatically to insert and remove **Person** objects from the employees array. Notice that these methods are inverses of each other:

```
- (void)insertObject:(Person *)p inEmployeesAtIndex:(int)index
{
    // Add the inverse of this operation to the undo stack
    NSUndoManager *undo = [self undoManager];
    [[undo prepareWithInvocationTarget:self]
                        removeObjectFromEmployeesAtIndex:index];
    if (![undo isUndoing]) {
        [undo setActionName:@"Insert Person"];
    }

    // Add the Person to the array
    [employees insertObject:p atIndex:index];
}

- (void)removeObjectFromEmployeesAtIndex:(int)index
{
    Person *p = [employees objectAtIndex:index];
    // Add the inverse of this operation to the undo stack
    NSUndoManager *undo = [self undoManager];
    [[undo prepareWithInvocationTarget:self] insertObject:p
                                    inEmployeesAtIndex:index];
    if (![undo isUndoing]) {
        [undo setActionName:@"Delete Person"];
    }
```

```
    [employees removeObjectAtIndex:index];
}
```

These methods will be called when the **NSArrayController** wishes to insert or remove **Person** objects (for example, when the Create New and Delete buttons send it **insert:** and **remove:** messages).

At this point, you have made it possible to undo deletions and insertions. Undoing edits will be a little trickier. Before tackling this task, build and run your application. Test the undo capabilities that you have at this point.

Key-Value Observing

In Chapter 6, we discussed key-value coding. To review, key-value coding is a way to read and change a variable's value using its name. *Key-value observing* allows you to be informed when these sorts of changes occur.

To enable undo capabilities for edits, you will want your document object to be informed of changes to the keys expectedRaise and personName for all of its **Person** objects.

A method in **NSObject** allows you to register to be informed of these changes:

```
- (void)addObserver:(NSObject *)observer
        forKeyPath:(NSString *)keyPath
           options:(NSKeyValueObservingOptions)options
           context:(void *)context;
```

You supply the object that should be informed as observer and the key path for which you wish to be informed about changes. The options variable defines what you would like to have included when you are informed about the changes. For example, you can be told about the old value (before the change) and the new value (after the change). The context variable is a pointer to data that you would like sent with the rest of the information. You can use it for whatever you wish. I typically leave it NULL.

When a change occurs, the observer is sent the following message:

```
- (void)observeValueForKeyPath:(NSString *)keyPath
                      ofObject:(id)object
                        change:(NSDictionary *)change
                       context:(void *)context;
```

The observer is told which key path changed in which object. Here change is a dictionary that (depending on the options you asked for when you registered as an observer) may contain the old value and/or the new value. Of course, it is sent the context pointer supplied when it was registered as an observer. I typically ignore context.

Undo for Edits

The first step is to register your document object to observe changes to its **Person** objects. Add the following methods to MyDocument.m:

```
- (void)startObservingPerson:(Person *)person
{
    [person addObserver:self
            forKeyPath:@"personName"
                options:NSKeyValueObservingOptionOld
                context:NULL];

    [person addObserver:self
            forKeyPath:@"expectedRaise"
                options:NSKeyValueObservingOptionOld
                context:NULL];
}

- (void)stopObservingPerson:(Person *)person
{
    [person removeObserver:self forKeyPath:@"personName"];
    [person removeObserver:self forKeyPath:@"expectedRaise"];
}
```

Call these methods every time a **Person** enters or leaves the document:

```
- (void)insertObject:(Person *)p inEmployeesAtIndex:(int)index
{
    // Add the inverse of this operation to the undo stack
    NSUndoManager *undo = [self undoManager];
    [[undo prepareWithInvocationTarget:self]
        removeObjectFromEmployeesAtIndex:index];
    if (![undo isUndoing]) {
        [undo setActionName:@"Insert Person"];
    }

    // Add the Person to the array
    [self startObservingPerson:p];
    [employees insertObject:p atIndex:index];
}
```

```
- (void)removeObjectFromEmployeesAtIndex:(int)index
{
    Person *p = [employees objectAtIndex:index];
    // Add the inverse of this operation to the undo stack
    NSUndoManager *undo = [self undoManager];
    [[undo prepareWithInvocationTarget:self] insertObject:p
                                    inEmployeesAtIndex:index];
    if (![undo isUndoing]) {
        [undo setActionName:@"Delete Person"];
    }
    [self stopObservingPerson:p];
    [employees removeObjectAtIndex:index];
}

- (void)setEmployees:(NSMutableArray *)array
{
    if (array == employees)
        return;

    NSEnumerator *e = [employees objectEnumerator];
    Person *person;
    while (person = [e nextObject]) {
        [self stopObservingPerson:person];
    }

    [employees release];
    [array retain];
    employees = array;

    e = [employees objectEnumerator];
    while (person = [e nextObject]) {
        [self startObservingPerson:person];
    }
}
```

Now, implement the method that does edits and is its own inverse:

```
- (void)changeKeyPath:(NSString *)keyPath
             ofObject:(id)obj
              toValue:(id)newValue
{
    // setValue:forKeyPath: will cause the key-value observing method
    // to be called, which takes care of the undo stuff
    [obj setValue:newValue forKeyPath:keyPath];
}
```

Implement the method that will be called whenever a **Person** object is edited, either by the user or by the **changeKeyPath:ofObject:toValue:** method. Note that it puts a call to **changeKeyPath:ofObject:toValue:** on the stack with the old value for the changed key.

```
- (void)observeValueForKeyPath:(NSString *)keyPath
                     ofObject:(id)object
                       change:(NSDictionary *)change
                      context:(void *)context
{
    NSUndoManager *undo = [self undoManager];
    id oldValue = [change objectForKey:NSKeyValueChangeOldKey];
    NSLog(@"oldValue = %@", oldValue);
    [[undo prepareWithInvocationTarget:self] changeKeyPath:keyPath
                                                  ofObject:object
                                                   toValue:oldValue];

    [undo setActionName:@"Edit"];
}
```

That should do it. Once you build and run your application, undo should work flawlessly.

Notice that as you make changes to the document, a dot appears in the red close button in the window's title bar to indicate that changes have been made but have not been saved. You will learn how to save them to a file in the next chapter.

For the More Curious: Windows and the Undo Manager

A view can add edits to the undo manager. **NSTextView**, for example, can put each edit that a person makes to the text onto the undo manager. How does the text view know which undo manager to use? First, it asks its delegate. **NSTextView** delegates can implement this method:

> - (NSUndoManager *)**undoManagerForTextView:**(NSTextView *)tv;

Next, it asks its window. **NSWindow** has a method for this purpose:

> - (NSUndoManager *)**undoManager**;

The window's delegate can supply an undo manager for the window by implementing the following method:

> - (NSUndoManager *)**windowWillReturnUndoManager:**(NSWindow *)window;

The undo/redo menu items reflect the state of the undo manager for the key window (Figure 7.5). (The key window is what most users call the "active window." Cocoa developers call it *key* because it is the one that will get the keyboard events if the user types.)

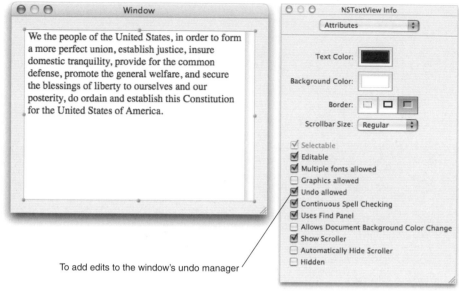

To add edits to the window's undo manager

Figure 7.5   NSTextView Inspector

Chapter 8

ARCHIVING

While an object-oriented program is running, a complex graph of objects is being created. It is often necessary to represent this graph of objects as a stream of bytes, a process called *archiving* (Figure 8.1). This stream of bytes can then be sent across a network connection or written into a file. For example, when you save a nib file, Interface Builder is archiving objects into a file. (Instead of "archiving," a Java programmer would call this process "serialization.")

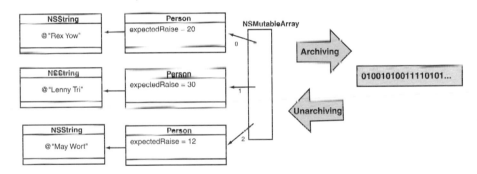

Figure 8.1 Archiving

When you need to recreate the graph of objects from the stream of bytes, you will *unarchive* it. For example, when your application starts up, it unarchives the objects from the nib file created by Interface Builder.

Although objects have both instance variables and methods, only the instance variables and the name of the class go into the archive. In other words, only data goes into the archive, not code. As a result, if one application archives an object and another application unarchives the same object, both applications must have the code for the class linked in. In the nib file, for example, you have used classes like **NSWindow** and **NSButton** from the AppKit framework. If you do not link your application against the AppKit framework, it will be unable to create the instances of **NSWindow** and **NSButton** that it finds in the archive.

There was once a shampoo ad that said, "I told two friends, and they told two friends, and they told two friends, and so on, and so on, and so on." The implication was that as long as you told your friends about the shampoo, everyone who matters would eventually wind up using the shampoo. Object archiving works in much the same way. You archive a root object, it archives the objects to which it is attached, they archive the objects to which they are attached, and so on, and so on, and so on. Eventually, every object that matters will be in the archive.

Archiving involves two steps. First, you need to teach your objects how to archive themselves. Second, you need to cause the archiving to occur.

The Objective-C language has a construct called a *protocol*, which is identical to the Java construct called an *interface*. That is, a protocol is a list of method declarations. When you create a class that implements a protocol, it promises to implement all the methods declared in the protocol.

NSCoder and NSCoding

One protocol is called **NSCoding**. If your class implements **NSCoding**, it promises to implement the following methods:

```
- (id)initWithCoder:(NSCoder *)coder;
```

```
- (void)encodeWithCoder:(NSCoder *)coder;
```

An **NSCoder** is an abstraction of a stream of bytes. You can write your data to a coder or read your data from a coder. The **initWithCoder:** method in your object will read data from the coder and save that data to its instance variables. The **encodeWithCoder:** method in your object will read its instance variables and write those values to the coder. In this chapter, you will implement both methods in your **Person** class.

NSCoder is actually an *abstract class*. You won't ever create instances of an abstract class. Instead, an abstract class has some capabilities that are intended to be inherited by subclasses. You will create instances of the concrete subclasses. Namely, you will use **NSKeyedUnarchiver** to read objects from a stream of data, and you will use **NSKeyedArchiver** to write objects to the stream of data.

Encoding

NSCoder has many methods, but most programmers find themselves using just a few of them repeatedly. Here are the methods most commonly used when you are encoding data onto the coder:

```
- (void)encodeObject:(id)anObject forKey:(NSString *)aKey
```

This method writes anObject to the coder and associates it with the key aKey. This will cause anObject's **encodeWithCoder:** method to be called (and they told two friends, and they told two friends...).

For each of the common C primitive types (like int and float), **NSCoder** has an encode method:

```
- (void)encodeBool:(BOOL)boolv forKey:(NSString *)key
```

```
- (void)encodeDouble:(double)realv forKey:(NSString *)key
```

```
- (void)encodeFloat:(float)realv forKey:(NSString *)key
```

```
- (void)encodeInt:(int)intv forKey:(NSString *)key
```

To add encoding to your **Person** class, add the following method to Person.m:

```
- (void)encodeWithCoder:(NSCoder *)coder
{
    [coder encodeObject:personName forKey:@"personName"];
    [coder encodeFloat:expectedRaise forKey:@"expectedRaise"];
}
```

If you looked at the documentation for **NSString**, you would see that it implements the **NSCoding** protocol. Thus, the personName knows how to encode itself.

All of the commonly used AppKit and Foundation classes implement the **NSCoding** protocol, with the notable exception of **NSObject**. Because **Person** inherits from **NSObject**, it doesn't call [super encodeWithCoder:coder]. If **Person**'s superclass *had* implemented the **NSCoding** protocol, the method would have looked like this:

```
- (void)encodeWithCoder:(NSCoder *)coder
{
    [super encodeWithCoder:coder];
    [coder encodeObject:personName forKey:@"personName"];
    [coder encodeFloat:expectedRaise forKey:@"expectedRaise"];
}
```

The call to the superclass's **encodeWithCoder:** method would give the superclass a chance to write its variables onto the coder. Thus, each class in the hierarchy writes only its instance variables (and not its superclass's instance variables) onto the coder.

Decoding

When decoding data from the coder, you will use the analogous decoding methods:

- (id)**decodeObjectForKey:**(NSString *)aKey

- (BOOL)**decodeBoolForKey:**(NSString *)key

- (double)**decodeDoubleForKey:**(NSString *)key

- (float)**decodeFloatForKey:**(NSString *)key

- (int)**decodeIntForKey:**(NSString *)key

If, for some reason, the stream does not include the data for a key, you will get zero for the result. For example, if the object did not write out data for the key "foo" when the stream was first written, the coder will return if it is later asked to decode a float for the key "foo". If the coder is asked to decode an object for the key "foo", it will return nil.

To add decoding to your **Person** class, add the following method to your Person.m file:

```
- (id)initWithCoder:(NSCoder *)coder
{
    [super init];
    [self setPersonName:[coder decodeObjectForKey:@"personName"]];
    [self setExpectedRaise:[coder decodeFloatForKey:@"expectedRaise"]];
    return self;
}
```

Once again, you did not call the superclass's implementation of **initWith-Coder:**, because **NSObject** doesn't have one. If **Person**'s superclass *had* implemented the **NSCoding** protocol, the method would have looked like this:

```
- (id)initWithCoder:(NSCoder *)coder
{
  [super initWithCoder:coder];
  [self setPersonName:[coder decodeObjectForKey:@"personName"]];
  [self setExpectedRaise:[coder decodeObjectForKey:@"expectedRaise"]];
  return self;
}
```

The attentive reader may now be saying, "Chapter 3 said that the designated initializer does all the work and calls the superclass's designated initializer. It said that all other initializers call the designated initializer. But **Person** has an **init** method, which is its designated initializer, and this new initializer doesn't call it." You are right. **initWithCoder:** is an exception to initializer rules.

You have now implemented the methods in the **NSCoding** protocol. To declare your **Person** class as implementing the **NSCoding** protocol, you will edit the Person.h file. Change the declaration of your class to look like this:

```
@interface Person : NSObject <NSCoding> {
```

Now try to compile the project. Fix any errors. You could run the application at this point, if you like. However, although you have taught **Person** objects to encode themselves, you haven't asked them to do so. Thus, you will see no change in the behavior of your application.

The Document Architecture

Applications that deal with multiple documents have a lot in common. All of them can create new documents, open existing documents, save or print open documents, and remind the user to save edited documents when he tries to close a window or quit the application. Apple supplies three classes that take care of most of the details for you: **NSDocumentController**, **NSDocument**, and **NSWindowController**. Together, these three classes constitute the *document architecture*.

The purpose of the document architecture relates to the Model-View-Controller design pattern discussed in Chapter 6. In RaiseMan, your subclass of **NSDocument** (with the help of **NSArrayController**) acts as the controller. It will have a pointer to the model objects, and will be responsible for the following duties:

- Saving the model data to a file
- Loading the model data from a file
- Displaying the model data in the views
- Taking user input from the views and updating the model

Info.plist and NSDocumentController

When Xcode builds an application, it includes a file called `Info.plist`. (Later in this chapter, you will change `Info.plist`.) When the application is launched, it reads from `Info.plist`, which tells it what type of files it works with. If it finds that it is a document-based application, it creates an instance of **NSDocumentController** (Figure 8.2). You will seldom have to deal with the document controller; it lurks in the background and takes care of a bunch of details for you. For example, when you choose the New or Save All menu item, the document controller handles the request. If you need to send messages to the document controller, you could get to it like this:

```
NSDocumentController *dc;
dc = [NSDocumentController sharedDocumentController];
```

The document controller has an array of document objects—one for each open document.

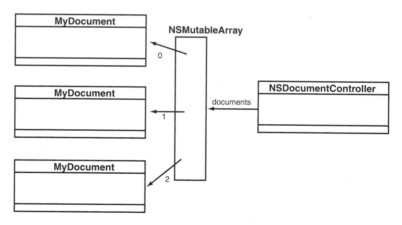

Figure 8.2   Document Controller

NSDocument

The document objects are instances of a subclass of **NSDocument**. In your RaiseMan application, for example, the document objects are instances of **MyDocument**. For many applications, you can simply extend **NSDocument** to do what you want; you don't have to worry about **NSDocumentController** or **NSWindowController** at all.

Saving

The menu items Save, Save As..., Save All, and Close are all different, but all deal with the same problem: getting the model into a file or file wrapper. (A file wrapper is a directory that looks like a file to the user.) To handle these menu items, your **NSDocument** subclass must implement one of three methods:

```
- (NSData *)dataRepresentationOfType:(NSString *)aType
```

Your document object supplies the model to go into the file as an **NSData** object. **NSData** is essentially a buffer of bytes. It is the easiest and most popular way to implement saving in a document-based application. Return nil if you are unable to create the data object and the user will get an alert sheet indicating that the save attempt failed. Notice that you are passed the type, which allows you to save the document in one of several possible formats. For example, if you wrote a graphics program, you might allow the user to save the image as a gif or a jpg file. When you are creating the data object, aType indicates the format that the user has requested for saving the document. If you are dealing with only one type of data, you may simply ignore aType.

```
- (NSFileWrapper *)fileWrapperRepresentationOfType:
                                            (NSString *)aType
```

Your document object returns the model as an **NSFileWrapper** object. It will be written to the filesystem in the location chosen by the user.

```
- (BOOL)writeToFile:(NSString *)filename
             ofType:(NSString *)type
```

Your document object is given the filename and the type. It is responsible for getting the model into the file. Return YES if the save is successful and NO if the save fails.

Loading

The Open..., Open Recent, and Revert To Saved menu items, although different, all deal with the same basic problem: getting the model from a file or file wrapper. To handle these menu items, your **NSDocument** subclass must implement one of three methods:

```
- (BOOL)loadDataRepresentation:(NSData *)docData
                        ofType:(NSString *)docType
```

Your document is passed an **NSData** object that holds the contents of the file that the user is trying to open. Return YES if you successfully create a model from the data. If you return NO, the user will get an alert panel telling him or her that the application was unable to read the file.

```
- (BOOL)loadFileWrapperRepresentation:(NSFileWrapper *)wrapper
                              ofType:(NSString *)docType
```

Your document reads the data from an **NSFileWrapper** object.

```
- (BOOL)readFromFile:(NSString *)filename
             ofType:(NSString *)docType
```

Your document object is passed the path. The document reads the data from the file.

After implementing one save method and one load method, your document will know how to read from and write to files. When opening a file, the document will read the document file before reading the nib file. As a consequence, you will not be able to send messages to the user interface objects immediately after loading the file (because they won't exist yet). To solve this problem, after the nib file is read, your document object is sent the following method:

```
- (void)windowControllerDidLoadNib:(NSWindowController *)x;
```

In your **NSDocument** subclass, you will implement this method to update the user interface objects as you did in Chapter 4.

If the user chooses Revert To Saved from the menu, the model is loaded but **windowControllerDidLoadNib:** is not called. You will, therefore, also have to update the user interface objects in the method that loads the data, just in case it was a revert operation. One common way to deal with this possibility is to check one of the outlets set in the nib file. If it is nil, the nib file has not been loaded and there is no need to update the user interface.

NSWindowController

The final class in the document architecture that we might discuss would be **NSWindowController**, but you will not initially need to worry about it. For each window that a document opens, it will typically create an instance of **NSWindow-Controller**. As most applications have only one window per document, the default behavior of the window controller is usually perfect. Nevertheless, you might want to create a custom subclass of **NSWindowController**. in the following situations:

- You need to have more than one window on the same document. For example, in a CAD program you might have a window of text that describes the solid and another window that shows a rendering of the solid.
- You want to put the user interface controller logic and model controller logic into separate classes.
- You want to create a window without a corresponding **NSDocument** object. You will do this in Chapter 9.

Saving and NSKeyedArchiver

Now that you have taught your object to encode and decode itself, you will use it to add saving and loading to your application. When it is time to save your people to a file, your **MyDocument** class will be asked to create an instance of **NSData**. Once your object has created and returned an **NSData** object, it will be automatically written to a file.

To create an **NSData** object, you will use the **NSKeyedArchiver** class. **NSKeyedarchiver** has the following class method:

```
+ (NSData *)archivedDataWithRootObject:(id)rootObject
```

This method archives the objects into the **NSData** object's buffer of bytes.

Once again, we return to the idea of "I told two friends, and they told two friends." When you encode an object, it will encode its objects, and they will encode their objects, and so on, and so on, and so on. What you will encode, then, is the employees array. It will encode the **Person** objects to which it has references. Each **Person** object (because you implemented **encodeWithCoder:**) will, in turn, encode the personName string and the expectedRaise float.

To add saving capabilities to your application, edit the method **dataRepresentationOfType:** so that it looks like this:

```
- (NSData *)dataRepresentationOfType:(NSString *)aType
{
    // End editing
    [personController commitEditing];

    // Create an NSData object from the employees array
    return [NSKeyedArchiver archivedDataWithRootObject:employees];
}
```

Loading and NSKeyedUnarchiver

Now you will add the ability to load files to your application. Once again, **NSDocument** has taken care of most of the details for you.

To do the unarchiving, you will use **NSKeyedUnarchiver**. **NSKeyedUnarchiver** has the following handy method:

```
+ (id)unarchiveObjectWithData:(NSData *)data
```

In your **MyDocument** class, edit your **loadDataRepresentation:ofType:** method to look like this:

```
- (BOOL)loadDataRepresentation:(NSData *)data ofType:(NSString *)aType
{
    NSLog(@"About to read data of type %@", aType);
    NSMutableArray *newArray;
    newArray = [NSKeyedUnarchiver unarchiveObjectWithData:data];

    if (newArray == nil) {
        return NO;
    } else {
        [self setEmployees:newArray];
        return YES;
    }
}
```

You could update the user interface after the nib file is loaded, but **NSArrayController** will handle it for you—the **windowControllerDidLoadNib:** method doesn't need to do anything. Leave it here for now because you will add to it in Chapter 10:

```
- (void)windowControllerDidLoadNib:(NSWindowController *)aController
{
    [super windowControllerDidLoadNib:aController];

}
```

Note that your document is asked which nib file to load when a document is opened or created. This method also needs no changing:

```
- (NSString *)windowNibName
{
    return @"MyDocument";
}
```

The window is automatically marked as edited when you make an edit, because you have properly enabled the undo mechanism. When you register your changes with the undo manager for this document, it will automatically mark the document as edited.

At this point, your application can read and write to files. Compile your application and try it out. Everything should work correctly, but all your files will have the extension "????". You need to define an extension for your application in the `Info.plist`.

Setting the Extension and Icon for the File Type

RaiseMan files will have the extension `.rsmn`, and `.rsmn` files will have an icon. First, find an `.icns` file and copy it into your project. A fine icon is found at `/Developer/Examples/AppKit/CompositeLab/BBall.icns`. Drag it from the Finder into the Groups and Files view of Xcode. Drop it in the Resources group (Figure 8.3).

Figure 8.3   Drag Icon into Project

Xcode will bring up a sheet. Make sure that you check Copy items into destination group's folder (Figure 8.4). This will copy the icon file into your project directory.

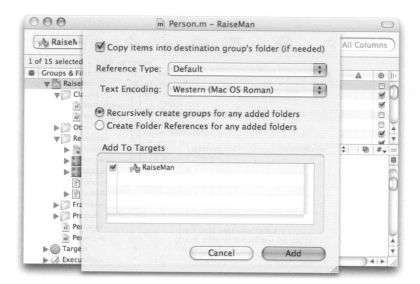

Figure 8.4 Make It a Copy

To set the document-type information, select the RaiseMan target in Xcode and open the info panel by choosing Show Inspector from the Project menu. Under the Properties tab, set the identifier for your application to be com.bignerdranch.RaiseMan. Set the Icon File to be BBall.icns. In the document types table view, set the name to be RaiseMan File. Set the Extensions to be rsmn. Set the icon for the file type to be BBall.icns. (You'll need to scroll the table to the right to see the Icon File column). See Figure 8.5.

Note that Xcode does incremental builds: Only edited files are recompiled. To accomplish this, it maintains many intermediate files between builds. To remove these intermediate files, you can clean the project by choosing Clean from the Build menu. In my experience, the changes that you have just made don't seem to take unless the project is cleaned and rebuilt.

Clean, build, and run your application. You should be able to save data to a file and read it in again. In Finder, the BBall.icns icon will be used as the icon for your .rsmn files.

An application is actually a directory. The directory contains the nib files, images, sounds, and executable code for the application. In Terminal, try the following:

```
> cd /Applications/TextEdit.app/Contents
> ls
```

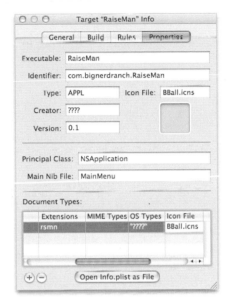

Figure 8.5 Specify Icon and Document Types

You will see three interesting things.

- The Info.plist file, which includes the information about the application, its file types, and associated icons. Finder uses this information.
- The MacOS/ directory, which contains the executable code.
- The Resources/ directory, which has the images, sounds, and nib files that the application uses. You will see localized resources for several different languages.

For the More Curious: Preventing Infinite Loops

The astute reader may be wondering: "If object A causes object B to be encoded, and object B causes object C to be encoded, and then object C causes object A to be encoded again, couldn't it just go around and around in an infinite loop?" It would, but **NSKeyedArchiver** was designed with this possibility in mind.

When an object is encoded, a unique token is also put onto the stream. Once archived, the object is added to the table of encoded objects under that token. When **NSKeyedArchiver** is told to encode the same object again, it simply puts a token in the stream.

When **NSKeyedUnarchiver** decodes an object from the stream, it puts both the object and its token in a table. The unarchiver finds a token with no associated data, so it knows to look up the object in the table instead of creating a new instance.

This idea led to the method in **NSCoder** that often confuses developers when they read the documentation:

```
- (void)encodeConditionalObject:(id)anObject forKey:(NSString *)aKey
```

This method is used when object A has a pointer to object B, but object A doesn't really care if B is archived. However, if *another* object *has* archived B, A would like the token for B put into the stream. If no other object has archived B, it will be treated like `nil`.

For example, if you were writing an **encodeWithCoder:** method for an **Engine** object (Figure 8.6), it might have an instance variable called `car` that is a pointer to the **Car** object that it is part of. If you are just archiving the **Engine**, you wouldn't want the entire **Car** archived. But if you were archiving the entire **Car**, you would want the `car` pointer set. In this case, you would make the **Engine** object encode the `car` pointer conditionally.

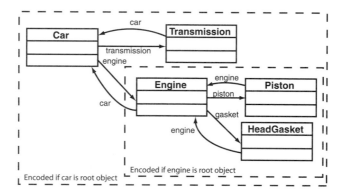

Figure 8.6   Conditional Encoding Example

For the More Curious: Versioning

As your application evolves, instance variables may be added and removed from your classes. The stream created by one version of your application may not be the same as the stream created by another version. How will you deal with this situation?

When an object is encoded, the name of the class and its version are added to the stream. To enable the developer to access this information, **NSCoder** has the following method:

```
- (unsigned)versionForClassName:(NSString *)className
```

Imagine that version 2 of the class **Person** had an instance variable called phone of type **NSString** but that version 1 did not. You could create a method like this:

```
- (id)initWithCoder:(NSCoder *)coder
{
    unsigned version;
    if (self = [super init]) {
        version = [coder versionForClassName:@"Person"];
        [self setPersonName:[coder decodeObjectForKey:@"personName"]];
        [self setExpectedRaise:
                        [coder decodeObjectForKey:@"expectedRaise"]];
        if (version > 1)
            [self setPhone:[coder decodeObjectForKey:@"phoneNumber"]];
        else
            // Set the phone number to a default value
            [self setPhone:@"(555)555-5555"];
    }
    return self;
}
```

How do you set the version of your class before it is encoded? **NSObject** declares the class method:

```
+ (void)setVersion:(int)theVersion
```

By default, the version is 0.

If you are using versioning, be sure to call **setVersion:** before any instances are encoded. One easy way to do so is via the class's **initialize** method. Just as **init** is sent to an instance to make sure that it is prepared for use, **initialize** is sent to a class to make sure that it is prepared for use. That is, before a class is used, it is automatically sent the message **initialize**.

A subclass inherits this method from its superclass. Thus, if you want the code executed only for this class (and not its subclasses), you will prefix it with an if statement:

```
+ (void)initialize
{
    // Am I the Person class?
    if (self == [Person class]) {
        [self setVersion:2];
    }
}
```

For the More Curious: Creating a Protocol

Creating your own protocol is very simple. Here is a protocol with two methods. It would typically be in a file called Foo.h.

```
@protocol Foo
- (void)bar:(int)x;
- (float)baz;
@end
```

If you had a class that wanted to implement the **Foo** protocol and the **NSCoding** protocol, it would look like this:

```
#import "Rex.h"
#import "Foo.h"

@interface Fido:Rex <Foo, NSCoding>
...etc...
@end
```

A class doesn't have to redeclare any method it inherits from its superclass, nor does it have to redeclare any of the methods from the protocols it implements. Thus, in our example, the interface file for the class **Fido** is not required to list any of the methods in **Rex** or **Foo** or **NSCoding**.

For the More Curious: Document-Based Applications Without Undo

The **NSUndoManager** for your application knows when unsaved edits have occurred. Also, the window is automatically marked as edited. But what if you've written an application and you are not registering your changes with the undo manager?

NSDocument keeps track of how many changes have been made. It has a method for this purpose:

- (void)**updateChangeCount:**(NSDocumentChangeType)change;

The NSDocumentChangeType can be one of the following: NSChangeDone, NSChangeUndone, or NSChangeCleared. NSChangeDone increments the change count, NSChangeUndone decrements the change count, and NSChangeCleared sets the change count to 0. The window is marked as dirty unless the change count is 0.

Chapter 9

Nib Files and NSWindowController

In RaiseMan, you are already using two nib files: MainMenu.nib and MyDocument.nib. MainMenu.nib is automatically loaded by **NSApplication** when the application first launches. MyDocument.nib is automatically loaded each time an instance of MyDocument is created. In this section, you will learn how to load nib files using **NSWindowController**.

Why would you want to load a nib file? Most commonly, your application will have several windows (such as a find panel and a preferences panel) that are used only occasionally. By putting off loading the nib until the window is needed, your application will launch faster. Furthermore, if the user never needs the window, your program will use less memory.

NSPanel

In this chapter, you will create a preferences panel. The panel will be an instance of **NSPanel**, which is a subclass of **NSWindow**. There really are not that many differences between a panel and a general window, but because a panel is meant to be auxiliary (as opposed to a document window), it acts a little differently.

- A panel can become the key window, but without becoming the main window. For example, when the user brings up a print panel, he can type into it (it is key), but the document the user was looking at remains the main window (that is what will be printed). **NSApplication** has a mainWindow outlet and a keyWindow outlet. Both outlets point at the same window unless a panel is involved; panels do not typically become the main window.
- If it has a close button, you can close a panel by pressing the Escape key.
- Panels do not appear in the window list in the Window menu. After all, if the user is looking for a window, the user is probably looking for a document, not a panel.

All windows have a Boolean variable called hidesOnDeactivate. If it is set to YES, the window will hide itself when the application is not active. Most document windows have this variable set to NO; most auxilary panels have it set to YES. This mechanism reduces screen clutter. You can set hidesOnDeactivate using the window inspector in Interface Builder.

Adding a Panel to the Application

The preferences panel that you are going to add will not do anything except appear for now. In Chapter 10, however, you will learn about user defaults. In that chapter, you will make the preferences panel actually do something.

The preferences panel will be in its own nib file. You will create a subclass of **NSWindowController** called **PreferenceController**. An instance of **PreferenceController** will act as the controller for the preferences panel. When creating an auxiliary panel, it is important to remember that you may want to reuse it in the next application. Creating a class to act just as a controller and a nib that contains only the panel makes it easier to reuse the panel in another application. Hip programmers would say, "By making the application more modular, we can maximize reuse." The modularity also makes it easier to divide tasks among several programmers. A manager can say, "Rex, you are in charge of the preferences panel. Only you may edit the nib file and the preference controller class."

The objects on the preferences panel will be connected to the preference controller. In particular, the preference controller will be the target of a color well and the check box. The preferences panel will appear when the user clicks on the Preferences... menu item. When running, it will look like Figure 9.1.

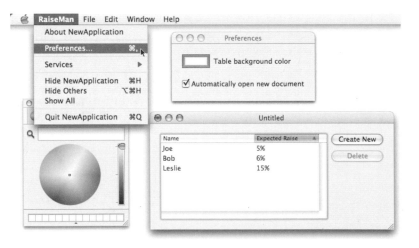

Figure 9.1 Completed Application

Figure 9.2 presents a diagram of the objects that you will create and the nib files in which they will reside.

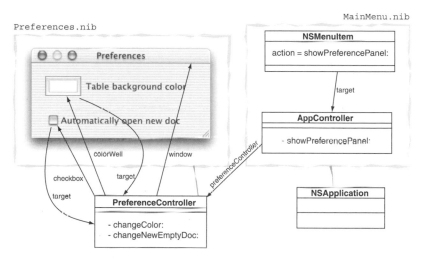

Figure 9.2   Object/Nib Diagram

MainMenu.nib

Open your project and create a new Objective-C class named **AppController**. Edit AppController.h to look like this:

```
#import <Cocoa/Cocoa.h>
@class PreferenceController;

@interface AppController : NSObject {
    PreferenceController *preferenceController;
}
- (IBAction)showPreferencePanel:(id)sender;

@end
```

Notice the Objective-C syntax:

```
@class PreferenceController;
```

This tells the compiler that there is a class **PreferenceController**. You can then make the declaration

```
    PreferenceController *preferenceController;
```

without importing the header file for **PreferenceController**. You could replace `@class PreferenceController;` with `#import "PreferenceController.h"`. This statement would import the header, and the compiler would learn that **PreferenceController** was a class. Because the `import` command requires the compiler to parse more files, `@class` will often result in faster builds.

Note that you must always import the superclass's header file, because the compiler needs to know which instance variables are declared in the superclass. In this case, `NSObject.h` is imported by `<Cocoa/Cocoa.h>`.

Setting Up the Menu Item

Save `AppController.h` and drag it from Xcode into `MainMenu.nib` in Interface Builder (Figure 9.3).

Figure 9.3   Parse AppController.h

You will see the **AppController** class in the nib's class browser (Figure 9.4).

Use the Classes menu to instantiate an instance of **AppController** (Figure 9.5).

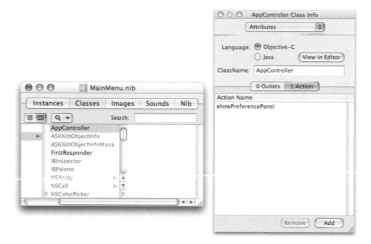

Figure 9.4   Outlets and Actions of AppController

Figure 9.5   Instantiate an Instance of AppController

Control-drag from the Preferences... menu item to the **AppController**. Make it the `target` and set the `action` to **showPreferencePanel:** (Figure 9.6).

Close the nib file.

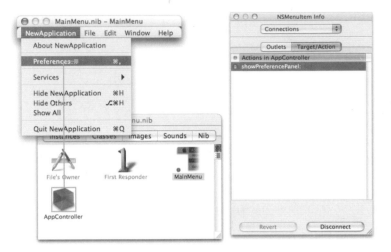

Figure 9.6   Set the Target of the Menu Item

AppController.m

Now you need to write the code for **AppController**. Make the contents of
AppController.m look like this:

```
#import "AppController.h"
#import "PreferenceController.h"

@implementation AppController

- (IBAction)showPreferencePanel:(id)sender
{
    // Is preferenceController nil?
    if (!preferenceController) {
        preferenceController = [[PreferenceController alloc] init];
    }
    [preferenceController showWindow:self];
}
- (void)dealloc
{
    [preferenceController release];
    [super dealloc];
}
@end
```

Notice that this file creates the instance of **PreferenceController** only once. If
the preferenceController variable is non-nil, it simply sends the message
showWindow: to the existing instance.

Preferences.nib

In Xcode, choose New File... from the File menu, and create a new Objective-C NSWindowController subclass. Name it **PreferenceController** (Figure 9.7).

Figure 9.7   Create Files for PreferenceController

Edit PreferenceController.h to look like this:

```
#import <Cocoa/Cocoa.h>

@interface PreferenceController : NSWindowController {
    IBOutlet NSColorWell *colorWell;
    IBOutlet NSButton *checkbox;
}
- (IBAction)changeBackgroundColor:(id)sender;
- (IBAction)changeNewEmptyDoc:(id)sender;
@end
```

In Interface Builder, create a new nib file. Choose Empty as the starting point (Figure 9.8).

Figure 9.8   Create a New Nib File

Save the new nib into the English.lproj directory in your project directory as Preferences.nib. When asked, insert the new nib into the project (Figure 9.9).

Figure 9.9   Add the Nib to the Project

Drag the PreferenceController.h file into the empty nib file (Figure 9.10).

Bring up the info panel, select File's Owner, and set its class to **PreferenceController** (Figure 9.11).

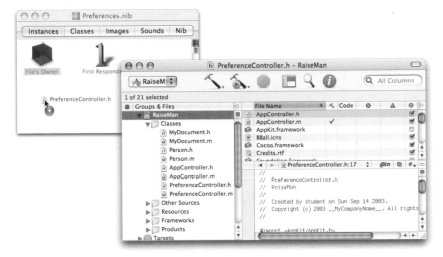

Figure 9.10   Parse PreferenceController.h

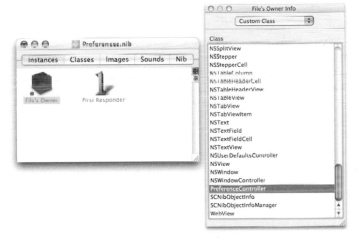

Figure 9.11   Set File's Owner to an Instance of PreferenceController

File's Owner

When a nib file is loaded into an application that has been running for a while, the objects that already exist need to establish some connection to the objects read from the nib file. File's Owner provides this connection. File's Owner is a placeholder in a nib file for an object that will already exist when the nib file is loaded. An object loading a nib file will provide the owner object. The owner is put into the place that File's Owner represents. In your application, the owner will be the instance of **PreferenceController** that was created by the **AppController**.

The use of File's Owner is confusing to many people. You will not instantiate **PreferenceController** in the nib file. Instead, you have just informed the nib file that the owner (which will be provided when the nib file is loaded) is a **PreferenceController**.

Lay Out the User Interface

Create a new panel by dragging a panel from the palette window and dropping it anywhere on the screen (Figure 9.12).

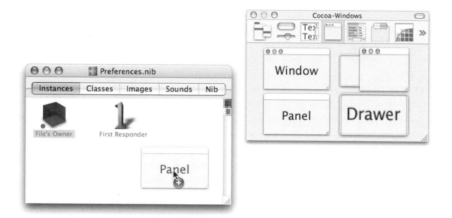

Figure 9.12   Create an Instance of NSPanel

Make the panel smaller and drop a color well and a check box on it. Label them as shown in Figure 9.13. (Check boxes have labels, but you will have to drag out a text field to label the color well.)

Figure 9.13   Completed Interface

Set the target of the color well to be File's Owner (your **PreferenceController**) and set the action to be **changeBackgroundColor:** (Figure 9.14).

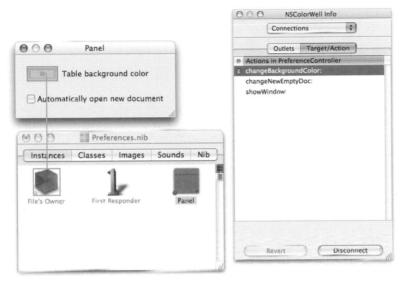

Figure 9.14   Set the Target of the Color Well

Also, make your **PreferenceController** be the target of the check box and set the action to be **changeNewEmptyDoc:**.

Set the `colorWell` outlet of File's Owner to the color well object. Set the `checkbox` outlet of File's Owner to the check box object. Set the `window` outlet of File's Owner to the panel (Figure 9.15).

Open the attributes inspector for the panel. Disable resizing.

Change the title on the window to Preferences. Save the nib file.

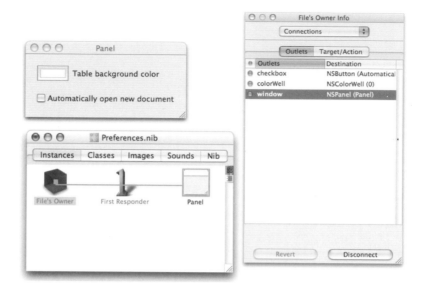

Figure 9.15   Set the Window Outlet of the File's Owner

PreferenceController.m

In Xcode, edit the PreferenceController.m to look like this:

```
#import "PreferenceController.h"

@implementation PreferenceController

- (id)init
{
    self = [super initWithWindowNibName:@"Preferences"];
    return self;
}

- (void)windowDidLoad
{
    NSLog(@"Nib file is loaded");
}

- (IBAction)changeBackgroundColor:(id)sender
{
    NSLog(@"Color changed: %@", [sender color]);
}

- (IBAction)changeNewEmptyDoc:(id)sender
{
    NSLog(@"Checkbox changed %d", [sender state]);
}

@end
```

Note that you set the name of the nib file to be loaded in the **init** method. This nib file will be loaded automatically when it is needed. The instance of **PreferenceController** will be substituted for the File's Owner in the nib file.

After the nib file is loaded, the **PreferenceController** will be sent **windowDidLoad**. It offers an opportunity (similar to **awakeFromNib** or **window-ControllerDidLoadNib:**) for the controller object to initialize the user interface objects that have been read from the nib file.

When sent **showWindow:** for the first time, the **NSWindowController** automatically loads the nib file and moves the window on screen and to the front. The nib file is loaded only once. When the user closes the preferences panel, it is moved off screen but not deallocated. The next time the user asks for the preferences panel, it is simply moved on screen.

The **changeBackgroundColor:** and **checkboxChanged:** methods are pretty boring right now—they simply print out a message. In Chapter 10, you will change them to update the user's defaults database.

Build and run the application. The new panel should appear, and altering the check box or color well should result in a message in the console (Figure 9.16).

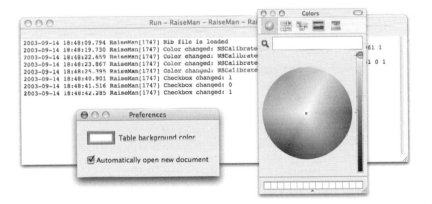

Figure 9.16 Completed Application

The first time a user encounters a color well, it may seem confusing. If you click on the edge of the color well, the edge becomes highlighted, the color panel appears, and the well is in "active" mode.

For the More Curious: NSBundle

A *bundle* is a directory of resources that may be used by an application. Resources include things like images, sounds, compiled code, and nib files. The class **NSBundle** is a very elegant way of dealing with bundles.

Your application is a bundle. In Finder, an application looks to the user like any other file, but it is really a directory filled with nib files, compiled code, and other resources. We call this directory the *main bundle* of the application.

Some resources in a bundle can be localized. For example, you could have two different versions of foo.nib, one for English speakers and one for French speakers. The bundle would have two subdirectories: English.lproj and French.lproj. You would put an appropriate version of foo.nib in each. When your application asks the bundle to load foo.nib, if the user has set the preferred language to French, the bundle will automatically load the French version of foo.nib. We will cover localization in Chapter 13.

To get the main bundle of an application, use the following code:

```
NSBundle *myBundle = [NSBundle mainBundle];
```

This is the most commonly used bundle. If you need to access resources in another directory, however, you could ask for the bundle at a certain path:

```
NSBundle *goodBundle;
goodBundle = [NSBundle bundleWithPath:@"~/.myApp/Good.bundle"];
```

Once you have an **NSBundle** object, you can ask it for its resources:

```
// Extension is optional
NSString *path = [goodBundle pathForImageResource:@"Mom"];
NSImage *momPhoto = [[NSImage alloc] initWithContentsOfFile:path];
```

A bundle may have a library of code. By asking for a class from the bundle, the bundle will link in the library and search for a class by that name:

```
Class newClass = [goodBundle classNamed:@"Rover"];
id newInstance = [[newClass alloc] init];
```

If you do not know the name of any classes in the bundle, you can simply ask for the principal class:

```
Class aClass = [goodBundle principalClass];
id anInstance = [[aClass alloc] init];
```

As you see, **NSBundle** is handy in many ways. In this section, the **NSBundle** was actually responsible (behind the scenes) for loading the nib file. If you wanted to load a nib file without an **NSWindowController**, you could do it like this:

```
BOOL successful = [NSBundle loadNibNamed:@"FindPanel"
                          owner:someObject];
```

Note that you would supply the object that will act as the File's Owner.

Challenge 1

Delete your color well and check box. Drop an **NSTabView** on the preferences panel. Put the color well under one tab, and put the check box under the other. Be sure to reconnect them.

Challenge 2

Create another nib file for a custom "About" panel. Use **NSBundle** to load it explicitly. To bring the window forward (and on screen if necessary), send it the message **makeKeyAndOrderFront:**.

Chapter 10

USER DEFAULTS

Many applications have preferences panels that allow the user to choose a preferred appearance or behavior. The user's choices go into the user defaults database in the user's home directory. Note that only the choices that vary from the factory defaults are saved in the user defaults database. If you go to ~/Library/Preferences, you can see your user defaults database. The files are in XML format; you can browse through them with a text editor.

The **NSUserDefaults** class allows your application to register the factory defaults, save the user's preferences, and read previously saved user preferences.

The color well that you dropped into the preferences window in Chapter 9 will determine the background color of the table view. When the user changes his or her preference, your application will write the new preference to the user defaults database. When your application creates a new document window, it will read from the user defaults database. As a consequence, only windows created after the change will be affected (Figure 10.1).

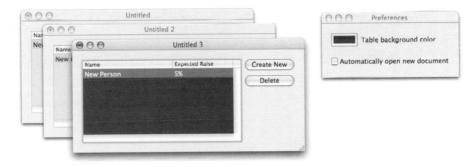

Figure 10.1   Completed Application

Also, have you noticed that every time you start the application, it brings up an untitled document? The Automatically open new document check box will allow the user to choose whether the untitled document should appear.

NSDictionary and NSMutableDictionary

Before you do anything with user defaults, we need to discuss the classes **NSDictionary** (Figure 10.2) and **NSMutableDictionary**. A dictionary is a collection of key-value pairs. The keys are strings, and the values are pointers to objects.

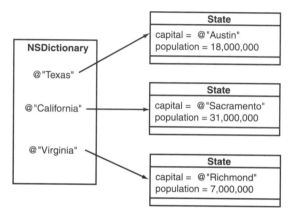

Figure 10.2   An Instance of NSDictionary

A string can be a key only once in a dictionary. When you want to know the value to which a key is bound, you will use the method **objectForKey:**.

```
anObject = [myDictionary objectForKey:@"foo"];
```

If the key is not in the dictionary, this method will return **nil**.

NSMutableDictionary is a subclass of **NSDictionary**. An instance of **NSDictionary** is created with all the keys and values it will ever have. You can query the object, but you cannot change it. **NSMutableDictionary**, on the other hand, allows you to add and remove keys and values.

NSDictionary

A dictionary is implemented as a hash table, so looking up keys is very fast. Here are a few of the most commonly used methods in the class **NSDictionary**:

- (NSArray *)**allKeys**

Returns a new array containing the keys in the dictionary.

- (unsigned)**count**

Returns the number of key-value pairs in the dictionary.

- (id)**objectForKey:**(NSString *)aKey

Returns the value associated with aKey, or returns nil if no value is associated with aKey.

- (NSEnumerator *)**keyEnumerator**

Enumerators are also known as *iterators* or *enumerations*. You can use them to step through all the members of a collection. The preceding method returns an enumerator that steps through all the keys in the dictionary. Here is how you would use one to list all of the key-value pairs in a dictionary:

```
NSString *s;
NSEnumerator *e = [myDict keyEnumerator];
while (s = [e nextObject]) {
    NSLog(@"key is %@, value is %@", s, [myDict objectForKey:s]);
}
```

- (NSEnumerator *)**objectEnumerator**

Returns an enumerator that steps through all the values in the dictionary. (The class **NSArray** also has a method **objectEnumerator**, which returns an enumerator that steps through the elements in the array.)

NSMutableDictionary

+ (id)**dictionary**

Creates an empty dictionary.

- (void)**removeObjectForKey:**(NSString *)aKey

Removes aKey and its associated value object from the dictionary.

- (void)**setObject:**(id)anObject **forKey:**(NSString *)aKey

Adds an entry to the dictionary, consisting of aKey and its corresponding value object anObject. The value object receives a retain message before being added to the dictionary. If aKey already exists in the receiver, the receiver's previous value object for that key is sent a release message and `anObject` takes its place.

NSUserDefaults

Every application comes with a set of defaults "from the factory." When a user edits his or her defaults, only the differences between the user's wishes and the factory defaults are stored in the user's defaults database. Thus, every time the application starts up, you need to remind it of the factory defaults. This operation is called *registering defaults*.

After registering, you will use the user defaults object to determine how the user wants the app to behave. This process is called *reading and using the defaults*. The data from the user's defaults database will be read automatically from the filesystem.

You will also create a preferences panel that will allow the user to set the defaults. The changes to the defaults object will be written automatically to the filesystem. This process is known as *setting the defaults* (Figure 10.3).

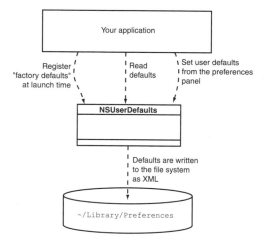

Figure 10.3   NSUserDefaults and the File System

Here are some commonly used methods that are implemented in **NSUserDefaults**:

    + (NSUserDefaults *)**standardUserDefaults**

Returns the shared defaults object.

- (void)**registerDefaults:**(NSDictionary *)dictionary

Registers the factory defaults for the application.

- (void)**setBool:**(BOOL)value   **forKey:**(NSString *)defaultName
- (void)**setFloat:**(float)value **forKey:**(NSString *)defaultName
- (void)**setInteger:**(int)value **forKey:**(NSString *)defaultName
- (void)**setObject:**(id)value **forKey:**(NSString *)defaultName

Methods for changing and saving a user's wishes.

- (BOOL)**boolForKey:**(NSString *)defaultName
- (float)**floatForKey:**(NSString *)defaultName
- (int)**integerForKey:**(NSString *)defaultName
- (id)**objectForKey:**(NSString *)defaultName

Methods for reading the defaults. If the user hasn't changed them, the factory defaults are returned.

- (void)**removeObjectForKey:**(NSString *)defaultName

Removes the user's preference, so that the application will return to using the factory defaults.

Precedence of Different Types of Defaults

We have talked about two levels of precedence: What the user writes to his or her defaults database overrides the factory defaults. Actually, several more levels of precedence exist. These levels of default settings are known as *domains*. Here are the domains used by an application, in order of priority:

Arguments: Passed on the command line. Most people start their applications by double-clicking on an icon instead of by working from the command line, so this feature is seldom used in a production app.

Application: What comes from the user's defaults database.

Global: What the user has set for his or her entire system.

Language: What is set based on the user's preferred language.

Registered defaults: The factory defaults for the app.

Setting the Identifier for the Application

What is the XML file in ~/Library/Preferences created for this application called? By default, it uses the identifier of the application that created it. You set this identifier in Chapter 8 to be com.bignerdranch.RaiseMan, so the filename will be com.bignerdranch.RaiseMan.plist.

Creating Keys for the Names of the Defaults

You will be registering, reading, and setting defaults in several different classes in your application. To make sure that you always use the same name, you should declare those strings in a single file and then simply #import that file into any file where you use the names.

There are several ways to do this (for example, you could use the C pre-processor's #define command), but most Cocoa programers use global variables for this purpose. Add the following lines to your PreferenceController.h file after the #import statement:

```
extern NSString *BNRTableBgColorKey;
extern NSString *BNREmptyDocKey;
```

Now actually define these variables in PreferenceController.m. Put them after the #import lines but before @implementation :

```
NSString *BNRTableBgColorKey = @"TableBackgroundColor";
NSString *BNREmptyDocKey = @"EmptyDocumentFlag";
```

Why would we declare global variables that simply contain a constant string? After all, you could just remember what the string was and type it in whenever you need it. The problem is that you might misspell the string. If the string is surrounded by quotes, the compiler will accept the misspelled string. In contrast, if you misspell the name of a global variable, the compiler will catch your error.

To keep the global variables from conflicting with another company's global variables, you have prefixed them with "BNR" (for Big Nerd Ranch). Global variables from Cocoa are prefixed with "NS." These prefixes are important only when you start using classes and frameworks developed by third parties. (Note that class names are also global. You might prefer to prefix all of your class names with "BNR" to keep them from conflicting with anyone else's classes.)

Registering Defaults

As mentioned near the end of Chapter 8, each class is sent the message **initialize** before any other message. To ensure that your defaults are registered early, you will override **initialize** in AppController.m:

```
+ (void)initialize {

    // Create a dictionary
    NSMutableDictionary *defaultValues = [NSMutableDictionary dictionary];

    // Archive the color object
    NSData *colorAsData = [NSKeyedArchiver archivedDataWithRootObject:
                                                [NSColor yellowColor]];

    // Put defaults in the dictionary
    [defaultValues setObject:colorAsData forKey:BNRTableBgColorKey];
    [defaultValues setObject:[NSNumber numberWithBool:YES]
                    forKey:BNREmptyDocKey];

    // Register the dictionary of defaults
    [[NSUserDefaults standardUserDefaults]
                                        registerDefaults: defaultValues],
    NSLog(@"registered defaults: %@", defaultValues);
}
```

Notice that we had to store the color as a data object. **NSColor** objects do not know how to write themselves out as XML, so we pack them into a data object that does. One group of classes does know how to write themselves out as XML, known as the *property list* classes: **NSString**, **NSArray**, **NSDictionary**, **NSCalendarDate**, **NSData**, and **NSNumber**. A property list comprises any combination of these classes. For example, a dictionary containing arrays of dates is a property list.

Let the User Edit the Defaults

Next, you will alter the **PreferenceController** class so that the preferences panel will actually cause the defaults database to get updated. Declare the following methods in PreferenceController.h:

```
- (NSColor *)tableBgColor;
- (BOOL)emptyDoc;
```

Make your `PreferenceController.m` file look like this:

```
#import "PreferenceController.h"

NSString *BNRTableBgColorKey = @"TableBackgroundColor";
NSString *BNREmptyDocKey = @"EmptyDocumentFlag";

@implementation PreferenceController

- (id)init
{
    self = [super initWithWindowNibName:@"Preferences"];
    return self;
}

- (NSColor *)tableBgColor
{
    NSUserDefaults *defaults;
    NSData *colorAsData;

    defaults = [NSUserDefaults standardUserDefaults];
    colorAsData = [defaults objectForKey:BNRTableBgColorKey];
    return [NSKeyedUnarchiver unarchiveObjectWithData:colorAsData];
}

- (BOOL)emptyDoc
{
    NSUserDefaults *defaults;

    defaults = [NSUserDefaults standardUserDefaults];
    return [defaults boolForKey:BNREmptyDocKey];
}

- (void)windowDidLoad
{
    [colorWell setColor:[self tableBgColor]];
    [checkbox setState:[self emptyDoc]];
}

- (IBAction)changeBackgroundColor:(id)sender
{
    NSColor *color = [sender color];
    NSData *colorAsData;
    colorAsData = [NSKeyedArchiver archivedDataWithRootObject:color];
    NSUserDefaults *defaults;
    defaults = [NSUserDefaults standardUserDefaults];
    [defaults setObject:colorAsData
                forKey:BNRTableBgColorKey];
}
```

```
- (IBAction)changeNewEmptyDoc:(id)sender
{
    [[NSUserDefaults standardUserDefaults] setBool:[sender state]
                                    forKey:BNREmptyDocKey];
}

@end
```

In the **windowDidLoad** method, you are reading the defaults and making the color well and check box reflect the current settings. In **changeBackground-Color:** and **changeNewEmptyDoc:**, you are updating the defaults database.

You should now be able to build and run your application. It will read and write to the defaults database, so the preferences panel will display the last color you chose and indicate whether the check box was on or off. You have not, however, actually done anything with this information yet, so the untitled document will continue to appear and the background of the table view will continue to be white.

Using the Defaults

Now you are going to use the defaults. First, you will make your **AppController** become a delegate of the **NSApplication** object and suppress the creation of an untitled document, depending on the user defaults. Then, in **MyDocument**, you will set the background color of the table view from the user defaults.

Suppressing the Creation of Untitled Documents

As before, there are two steps to creating a delegate: implementing the delegate method and setting the **delegate** outlet to point to the object (Figure 10.4).

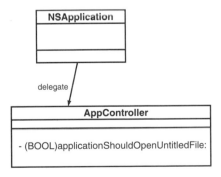

Figure 10.4   Delegate Suppresses Creation of Untitled Documents

Before automatically creating a new untitled document, the **NSApplication** object will send the message **applicationShouldOpenUntitledFile:** to its delegate. In AppController.m, add the following method:

```
- (BOOL)applicationShouldOpenUntitledFile:(NSApplication *)sender
{
    NSLog(@"applicationShouldOpenUntitledFile:");
    return [[NSUserDefaults standardUserDefaults]
                              boolForKey:BNREmptyDocKey];
}
```

To make your **AppController** the delegate of the **NSApplication** object, open the MainMenu.nib file, and control-drag from the File's Owner (which represents the **NSApplication** object) to your **AppController**. Set the delegate outlet (Figure 10.5).

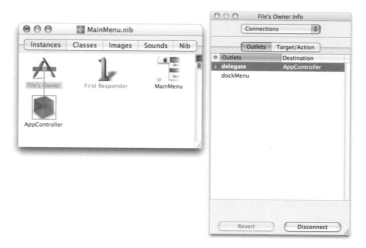

Figure 10.5   Select the delegate Outlet

Setting the Background Color on the Table View

After the nib file for a new document window has been successfully unarchived, your **MyDocument** object is sent the message **windowControllerDidLoadNib:**. At that moment, you can update the background color of the table view.

Of course, you will need an outlet to the table view. Add one in MyDocument.h:

```
@interface MyDocument : NSDocument
{
    IBOutlet NSArrayController *personController;
```

```
IBOutlet NSTableView *tableView;
NSMutableArray *employees;
}
```

To set the outlet, open MyDocument.nib, and drag in MyDocument.h. Control-drag from the File's Owner to the **NSTableView**. In the inspector, set the outlet named tableView, as shown in Figure 10.6.

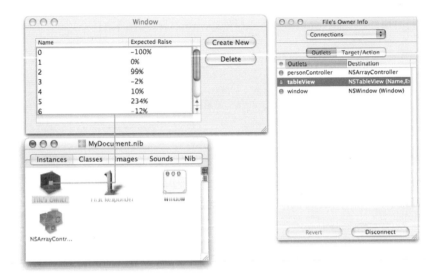

Figure 10.6   Select the tableView Outlet

You should already have this method in MyDocument.m; just edit it to look like this:

```
- (void)windowControllerDidLoadNib:(NSWindowController *)aController
{
    NSData *colorAsData;
    [super windowControllerDidLoadNib:aController];
    colorAsData = [[NSUserDefaults standardUserDefaults]
                            objectForKey:BNRTableBgColorKey];

    // Because of a Cocoa bug introduced in 10.3.0, this change
    // doesn't become visible on some systems until after a row has
    // been added to the table view
    [tableView setBackgroundColor:
            [NSKeyedUnarchiver unarchiveObjectWithData:colorAsData]];
}
```

Also, make sure that you import `PreferenceController.h` at the beginning of `MyDocument.m` so that you can use the global variables that are declared there.

Build and run your application.

For the More Curious: Reading and Writing Defaults from the Command Line

The user defaults database is found in `~/Library/Preferences/`. To edit it from the command line, you use a tool called *defaults*. For example, to see your defaults for Xcode, you can bring up the terminal and enter the following command:

```
defaults read com.apple.Xcode
```

You should see all of your defaults for Xcode. The first few lines of mine look like this:

```
{
    DocViewerHasSetPrefs = YES;
    NSNavBrowserPreferedColumnContentWidth = 155;
    NSNavLastCurrentDirectoryForOpen = "~/RaiseMan";
    NSNavLastRootDirectoryForOpen = "~";
    NSNavPanelExpandedSizeForOpenMode = "{518, 400}";
    NSNavPanelFileListModeForOpenMode = 1;
```

You can also write to the defaults database. To set Xcode's default directory in the **NSOpenPanel** to the /Users directory, you could enter this:

```
defaults write com.apple.Xcode NSNavLastRootDirectoryForOpen /Users
```

Try this:

```
defaults read com.bignerdranch.RaiseMan
```

To see your global defaults, enter this:

```
defaults read -globalDefaults
```

Challenge

Add a button to the preferences panel that will remove all of the user's defaults. Label the button Reset Preferences.

Chapter 11

USING NOTIFICATIONS

A user may have several RaiseMan documents open when he decides that it is too hard to read them with a purple background. The user opens the preferences panel, changes the background color, but then is disappointed to find that the color of the existing windows doesn't change. When the user sends you an e-mail about this problem, you reply, "The defaults are read only when the document window is created. Just save the document, close it, and open it again." In response, the user sends you a mean e-mail. It would be better to update all of the existing windows. But how many are there? Will you have to keep a list of all open documents?

What Notifications Are

The task is actually much easier than that. Every running application has an instance of **NSNotificationCenter**. The **NSNotificationCenter** functions much like a bulletin board. Objects register as interested in certain notifications ("Please write me if anyone finds a lost dog"); we call the registered object an *observer*. Other objects can then post notifications to the center ("I have found a lost dog"). That notification is subsequently forwarded to all objects that are registered as interested. We call the object that posted the notification a *poster*.

Lots of standard Cocoa classes post notifications: Windows send notifications that they have changed size. When the selection of a table view changes, the table view sends a notification. The notifications sent by standard Cocoa objects are listed in the online documentation.

In our example, you will register all of your **MyDocument** objects as observers. Your preference controller will post a notification when the user chooses a new color. When sent the notification, the **MyDocument** objects will change the background color.

Before the **MyDocument** object is deallocated, you must remove it from the notification center's list of observers. Typically, this is done in the **dealloc** method.

What Notifications Are Not

When programmers first hear about the notification center, they sometimes think it is a form of interprocess communications. They think, "I will create an observer in one application and post notifications from an object in another." This scheme doesn't work, however: A notification center allows objects in an application to send notifications to other objects *in that same application.* Notifications do not travel between applications.

NSNotification

Notification objects are very simple. A notification is like an envelope into which the poster will place information for the observers. It has two important instance variables: name and object. Nearly always, object is a pointer to the object that posted the notification. (It is analogous to a return address.)

Thus, the notification also has two interesting methods:

```
- (NSString *)name
- (id)object
```

NSNotificationCenter

The **NSNotificationCenter** is the brains of the operation. It allows you to do three things:

- Register observer objects.
- Post notifications.
- Unregister observers.

Here are some commonly used methods implemented by **NSNotification-Center**:

+ (NSNotificationCenter *)**defaultCenter**

Returns the notification center.

- (void)**addObserver:**(id)anObserver
          selector:(SEL)aSelector
              name:(NSString *)notificationName
            object:(id)anObject

Registers anObserver to receive notifications with the name notificationName and containing anObject (Figure 11.1). When a notification of
the name notificationName containing the object anObject is posted,
anObserver is sent an aSelector message with this notification as the
argument:

- If notificationName is nil, the notification center sends the observer
  all notifications with an object matching anObject.
- If anObject is nil, the notification center sends the observer all notifications with the name notificationName.

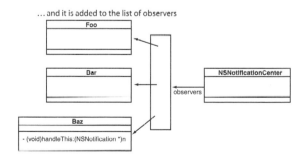

Figure 11.1   Registering for Notifications

The observer is *not* retained by the notification center. Notice that the method takes a selector.

- (void)**postNotification:**(NSNotification *)notification

Posts a notification to the notification center (Figure 11.2).

- (void)**postNotificationName:**(NSString *)aName
                         object:(id)anObject

Creates and posts a notification.

- (void)**removeObserver:**(id)observer

Removes observer from the list of observers.

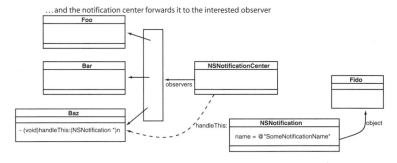

Figure 11.2   Posting a Notification

Posting a Notification

Posting a notification is the easiest step, so you will start there. When your
PreferenceController object receives a **changeBackgroundColor:**
message, it will post a notification with the new color. Name the notification
@"BNRColorChanged". (Experienced programmers put a prefix on the
notification so that it doesn't conflict with other notifications that may be
flying around the application.) Make your **changeBackgroundColor:** method
in PreferenceController.m look like this:

```
- (IBAction)changeBackgroundColor:(id)sender
{
    NSColor *color = [sender color];
    NSData *colorAsData;
    colorAsData = [NSKeyedArchiver archivedDataWithRootObject:color];
    [[NSUserDefaults standardUserDefaults] setObject:colorAsData
                                    forKey:BNRTableBgColorKey];

    NSNotificationCenter *nc;
    nc = [NSNotificationCenter defaultCenter];
    NSLog(@"Sending notification BNRColorChanged");
    [nc postNotificationName:@"BNRColorChanged" object:self];
}
```

Registering as an Observer

To register as an observer, you must supply several things: the object that is the
observer, the names of the notifications in which it is interested, and the message
that you want sent when an interesting notification arrives. You can also specify
that you are interested only in notifications with a certain object attached to
them. (Remember that this is often the object that posted the notification. Thus,
when you specify that you want resize notifications with a certain window
attached, you are saying that you are interested only in the resizing of that
particular window.)

Edit your **MyDocument** class's **init** method as follows:

```
- (id)init
{
    if (self = [super init]) {
        employees = [[NSMutableArray alloc] init];
        NSNotificationCenter *nc;
        nc = [NSNotificationCenter defaultCenter];
        [nc addObserver:self
                selector:@selector(handleColorChange:)
```

```
            name:@"BNRColorChanged"
        object:nil];
    NSLog(@"Registered with notification center");
    }
    return self;
}
```

Unregistering the Observer

Remember to remove your document from the notification center if it is closed. Edit the **dealloc** method in MyDocument.m as follows:

```
- (void)dealloc
{
    [self setEmployees:nil];

    NSNotificationCenter *nc;
    nc = [NSNotificationCenter defaultCenter];
    [nc removeObserver:self];
    NSLog(@"Unregistered with notification center: %@",
                                                [self fileName]);
    [super dealloc];
}
```

Handling the Notification When It Arrives

When the notification arrives, the method **handleColorChange:** is called. Add this method to your MyDocument.m file:

```
- (void)handleColorChange:(NSNotification *)note
{
    NSLog(@"Received notification: %@", note);
    PreferenceController *sender = [note object];
    NSColor *newColor = [sender tableBgColor];

    // Due to bug in 10.3.0,  this change will not be visible
    // on some systems unless the table view has at least one row.
    [tableView setBackgroundColor:newColor];
    [tableView setNeedsDisplay:YES];
}
```

Build and run the application. Open several windows and change the preferred background color. Note that all of them receive the notification and change color immediately.

For the More Curious: Delegates and Notifications

If an object has made itself the delegate of some standard Cocoa object, it is probably interested in receiving notifications from that object as well. For example, if you have implemented a delegate to handle the **windowShouldClose:** delegate method for a window, that same object is likely to be interested in the NSWindowDidResizeNotification from that same window.

If a standard Cocoa object has a delegate and posts notifications, the delegate is automatically registered as an observer for the methods it implements. If you are implementing such a delegate, how would you know what to call the method?

The naming convention is simple: Start with the name of the notification. Remove the "NS" from the beginning and make the first letter lowercase. Remove the "Notification" from the end. Add a colon. For example, to be notified that the window has posted an NSWindowDidResizeNotification, the delegate would implement the following method:

- (void)**windowDidResize:**(NSNotification *)aNotification

This method will be called automatically after the window resizes. You can also find this method listed in the documentation and header files for the class **NSWindow.**

For the More Curious: The userInfo Dictionary

If you wanted to include more than just the poster with the notification, you would use the user info dictionary. Every notification has a variable called userInfo that can be attached to an **NSDictionary** filled with other information that you want to pass to the observers:

```
NSDictionary *d = [NSDictionary dictionaryWithObject:@"867-5309"
                                              forKey:@"phoneNumber"];
NSNotification *n = [NSNotification notificationWithName:@"BNRFoo"
                                                 object:self
                                               userInfo:d];
[[NSNotificationCenter defaultCenter] postNotification:n];
```

On the other end, the receiver of the notification can use the data in the
userInfo dictionary:

```
- (void)myMethod:(NSNotification *)note
{
    NSString *thePhoneNumber;
    thePhoneNumber = [[note userInfo] objectForKey:@"phoneNumber"];
}
```

Just as you defined global variables to hold onto constant strings in Chapter 10
so that the compiler would catch your misspellings, most programmers define
global variables for the names of their notifications and the keys in their user info
dictionary.

Challenge 1

Make your application beep when it gives up its active status. **NSApplication**
posts an NSApplicationDidResignActiveNotification notification. Your
AppController is a delegate of **NSApplication**. **NSBeep()** will cause a system
beep.

Challenge 2

In **PreferenceController**, put the new color into the user info dictionary of the
BNRColorChanged notification. When **MyDocument** receives the notification, have
it read the new color out of the user info dictionary instead of calling back to the
PreferenceController.

Chapter 12
USING ALERT PANELS

Occasionally, you will want to warn the user about something by means of an alert panel. Alert panels are easy to create. While most things in Cocoa are object-oriented, showing an alert panel is typically done with a C function: **NSRunAlertPanel()**. Here is the declaration:

```
int NSRunAlertPanel(NSString *title, NSString *msg,
      NSString *defaultButton, NSString *alternateButton,
      NSString *otherButton, ...);
```

The code:

```
int choice = NSRunAlertPanel(@"Fido", @"Rover",
                             @"Rex", @"Spot", @"Fluffy");
```

would result in the alert panel shown in Figure 12.1.

Figure 12.1   Example Alert Panel

Note that the icon on the panel will be the icon for the responsible application. The second and third buttons are optional. To prevent a button from appearing, replace its label with nil.

The **NSRunAlertPanel()** function returns an int that indicates which button the user clicked. There are global variables for these constants: NSAlertDefaultReturn, NSAlertAlternateReturn, and NSAlertOtherReturn.

Note that **NSRunAlertPanel()** takes a variable number of arguments. The second string may include printf-like tokens. Values supplied after the otherButton label will be substituted in. Thus the code

```
int choice = NSRunAlertPanel(@"Fido", @"Rover is %d",
                            @"Rex", @"Spot", nil, 8);
```

would result in the alert panel shown in Figure 12.2.

Figure 12.2   Another Example Alert Panel

Alert panels run *modally*; that is, other windows in the application don't receive events until the alert panel has been dismissed.

Make the User Confirm the Deletion

If the user clicks the delete button, an alert panel should display before the records are deleted (Figure 12.3).

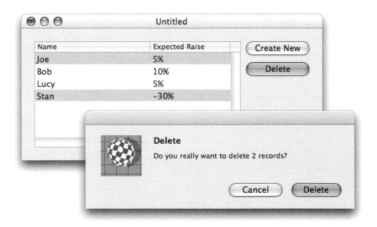

Figure 12.3   Completed Application

To enable this behavior, open MyDocument.nib, select the table view, and open the inspector. Allow the user to make multiple selections (Figure 12.4).

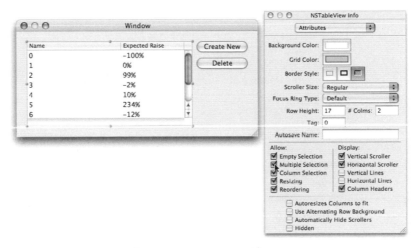

Figure 12.4   Inspect TableView

You now want the Delete button to send a message to **MyDocument**, which will ask the user to confirm the deletion. If the user confirms this choice, **MyDocument** will send the **remove:** message to the array controller to remove the selected **Person** objects.

In Xcode, open the MyDocument.h file and add the method that will be triggered by the Delete button:

```
@interface MyDocument : NSDocument
{
    IBOutlet NSArrayController *personController;
    NSMutableArray *employees;
}
- (void)insertObject:(Person *)p inEmployeesAtIndex:(int)index;
- (void)removeObjectFromEmployeesAtIndex:(int)index;
- (void)setEmployees:(NSMutableArray *)array;
- (void)remove:(id)sender;
@end
```

Implement the **remove:** method in MyDocument.m:

```
- (void)remove:(id)sender
{
    NSArray *selectedPeople = [personController selectedObjects];
```

```
    // Run an alert panel
    int choice = NSRunAlertPanel(@"Delete",
                        @"Do you really want to delete %d records?",
                        @"Delete", @"Cancel", nil,
                        [selectedPeople count]);

    // If the user chose Yes, tell the array controller to
    // delete the people
    if (choice == NSAlertDefaultReturn) {
        [personController remove:sender];
    }
}
```

Drag the MyDocument.h file from the Xcode project into the MyDocument.nib window. Disconnect the target outlet of the Delete button, and control-drag from the button to the File's Owner icon to make the File's Owner be the new target. Set the action to **remove:**.

Build and run your application.

As you can see, **NSRunAlertPanel()** is very easy to use, but rather limiting. If you need more control over your alert panel, use the class **NSAlert**. **NSAlert** allows you to change the icon, have more than three buttons, run the alert as a sheet, and offer customized help.

Challenge

Add another button to the alert panel that says Keep, but no raise. Instead of deleting the employees, this button will simply set the raises of the selected employees to zero.

Chapter 13
LOCALIZATION

If the application you create is useful, you will want to share it with all the people of the world. Unfortunately, we don't all speak the same language. Suppose you wish to make your RaiseMan application available to French speakers. We would say, "You are going to *localize* RaiseMan for French speakers."

If you are creating an application for the world, you should plan on localizing it for at least the following languages: English, French, Spanish, German, Dutch, Italian, and Japanese. Clearly, you do not want to have to rewrite the entire app for each language. In fact, our goal is to ensure that you don't have to rewrite any Objective-C code for each language. That way all the nations of the world can use a single executable in peace and harmony.

Instead of creating multiple executables, you will localize resources and create string tables. Inside your project directory, an English.lproj directory holds all the resources for English speakers: nib files, images, and sounds. To localize the app for French speakers, you will add a French.lproj directory. The nibs, images, and sounds in this directory will be appropriate for French speakers. At runtime, the app will automatically use the version of the resource appropriate to the user's language preference.

What about the places in your application where you use the language programmatically? For example, in MyDocument.m, you have the following line of code:

```
int choice = NSRunAlertPanel(@"Delete",
                        @"Do you really want to delete %d records?",
                        @"Delete", @"Cancel", nil,
                        [selectedPeople count]);
```

That alert panel is not going to bring about world peace. For each language, you will have a table of strings. You will ask **NSBundle** to look up the string, and it will automatically use the version appropriate to the user's language preference (Figure 13.1).

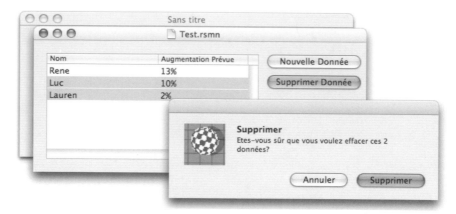

Figure 13.1   Completed Application

Localizing a Nib File

In Xcode, select—but do not open—MyDocument.nib and bring up the info panel. Click the Add Localization button (Figure 13.2).

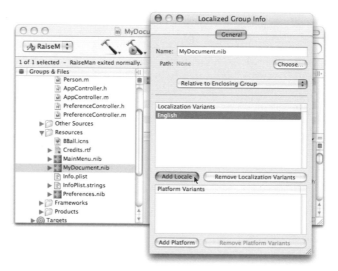

Figure 13.2   Create a French Version of MyDocument.nib

You will be prompted for a locale. Choose French.

If you look in Finder, you will see that a copy of `English.lproj/`
`MyDocument.nib` has been created in `French.lproj`. You will francophize this
copy. In Xcode, under the Resources group, you will have two versions of
`MyDocument.nib`: English and French, as shown in Figure 13.3. Double-click on
the French version to open it in Interface Builder.

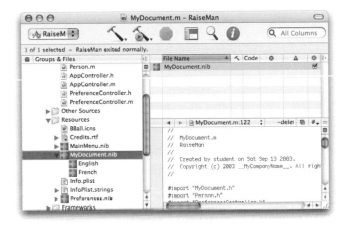

Figure 13.3   Completed Application

Make your window look like Figure 13.4.

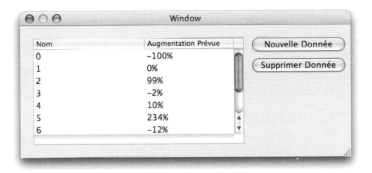

Figure 13.4   Completed Interface

To type in characters with accents, you will need to use the option key. For
example, to type "é", type the "e", while holding down the option key, and then
type "e" again. (In the International page of System Preferences, you can add the
Keyboard Viewer to your input menu. If you are using a lot of unusual characters,
the Keyboard Viewer can help you learn which key combinations create which
characters.)

At this point, you have created a localized resource. Notice that if you make a lot of changes to your program, you may need to update both nib files (the French version and the English version). For this reason, it is a good idea to wait until the application is completed and tested before localizing it.

Build your app. Before running it, bring up the International page of the System Preferences application. Set Français as your preferred language. Now run your application. Note that the French version of the nib is used automatically.

String Tables

For each language, you can create several string tables. A string table is a file with the extension `.strings`. For example, if you had a find panel, you might create a `Find.strings` file for each language. This file would have the phrases used by the find panel, such as "None found."

The string table is just a collection of key-value pairs. The key and the value are strings surrounded by quotes, and the pair is terminated with a semicolon:

```
"Key1" = "Value1";
"Key2" = "Value2";
```

To find a value for a given key, you use **NSBundle**:

```
NSBundle *main;
NSString *aString;

main = [NSBundle mainBundle];
aString = [main localizedStringForKey:@"Key1"
                                value:@"DefaultValue1"
                                table:@"Find"];
```

This would search for the value for "Key1" in the `Find.strings` file. If it is not found in the user's preferred language, the second-favorite language is searched, and so on. If the key is not found in any of the user's languages, "DefaultValue1" is returned. If you do not supply the name of the table, `Localizable` is used. Most simple applications just have one string table for each language: `Localizable.strings`.

Creating String Tables

To create a `Localizable.strings` file for English speakers, choose the New File... menu item in Xcode. Create an empty file, and name it `Localizable.strings`. Save it in the `English.lproj` directory (Figure 13.5).

Figure 13.5   Create an English String Table

Edit the new file to have the following text:

```
"Delete" = "Delete";
"SureDelete" = "Do you really want to delete %d records?";
"Cancel" = "Cancel";
```

Save it.

Now create a localized version of that file for French. Select the English version of the `Localizable.strings` file in Xcode, bring up the info panel, and create a localized variant (Figure 13.6).

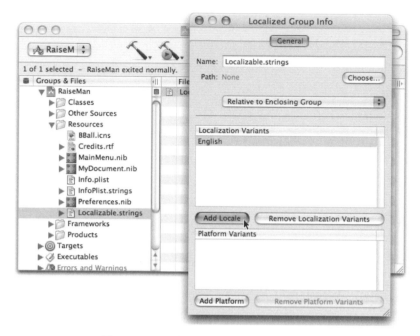

Figure 13.6   Create a French String Table

Edit the file to look like this:

```
"Delete" = "Supprimer";
"SureDelete" =
     "Etes-vous sûr que vous voulez effacer ces %d données?";
"Cancel" = "Annuler";
```

(To create the "u" with the circumflex, type "i" while holding down the option key, and then type "u". To type "é", type "e" while holding down the option key, and then type "e" again.)

When saving a file with unusual characters, you should use the Unicode (UTF-8) file encoding. While the French Localizable.strings file is active in Xcode, choose Unicode from the File Encodings submenu in the Format menu (Figure 13.7). (If you are presented with a panel asking if you wish to convert the file to UTF-8, click the button labeled Convert.)

Save the file.

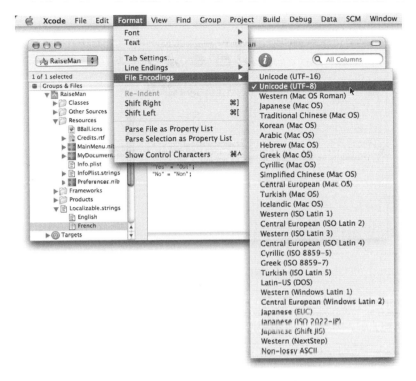

Figure 13.7 Change the File Encoding

Using the String Table

In an app with just one string table, you would probably do this:

```
NSString *deleteString;
deleteString = [[NSBundle mainBundle]
                localizedStringForKey:@"Delete"
                                value:@"Delete?"
                                table:nil];
```

Fortunately, there is a macro defined in `NSBundle.h` for this purpose:

```
#define NSLocalizedString(key, comment)
        [[NSBundle mainBundle] localizedStringForKey:(key)
                                              value:@""
                                              table:nil]
```

(Notice that the comment is completely ignored by this macro. It is, however, used by a tool called *genstrings*, which scans through your code for calls to the macro NSLocalizedString and creates a skeleton string table. This string table includes the comment.)

In MyDocument.m, find the place where you run the alert panel. Replace that line with this one:

```
int choice = NSRunAlertPanel
    (NSLocalizedString(@"Delete", @"Delete"),
    NSLocalizedString(@"SureDelete",
                    @"Do you really want to delete %d records?"),
    NSLocalizedString(@"Delete", @"Delete"),
    NSLocalizedString(@"Cancel", @"Cancel"),
    nil,
    [selectedPeople count]);
```

Build the app. Change your preferred language back to French in System Preferences, and run the app again. When you delete a row from the table, you should get an alert panel in French.

For the More Curious: nibtool

Clearly, as you develop and localize many applications, you will develop a set of common translations. It would be handy to have an automated way to get the translated strings into a nib file. This is one of several uses for nibtool.

The nibtool command, which is run from the terminal, can list the classes or objects in a nib file. It can also dump the localizable strings into a plist. Here is how you would dump the localizable strings from the English.lproj/MyDocument.nib file into a file named Doc.strings:

```
> cd RaiseMan/English.lproj
> nibtool -L MyDocument.nib > Doc.strings
```

The resulting Doc.strings file would look something like this:

```
/* NSButton (Delete Record) : <title:Delete Record> (oid:24) */
"Delete Record" = "Delete Record";

/* NSTableColumn : <title:Expected Raise> (oid:53) */
"Expected Raise" = "Expected Raise";

/* NSTableColumn : <title:Name> (oid:54) */
"Name" = "Name";

/* NSButton (New Empty) : <title:New Empty> (oid:23) */
```

```
"New Empty" = "New Empty";

/* NSWindow (Window) : <title:Window> (oid:5) */
"Window" = "Window";
```

To create a Spanish dictionary for this nib file, you could edit the file to look like this:

```
/* NSButton (Delete Record) : <title:Delete Record> (oid:24) */
"Delete Record" = "Borrar Archivo";

/* NSTableColumn : <title:Expected Raise> (oid:53) */
"Expected Raise" = "Aumento Esperado";

/* NSTableColumn : <title:Name> (oid:54) */
"Name" = "Nombre";

/* NSButton (New Empty) : <title:New Empty> (oid:23) */
"New Empty" = "Crear Nuevo Archivo";

/* NSWindow (Window) : <title:Window> (oid:5) */
"Window" = "Ventana";
```

To substitute the strings in a nib file with their Spanish equivalents from this dictionary, you could create a new nib file like this:

```
> mkdir ../Spanish.lproj
> nibtool -d Doc.strings -w ../Spanish.lproj/MyDocument.nib
MyDocument.nib
```

To learn more about nibtool, use Unix's man command:

```
> man nibtool
```

For the More Curious: Explicit Ordering of Tokens in Format Strings

As text is moved from language to language, besides the words changing, the order of the words changes. For example, in one language the words may be laid out like this: "Ted wants a scooter." In another, the order might be "A scooter is what Ted wants." Suppose you try to localize the format string to be used like this:

```
NSString * theFormat = NSLocalizedString(@"Wants", @"%@ wants a %@");
NSString *x = [NSString stringWithFormat:theFormat, @"Ted",
@"Scooter"];
```

For the first language,

```
"Wants" = "%@ wants a %@";
```

will work fine.

For the second language, you would need to explicitly indicate the index of the token you want to insert. This is done with a number and the dollar sign:

```
"Wants =   "A %2$@ is what %1$@ wants".
```

Chapter 14

CUSTOM VIEWS

All visible objects in an application are either windows or views. In this chapter, you will create a subclass of **NSView**. From time to time, you may need to create a custom view to do custom drawing or event handling. Even if you do not plan to do custom drawing or event handling, by learning how to create a new view class, you will learn a lot about how Cocoa works.

Windows are instances of the class **NSWindow**. Each window has a collection of views, each of which is responsible for a rectangle of the window. The view draws inside that rectangle and handles mouse events that occur there. A view may also handle keyboard events. You have worked with several subclasses of **NSView** already: **NSButton**, **NSTextField**, **NSTableView**, and **NSColorWell** are all views. (Note that a window is not a subclass of **NSView**.)

The View Hierarchy

Views are arranged in a hierarchy (Figure 14.1). The window has a content view that completely fills its interior. The content view usually has several subviews. Each subview may have subviews of its own. Every view knows its superview, its subviews, and the window it lives on.

Here are the relevant methods from **NSView**:

```
- (NSView *)superview;
- (NSArray *)subviews;
- (NSWindow *)window;
```

Any view can have subviews, but most don't. The following five views commonly have subviews:

- The content view of a window.
- **NSBox**. The contents of a box are its subviews.

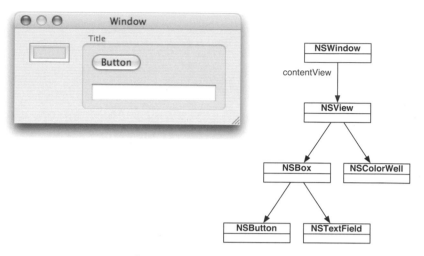

Figure 14.1   Views Hierarchy

- **NSScrollView**. If a view appears in a scroll view, it is a subview of the scroll view. The scroll bars are also subviews of the scroll view.
- **NSSplitView**. Each view in a split view is a subview (Figure 14.2).

Figure 14.2   A Scroll View in a Split View

- **NSTabView**. As the user chooses different tabs, different subviews are swapped in and out (Figure 14.3).

Figure 14.3   A Tab View

Get a View to Draw Itself

In this section, you will create a very simple view that will appear and paint itself green. It will look like Figure 14.4.

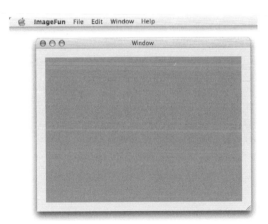

Figure 14.4   Completed Application

Create a new project of type Cocoa Application (Figure 14.5). Name it ImageFun.

Figure 14.5 Choose Project Type

After the new project is created, open MainMenu.nib, and select **NSView** in the classes browser (Figure 14.6).

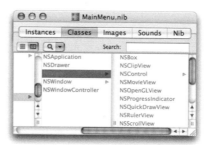

Figure 14.6 Select NSView

Press Enter to create a subclass, and name it **StretchView** (Figure 14.7).

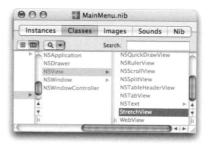

Figure 14.7 Create the StretchView Class

Create the files for **StretchView** (Figure 14.8).

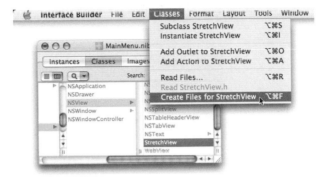

Figure 14.8   Create the Files for the StretchView Class

Save the files in the project directory.

Create an Instance of a View Subclass

Next, you will create an instance of your class by dragging out a CustomView placeholder and dropping it on the window (Figure 14.9).

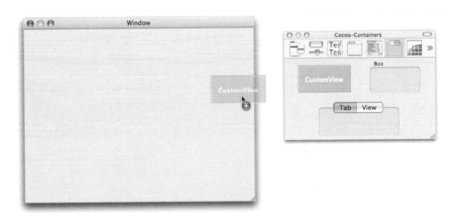

Figure 14.9   Drop a View on the Window

Resize the view to fill most of the window. Open the info panel and set the class of the view to be **StretchView** (Figure 14.10).

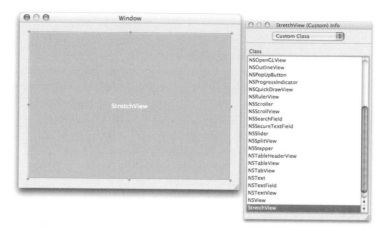

Figure 14.10   Set the Class of the View to StretchView

Notice that creating an instance of a view is different from creating an instance of a controller object like **AppController**. To create an instance of **AppController** in Chapter 2, you used the Instantiate menu item. When creating a view, you must attach it to a window and give it a size and location in that window.

Size Info

Your **StretchView** object is a subview of the window's content view. This point raises an interesting question: What happens to the view when the superview resizes? A page in the info panel allows you to specify that behavior. Open the size info panel, and set it as shown in Figure 14.11. Now it will grow and shrink as necessary to keep the distance from its edges to the edges of its superview constant.

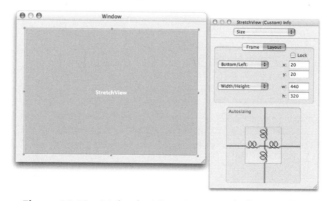

Figure 14.11   Make the View Resize with the Window

If you wanted the view to stay the same size, you could let the distance between the edges of the view and the edges of the superview grow and shrink. In this exercise, you do not want this behavior. But in a parallel universe where you did, the inspector would look like Figure 14.12.

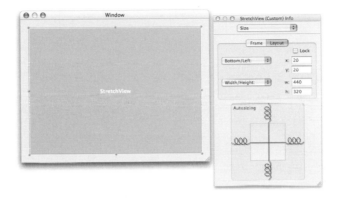

Figure 14.12 Not This!

Save and close the nib file.

drawRect:

When a view needs to draw itself, it is sent the message **drawRect:** with the rectangle that needs to be drawn or redrawn. The method is called automatically—you never need to call it directly. Instead, if you know that a view needs redrawing, you send the view the **setNeedsDisplay:** message:

```
[myView setNeedsDisplay:YES];
```

This message informs myView that it is "dirty." After the event has been handled, the view will be redrawn.

Before calling **drawRect:**, the system *locks focus* on the view. Each view has its own graphics context, which includes things like the view's coordinate system, its current color, its current font, and the clipping rectangle. When the focus is locked on a view, the view's graphics context is active. When the focus is unlocked, the graphics context is no longer active. Whenever you issue drawing commands, they will be executed in the current graphics context.

You can use **NSBezierPath** to draw lines, circles, curves, and rectangles. You can use **NSImage** to create composite images on the view. In this example, you will fill the entire view with a green rectangle.

Open StretchView.m and add the following code to the **drawRect:** method:

```
- (void)drawRect:(NSRect)rect
{
    NSRect bounds = [self bounds];
    [[NSColor greenColor] set];
    [NSBezierPath fillRect:bounds];
}
```

As shown in Figure 14.13, NSRect is a struct with two members: origin, which is an NSPoint, and size, which is an NSSize.

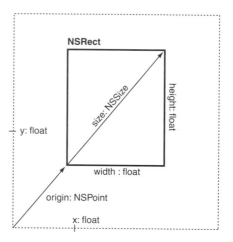

Figure 14.13   NSRect, NSSize, and NSPoint

NSSize is a struct with two members: width and height (both floats).

NSPoint is a struct with two members: x and y (both floats).

For performance reasons, structs are used in a few places instead of Objective-C classes. For completeness, here is the list of all the structs in Cocoa that you are likely to use: NSSize, NSPoint, NSRect, NSRange, NSDecimal, NSZone, and NSAffineTransformStruct. NSRange is used to define subranges. NSDecimal describes numbers with very specific precision and rounding behavior. NSZone specifies pages of virtual memory. NSAffineTransformStruct describes linear transformations of graphics.

Notice that your view knows its location as an NSRect called bounds. In this method, you fetched the bounds rectangle, set the current color to green, and filled the entire bounds rectangle with the current color.

The NSRect that is passed as an argument to the view is the region that is "dirty" and needs redrawing. It may be less than the entire view. If you are doing very time-consuming drawing, redrawing only the dirty rectangle may speed up your application considerably.

Notice that **setNeedsDisplay:** will trigger the entire visible region of the view to be redrawn. If you wish to be more precise about which part of the view needs redrawing, use **setNeedsDisplayInRect:** instead:

```
NSRect dirtyRect;
dirtyRect = NSMakeRect(0, 0, 50, 50);
[myView setNeedsDisplayInRect:dirtyRect];
```

Build and run your app. Try resizing the window.

Drawing with NSBezierPath

If you want to draw lines, ovals, curves, or polygons, you can use **NSBezierPath**. In this chapter, you have already used the **NSBezierPath**'s **fillRect:** class method to color your view. In this section, you will use **NSBezierPath** to draw lines connecting random points (Figure 14.14).

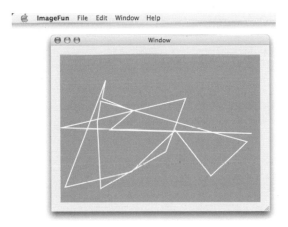

Figure 14.14 Completed Application

The first thing you will need is an instance variable to hold the instance of **NSBezierPath**. You will also create an instance method that returns a random point in the view. Open StretchView.h and make it look like this:

```
#import <Cocoa/Cocoa.h>

@interface StretchView : NSView
{
    NSBezierPath *path;
}
- (NSPoint)randomPoint;

@end
```

In StretchView.m, you will override **initWithFrame:**. As the designated initializer for **NSView**, **initWithFrame:** will be called automatically when an instance of your view is created. In your version of **initWithFrame:**, you will create the path object and fill it with lines to random points. Make StretchView.m look like this:

```
#import "StretchView.h"

@implementation StretchView

- (id)initWithFrame:(NSRect)rect
{
    int i;
    NSPoint p;

    if (self = [super initWithFrame:rect]) {
      // Seed the random number generator
      srandom(time(NULL));

      // Create a path object
      path = [[NSBezierPath alloc] init];
      [path setLineWidth:3.0];
      p = [self randomPoint];
      [path moveToPoint: p];
      for (i = 0; i < 15; i++) {
          p = [self randomPoint];
          [path lineToPoint: p];
      }
      [path closePath];
    }
    return self;
}
```

```
// randomPoint returns a random point inside the view
- (NSPoint)randomPoint
{
    NSPoint result;
    NSRect r;
    int width, height;
    r = [self bounds];
    width = round(r.size.width);
    height = round (r.size.height);
    result.x = (random() % width) + r.origin.x;
    result.y = (random() % height) + r.origin.y;
    return result;
}

- (void)drawRect:(NSRect)rect
{
    NSRect bounds = [self bounds];

    // Fill the view with green
    [[NSColor greenColor] set];
    [NSBezierPath fillRect: bounds];

    // Draw the path in white
    [[NSColor whiteColor] set];
    [path stroke];
}

- (void)dealloc
{
    [path release];
    [super dealloc];
}
@end
```

Build and run your app.

NSScrollView

In the art world, a larger work is typically more expensive than a smaller one of equal quality. Your beautiful view is lovely, but it would be more valuable if it were larger. How can it be larger, yet still fit inside that tiny window? You are going to put it in a scroll view (Figure 14.15).

A scroll view has three parts: the document view, the content view, and the scroll bars. In this example, your view will become the document view. It will be displayed in the content view, which is an instance of **NSClipView**.

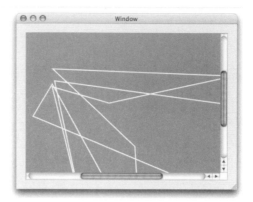

Figure 14.15   Completed Application

It looks tricky, but this change is actually very simple to make. In fact, it requires no code at all. Open `MainMenu.nib` in Interface Builder. Select the view, and choose Make subviews of Scroll View from the Layout menu (Figure 14.16).

Figure 14.16   Group StretchView in Scroll View

As the window resizes, you want the scroll view to resize, but you do not want your document to resize. Open the info panel, select the scroll view, and set the size inspector so that it resizes with the window (Figure 14.17).

Note the width and height of the view.

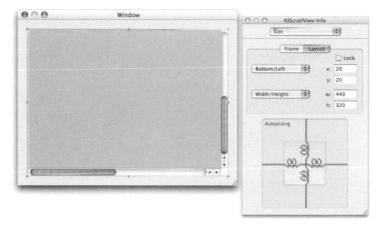

Figure 14.17 Make Scroll View Resize with Window

To select the document view, double-click inside the scroll view. You should see the title of the info panel change to StretchView (Custom) Info. Make the view about twice as wide and twice as tall as the scroll view. Set the size inspector so that the view will not resize (Figure 14.18). Build the application and run it.

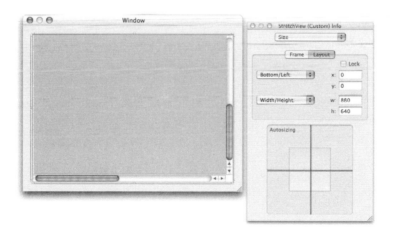

Figure 14.18 Make StretchView Larger and Non-resizing

For the More Curious: Cells

NSControl inherits from **NSView**. **NSView** (with its graphics context) is a relatively large and expensive object to create. When the **NSButton** class was first created, the first thing someone did was to create a calculator with 10 rows and 10 columns of buttons. The performance was less than it could have been because of the 100 tiny views. Later, someone had the clever idea of moving the brains of the button into another object (not a view) and creating one big view (called an **NSMatrix**) that would act as the view for all 100 button brains. The class for the button brains was called **NSButtonCell** (Figure 14.19).

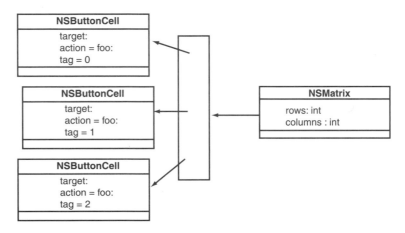

Figure 14.19   NSMatrix

In the end, **NSButton** became just a view that had an **NSButtonCell**. The button cell does everything, and **NSButton** simply claims a space in the window (Figure 14.20).

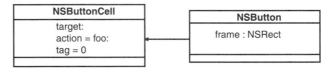

Figure 14.20   NSButton and NSButtonCell

Similarly, **NSSlider** is a view with an **NSSliderCell**, and **NSTextField** is a view with an **NSTextFieldCell**. **NSColorWell**, by contrast, has no cell.

To create an instance of **NSMatrix** in Interface Builder, you drop a control with a cell onto the window and option-drag as if resizing until the matrix has the correct number of rows and columns (Figure 14.21).

Figure 14.21   A Matrix of Buttons

An **NSMatrix** has a target and an action. A cell may also have a target and an action. If the cell is activated, the cell's target and action are used. If the target and action of the selected cell are not set, the matrix's target and action will be used.

When dealing with matrices, you will often ask which cell was activated. Cells can also be given a tag.

```
- (IBAction)myAction:(id)sender {
    id theCell = [sender selectedCell];
    int theTag = [theCell tag];
    ...
}
```

The cell's tag can be set in Interface Builder.

Cells are used in several other types of objects. The data in an **NSTableView**, for example, is drawn by cells.

For the More Curious: isFlipped

Both PDF and Postscript use the standard Cartesian coordinate system, where y increases as you move up the page. Quartz follows this model by default. The origin is usually at the lower-left corner of the view.

For some types of drawing, the math becomes easier if the upper-left corner is the origin and y increases as you move down the page. We say that such a view is *flipped*.

To flip a view, you override **isFlipped** in your view class to return YES:

```
- (BOOL)isFlipped
{
    return YES;
}
```

While we are discussing the coordinate system, note that *x*- and *y*-coordinates are measured in *points*. A point is typically defined as "72.0 points = 1 inch." In reality, by default "1.0 point = 1 pixel" on your screen. You can, however, change the size of a point by changing the coordinate system:

```
// Make everything in the view twice as large
NSSize newScale;
newScale.width = 2.0;
newScale.height = 2.0;
[myView scaleUnitSquareToSize:newScale];
[myView setNeedsDisplay:YES];
```

Challenge

NSBezierPath can also draw Bezier curves. Replace the straight lines with randomly curved ones. (*Hint:* Look in NSBezierPath.h.)

Chapter 15

IMAGES AND MOUSE EVENTS

In Chapter 14, you drew lines connecting random points. A more interesting application would have been to write some sort of a drawing application. To write this sort of application, you will need to be able to get and handle mouse events.

NSResponder

NSView inherits from **NSResponder**. All of the event-handling methods are declared in **NSResponder**. We will discuss keyboard events in Chapter 16. For now, we are interested just in mouse events. **NSResponder** declares these methods:

```
- (void)mouseDown:(NSEvent *)theEvent;
- (void)rightMouseDown:(NSEvent *)theEvent;
- (void)otherMouseDown:(NSEvent *)theEvent;
- (void)mouseUp:(NSEvent *)theEvent;
- (void)rightMouseUp:(NSEvent *)theEvent;
- (void)otherMouseUp:(NSEvent *)theEvent;
- (void)mouseDragged:(NSEvent *)theEvent;
- (void)scrollWheel:(NSEvent *)theEvent;
- (void)rightMouseDragged:(NSEvent *)theEvent;
- (void)otherMouseDragged:(NSEvent *)theEvent;
```

Notice that the argument is always an **NSEvent** object.

NSEvent

An event object has all the information about what the user did to trigger the event. When you are dealing with mouse events, you might be interested in the following methods:

```
- (NSPoint)locationInWindow
```

This method returns the location of the mouse event.

```
- (unsigned int)modifierFlags
```

The integer tells you which modifier keys the user is holding down on the keyboard. This enables the programmer to tell a control-click from a shift-click, for example. The code would look like this:

```
- (void)mouseDown:(NSEvent *)e
{
    unsigned int flags;
    flags = [e modifierFlags];
    if (flags & NSControlKeyMask) {
        ...handle control click...
    }
    if (flags & NSShiftKeyMask) {
        ...handle shift click...
    }
}
```

Here are the constants that you will AND (&) against the modifier flags:

NSAlphaShiftKeyMask

NSShiftKeyMask

NSControlKeyMask

NSAlternateKeyMask

NSCommandKeyMask

NSNumericPadKeyMask

NSHelpKeyMask

NSFunctionKeyMask

```
- (NSTimeInterval)timestamp
```

This method gives the time interval in seconds between the time the machine booted and the time of the event. NSTimeInterval is a `double`.

```
- (NSWindow *)window
```

This method returns the window associated with the event.

```
- (int)clickCount
```

Was it a single-, double-, or triple-click?

```
- (float)pressure
```

If the user is using an input device that gives pressure (a tablet, for example), this method returns the pressure. It is between 0 and 1.

```
- (float)deltaX;
- (float)deltaY;
- (float)deltaZ;
```

These methods give the change in the position of the mouse or scroll wheel.

Getting Mouse Events

To get mouse events, you need to override the mouse event methods in StretchView.m:

```
- (void)mouseDown:(NSEvent *)event
{
    NSLog(@"mouseDown: %d", [event clickCount]);
}
- (void)mouseDragged:(NSEvent *)event
{
    NSLog(@"mouseDragged:");
}
- (void)mouseUp:(NSEvent *)event
{
    NSLog(@"mouseUp:");
}
```

Build and run your application. Try double-clicking, and check the click count. Note that the first click is sent and then the second click. The first click has a click count of 1; the second click has a click count of 2.

Using NSOpenPanel

It would be fun to composite an image onto the view, but first you need to create a controller object that will read the image data from a file. This is a good opportunity to learn how to use **NSOpenPanel**. Note that the RaiseMan application used the **NSOpenPanel**, but it was done automatically by the **NSDocument** class. Here you will use the **NSOpenPanel** explicitly. Figure 15.1 shows what your application will look like while the open panel is active. Figure 15.2 shows what it will look like once the user has chosen an image. The slider at the bottom of the window will control how opaque the image is.

Figure 15.3 shows the object diagram.

Figure 15.1   NSOpenPanel

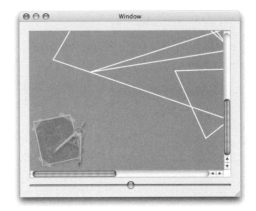

Figure 15.2   Completed Application

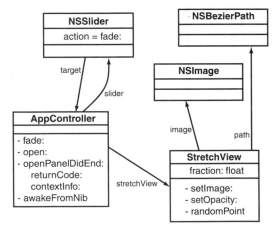

Figure 15.3   Object Diagram

Change the Nib File

Open the nib file and create a new subclass of **NSObject** called **AppController**. Create two outlets called stretchView (of type **StretchView**) and slider (of type **NSSlider**). Create two actions: **open:** and **fade:** (Figure 15.4). Create files for the **AppController** class.

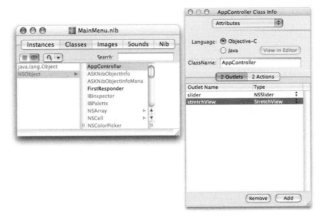

Figure 15.4 Create AppController Class

In the Classes menu, use Instantiate AppController to create an instance of your new class (Figure 15.5).

Figure 15.5 Create an Instance of AppController

Control-drag from the **AppController** to the **StretchView** and connect the stretchView outlet (Figure 15.6).

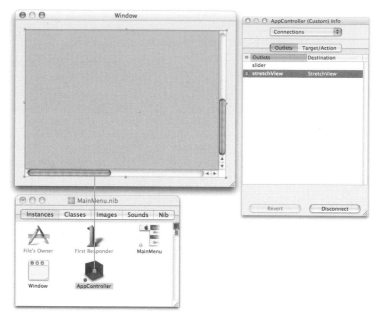

Figure 15.6   Connect the stretchView Outlet

Drop a slider on the window. In the inspector, set its range from 0 to 1. Also, check the box labeled Continuously send action while sliding. This slider will control how opaque the image is (Figure 15.7).

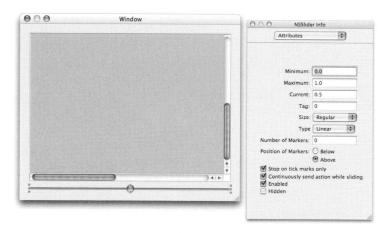

Figure 15.7   Inspect the Slider

Connect the slider outlet to the instance of **NSSlider** (Figure 15.8).

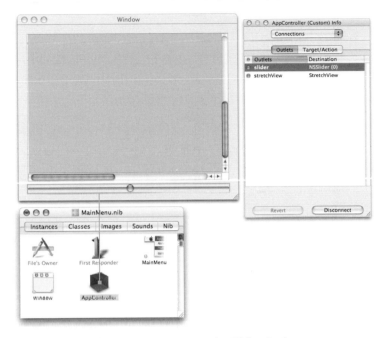

Figure 15.8   Connect the Slider Outlet

Set the target of the slider to be the **AppController**. Its action will be **fade:** (Figure 15.9).

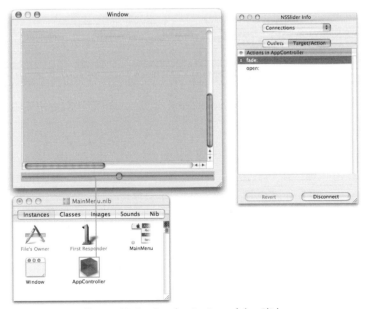

Figure 15.9   Set the Action of the Slider

Look at the main menu in your nib. Open the File menu and delete all menu items except Open. Control-drag to connect the menu item to the **AppController**'s **open:** action (Figure 15.10). Save the file.

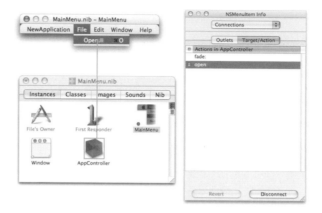

Figure 15.10   Connect the Menu Item

awakeFromNib Versus init

When your nib file is loaded, three things will happen (in this order) to your **AppController** object (and any other object in the nib file):

1. It will be allocated and sent the message **init**. (Views will be sent **initWithFrame:**.)
2. Its outlets will be set.
3. It will be sent **awakeFromNib**.

Note that **init** is sent before the outlets of the object are set. Thus, you cannot send messages to any of the other objects from the nib file in the **init** method. You can, however, send them messages in the **awakeFromNib** method.

Edit the Code

Edit AppController.h and add the following line:

```
#import <Cocoa/Cocoa.h>
@class StretchView;
```

Edit AppController.m:

```
#import "AppController.h"
#import "StretchView.h"

@implementation AppController

- (void)awakeFromNib
{
    // Make sure the slider and the stretch view
    // agree on the initial opacity
    [slider setFloatValue:0.5];
    [stretchView setOpacity:0.5];
}
- (IBAction)fade:(id)sender
{
    // The sender is the slider
    [stretchView setOpacity:[sender floatValue]];
}

- (void)openPanelDidEnd:(NSOpenPanel *)openPanel
              returnCode:(int)returnCode
             contextInfo:(void *)x
{
    NSString *path;
    NSImage *image;

    // Did they choose "Open"?
    if (returnCode == NSOKButton) {
        path = [openPanel filename];
        image = [[NSImage alloc] initWithContentsOfFile:path];
        [stretchView setImage:image];
        [image release];
    }
}

- (IBAction)open:(id)sender
{
    NSOpenPanel *panel = [NSOpenPanel openPanel];

    // Run the open panel
    [panel beginSheetForDirectory:nil
                             file:nil
                            types:[NSImage imageFileTypes]
                   modalForWindow:[stretchView window]
                    modalDelegate:self
                    didEndSelector:
          @selector(openPanelDidEnd:returnCode:contextInfo:)
                      contextInfo:NULL];
}

@end
```

Notice the line where you start the sheet. This is a very handy method:

```
- (void)beginSheetForDirectory:(NSString *)path
                          file:(NSString *)name
                         types:(NSArray *)types
                 modalForWindow:(NSWindow *)docWindow
                 modalDelegate:(id)delegate
                 didEndSelector:(SEL)didEndSelector
                   contextInfo:(void *)contextInfo
```

This method brings up an open panel as a sheet attached to the docWindow. The didEndSelector should have the following signature:

```
- (void)openPanelDidEnd:(NSWindow *)sheet
             returnCode:(int)returnCode
            contextInfo:(void *)contextInfo;
```

It should be implemented in the modal delegate. The path is the place where the file browser will open initially. The name is the name of the file that will be chosen initially. Both the path and the name may be nil.

Composite an Image onto Your View

You will also need to change **StretchView** so that it uses the opacity and image. First, declare variables and methods in your StretchView.h file:

```
#import <Cocoa/Cocoa.h>

@interface StretchView : NSView
{
    NSBezierPath *path;
    NSImage *image;
    float opacity;
}
- (void)setImage:(NSImage *)newImage;
- (void)setOpacity:(float)x;
- (NSPoint)randomPoint;

@end
```

Now implement these methods in your StretchView.m file:

```
- (void)setImage:(NSImage *)newImage
{
    [newImage retain];
    [image release];
    image = newImage;
```

```
    [self setNeedsDisplay:YES];
}
- (void)setOpacity:(float)x
{
    opacity = x;
    [self setNeedsDisplay:YES];
}
```

At the end of each of the methods, you inform the view that it needs to redraw itself.

Also in `StretchView.m`, you need to add compositing of the image to the **drawRect:** method:

```
- (void)drawRect:(NSRect)rect
{
    NSRect bounds = [self bounds];
    [[NSColor greenColor] set];
    [NSBezierPath fillRect:bounds];
    [[NSColor whiteColor] set];
    [path stroke];
    if (image) {
        NSRect imageRect;
        NSRect drawingRect;
        imageRect.origin = NSZeroPoint;
        imageRect.size = [image size];
        drawingRect = imageRect;
        [image drawInRect:drawingRect
                 fromRect:imageRect
                operation:NSCompositeSourceOver
                 fraction:opacity];
    }
}
```

Notice that the **drawInRect:fromRect:operation:fraction:** method composites the image onto the view. The fraction determines the image's opacity.

In the name of tidiness, be sure to release the image in your view's **dealloc** method:

```
- (void)dealloc
{
    [image release];
    [path release];
    [super dealloc];
}
```

Build and run your application. You will find a few images in /Developer/ Examples/AppKit/Sketch . When you open an image, it will appear in the lower-left corner of your **StretchView** object.

The View's Coordinate System

The final bit of fun comes from being able to choose the location and dimensions of the image based on the user's dragging. The mouse down will indicate one corner of the rectangle where the image will appear, and the mouse up will indicate the opposite corner. The final application will look something like Figure 15.11.

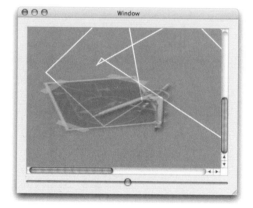

Figure 15.11   Completed Application

Each view has its own coordinate system. By default, (0, 0) is in the lower-left corner. This is consistent with PDF and PostScript. You can change the coordinate system of the view if you wish. You can move the origin, change the scale, or rotate the coordinates. The window also has a coordinate system.

If you have two views, a and b, and you need to translate an NSPoint p from b's coordinate system to a's coordinate system, it would look like this:

```
NSPoint q = [a convertPoint:p fromView:b];
```

If b is nil, the point is converted from the window's coordinate system.

Mouse events have their locations in the window's coordinate system, so you will nearly always have to convert the point to the local coordinate system. You are going to create variables to hold onto the corners of the rectangle where the image will be drawn.

Add these instance variables to StretchView.h:

```
NSPoint downPoint;
NSPoint currentPoint;
```

downPoint will be the location of the **mouseDown:**. currentPoint will be updated by **mouseDragged:** and **mouseUp:**.

Edit the mouse event-handling methods to update downPoint and currentPoint:

```
- (void)mouseDown:(NSEvent *)event
{
    NSPoint p = [event locationInWindow];
    downPoint = [self convertPoint:p fromView:nil];
    currentPoint = downPoint;
    [self setNeedsDisplay:YES];
}

- (void)mouseDragged:(NSEvent *)event
{
    NSPoint p = [event locationInWindow];
    currentPoint = [self convertPoint:p fromView:nil];
    [self setNeedsDisplay:YES];
}

- (void)mouseUp:(NSEvent *)event
{
    NSPoint p = [event locationInWindow];
    currentPoint = [self convertPoint:p fromView:nil];
    [self setNeedsDisplay:YES];
}
```

Add a method to calculate the rectangle based on the two points:

```
- (NSRect)currentRect
{
    float minX = MIN(downPoint.x, currentPoint.x);
    float maxX = MAX(downPoint.x, currentPoint.x);
    float minY = MIN(downPoint.y, currentPoint.y);
    float maxY = MAX(downPoint.y, currentPoint.y);

    return NSMakeRect(minX, minY, maxX-minX, maxY minY);
}
```

(I don't know why, but many people mistype that last method. Look at yours once more before going on. If you get it wrong, the results are disappointing.)

Declare the **currentRect** method in StretchView.h.

So that the user will see something even if he has not dragged, initialize downPoint and currentPoint in the **setImage:** method:

```
- (void)setImage:(NSImage *)newImage
{
    [newImage retain];
    [image release];
    image = newImage;
    NSSize imageSize;
    imageSize = [newImage size];
    downPoint = NSZeroPoint;
    currentPoint.x = downPoint.x + imageSize.width;
    currentPoint.y = downPoint.y + imageSize.height
    [self setNeedsDisplay:YES];
}
```

In the **drawRect:** method, composite the image inside the rectangle:

```
- (void)drawRect:(NSRect)rect
{
    NSRectbounds = [selfbounds];
    [[NSColor greenColor] set];
    [NSBezierPath fillRect:[bounds]];
    [[NSColor whiteColor] set];
    [path stroke];
    if (image) {
        NSRect imageRect;
        NSRect drawingRect;
        imageRect.origin.x = NSZeroPoint;
        imageRect.size = [image size];
        drawingRect = [self currentRect];
        [image drawInRect:drawingRect
                 fromRect:imageRect
                operation:NSCompositeSourceOver
                 fraction:opacity];
    }
}
```

Build and run your application. Notice that the view doesn't scroll when you drag past the edge. It would be nice if the scroll view would move to allow users to see where they have dragged to, a technique known as *autoscrolling*. In the next section, you will add autoscrolling to your application.

Autoscrolling

To add autoscrolling to your application, you will send the message **autoscroll:** to the clip view when the user drags. You will include the event as

an argument. Open StretchView.m and add the following line to the
mouseDragged: method:

```
- (void)mouseDragged:(NSEvent *)event
{
    NSPoint p = [event locationInWindow];
    currentPoint = [self convertPoint:p fromView:nil];
    [[self superview] autoscroll:event];
    [self setNeedsDisplay:YES];
}
```

Build and run your application.

Notice that autoscrolling happens only as you drag. For smoother autoscrolling,
most developers will create a timer that sends the view the **autoscroll:** method
periodically while the user is dragging. Timers are discussed in Chapter 21.

For the More Curious: NSImage

In most cases, it suffices to read in an image, resize it, and composite it onto a
view, as you did in this exercise.

An **NSImage** object has an array of representations. For example, your image
might be a drawing of a cow. That drawing can be in PDF, a color bitmap, and a
black-and-white bitmap. Each of these versions is an instance of a subclass of
NSImageRep. You can add representations to and remove representations from
your image. When you sit down to rewrite Adobe Photoshop, you will be
manipulating the image representations.

Here is a list of the subclasses of **NSImageRep**:

- NSBitmapImageRep
- NSEPSImageRep
- NSPICTImageRep
- NSCachedImageRep
- NSCustomImageRep
- NSPDFImageRep

Although **NSImageRep** has only five subclasses, it is important to note that
NSImage knows how to read approximately two dozen types of image files,
including all of the common formats: PICT, GIF, JPG, PNG, PDF, BMP, TIFF,
and so on.

Challenge

Create a new document-based application that allows the user to draw ovals in arbitrary locations and sizes. **NSBezierPath** has the following method:

```
+ (NSBezierPath *)bezierPathWithOvalInRect:(NSRect)rect;
```

If you are feeling ambitious, add the ability to save and read files.

If you are feeling extra ambitious, add undo capabilities.

Chapter 16

RESPONDERS AND KEYBOARD EVENTS

When the user types, where are the corresponding events sent? First, the window manager gets the event and forwards it to the active application. The active application forwards the keyboard events to the key window. The key window forwards the event to the "active" view. Which view, then, is the active one? Each window has an outlet called firstResponder that points to one view of that window. That view is the "active" one for that window. For example, when you click on a text field, it becomes the firstResponder of that window (Figure 16.1).

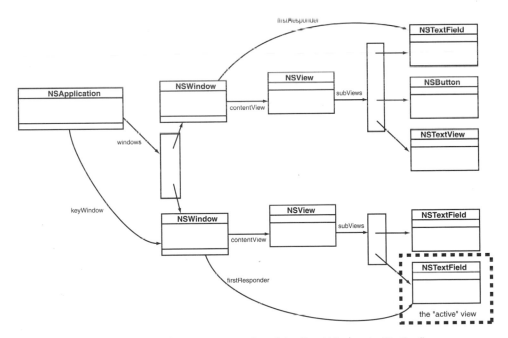

Figure 16.1   The First Responder of the Key Window Is "Active"

When the user tries to change the `firstResponder` to another view (by tabbing or clicking the other view), the views go through a certain ritual before `firstResponder` outlet is changed. First, the view that may become the `firstResponder` is asked if it accepts first-responder status. If it returns NO, that means the view is not interested in keyboard events. For example, you can't type into a slider, so it refuses to accept first-responder status. If the view does accept first-responder status, the view that is currently the first responder is asked if it resigns its role as the first responder. If the editing is not done, the view can refuse to give up first-responder status. For example, if the user had not typed in his or her entire phone number, the text field could refuse to resign this status. Finally, the view is told that it is becoming the first responder. Often, this triggers a change in its appearance (Figure 16.2).

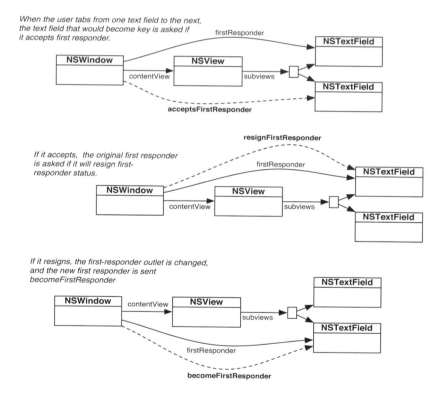

Figure 16.2   Becoming the First Responder

Note that each window has its own first responder. Several windows may be open, but only the first responder of the key window gets the keyboard events.

NSResponder

We are interested in the following methods that are inherited from
NSResponder:

- (BOOL)**acceptsFirstResponder**

Overridden by a subclass to return YES if it handles keyboard events.

- (BOOL)**resignFirstResponder**

Asks the receiver if it is willing to give up first-responder status.

- (BOOL)**becomeFirstResponder**

Notifies the receiver that has become first responder in its **NSWindow**.

- (void)**keyDown:**(NSEvent *)theEvent

Informs the receiver that the user has pressed a key.

- (void)**keyUp:**(NSEvent *)theEvent

Informs the receiver that the user has released a key.

- (void)**flagsChanged:**(NSEvent *)theEvent

Informs the receiver that the user has pressed or released a modifier key
(Shift, Control, or so on).

NSEvent

We discussed **NSEvent** in terms of mouse events in Chapter 15. Here are some of
the methods commonly used when getting information about a keyboard event:

- (NSString *)**characters**

Returns the characters created by the event.

- (BOOL)**isARepeat**

Returns YES if the key event is a repeat caused by the user holding the key down; returns NO if the key event is new.

- (unsigned short)**keyCode**

Returns the code for the keyboard key that caused the event. Its value is hardware dependent.

- (unsigned int)**modifierFlags**

Returns an integer bit field indicating the modifier keys in effect for the receiver. For information about what the bits of the integer mean, refer to the discussion in Chapter 15.

Create a New Project with a Custom View

Create a new project of type Cocoa Application. Name it TypingTutor.

Edit the Nib File

Open MainMenu.nib. Select **NSView** in the classes browser (Figure 16.3).

Figure 16.3   Select NSView

Create a subclass and name it **BigLetterView** (Figure 16.4).

Create the files for **BigLetterView** (Figure 16.5).

Save the files in the project directory.

Figure 16.4 Create the Subclass BigLetterView

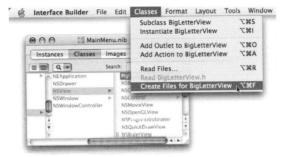

Figure 16.5 Create the Files for BigLetterView

Lay Out the Interface

Now create an instance of your class by dragging out a CustomView placeholder and dropping it on the window (Figure 16.6).

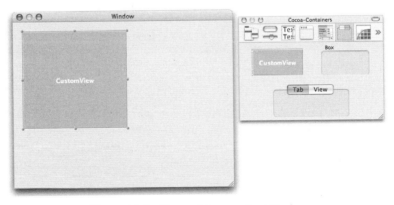

Figure 16.6 Drop a View on the Window

Open the inspector and set the class of the view to be **BigLetterView** (Figure 16.7).

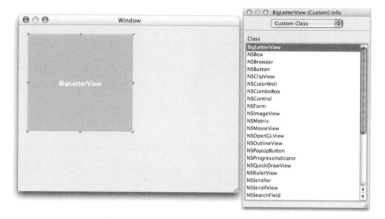

Figure 16.7   Set the Class of the View to BigLetterView

Size Info

Select the new view, open the size info panel, and set it as shown in Figure 16.8. Now it will keep constant its distance from the upper-left corner of its superview. That is, it will grow and shrink with the superview.

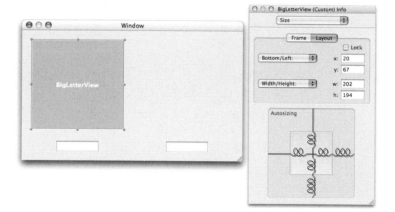

Figure 16.8   Set Size Info

Really small windows will mess up your nice resizing, so open the size info panel for the window and click the Current button in the Min Size box. That will prevent the user from making the window any smaller.

Drop two text fields on the window (Figure 16.9).

Figure 16.9   Completed Interface

Make Connections

Now you need to create the loop of key views for your window. That is, you are setting the order in which the views will be selected as the user tabs from one element to the next. The order will be the text field on the left, the text field on the right, the **BigLetterView**, and then back to the text field on the left.

Set the left-hand text field's nextKeyView to be the right-hand text field (Figure 16.10).

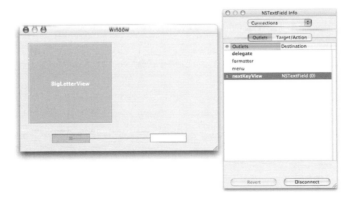

Figure 16.10   Set nextKeyView of Left-Hand Text Field

Set the right-hand text field's nextKeyView to be the **BigLetterView** (Figure 16.11).

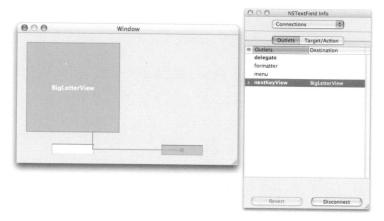

Figure 16.11 Set nextKeyView of Right-Hand Text Field

Finally, set the nextKeyView of the **BigLetterView** to be the left-hand text field (Figure 16.12). This will enable the user to tab between the three views. Shift-tabbing will move the selection in the opposite direction.

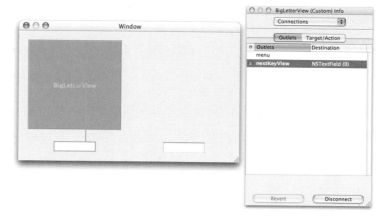

Figure 16.12 Set nextKeyView of the BigLetterView

Which view, then, should be the firstResponder when the window first appears? To make the **BigLetterView** be the initialFirstResponder of the window, drag from the window to the text field and set the initialFirst Responder outlet (Figure 16.13).

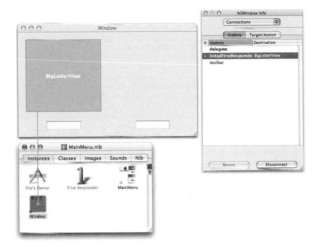

Figure 16.13   Set the initialFirstResponder of the Window

Save and close the nib file.

Write the Code

In this section, you will make your **BigLetterView** respond to key events. You will also make it accept first-responder status. The characters typed by the user will appear in the console. The completed application will look like Figure 16.14.

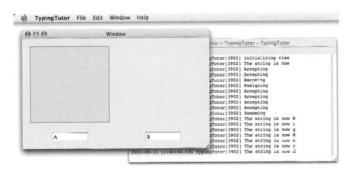

Figure 16.14   Completed Application

In BigLetterView.h

Your **BigLetterView** will have two instance variables and accessor methods for those variables. The bgColor variable will identify the background color of the view and will be an **NSColor** object. The string variable will hold on to the letter that the user most recently typed and will be an **NSString** object.

```
#import <Cocoa/Cocoa.h>

@interface BigLetterView : NSView
{
    NSColor *bgColor;
    NSString *string;
}

- (void)setBgColor:(NSColor *)c;
- (NSColor *)bgColor;
- (void)setString:(NSString *)c;
- (NSString *)string;

@end
```

In BigLetterView.m

The designated initializer for a view is **initWithFrame:**. In this method, you will call the superclass's **initWithFrame:** method and initialize bgColor and string to default values. Add the following method to BigLetterView.m:

```
- (id)initWithFrame:(NSRect)rect
{
    if (self = [super initWithFrame:rect]) {
        NSLog(@"initializing view");
        [self setBgColor:[NSColor yellowColor]];
        [self setString:@" "];
    }
    return self;
}
```

Create accessor methods for bgColor and string:

```
- (void)setBgColor:(NSColor *)c
{
    [c retain];
    [bgColor release];
    bgColor = c;
    [self setNeedsDisplay:YES];
}

- (NSColor *)bgColor
{
    return bgColor;
}
```

```
- (void)setString:(NSString *)c
{
    c = [c copy];
    [string release];
    string = c;
    NSLog(@"The string is now %@", string);
}

- (NSString *)string
{
    return string;
}
```

Add the following code to the **drawRect:** method. It will fill the view with
bgColor. If the view is the window's firstResponder, it will stroke a black
rectangle around its bounds to show the user that it will be the view receiving
keyboard events:

```
- (void)drawRect:(NSRect)rect
{
    NSRect bounds = [self bounds];
    [bgColor set];
    [NSBezierPath fillRect:bounds];

    // Am I the window's first responder?
    if ([[self window] firstResponder] == self) {
        [[NSColor keyboardFocusIndicatorColor] set];
        [NSBezierPath setDefaultLineWidth:4.0];
        [NSBezierPath strokeRect:bounds];
    }
}
```

The system can optimize your drawing a bit if it knows that the view is
completely opaque. Override *NSView's isOpaque* method.

```
- (BOOL)isOpaque
{
    return YES;
}
```

The methods to become firstResponder are as follows:

```
- (BOOL)acceptsFirstResponder
{
    NSLog(@"Accepting");
    return YES;
}

- (BOOL)resignFirstResponder
{
    NSLog(@"Resigning");
    [self setNeedsDisplay: YES];
    return YES;
}
```

```
- (BOOL)becomeFirstResponder {
    NSLog(@"Becoming");
    [self setNeedsDisplay: YES];
    return YES;
}
```

Once the view becomes the first responder, it will handle key events. For most **keyDowns**, the view will simply change `string` to be whatever the user typed. If, however, the user presses Tab or Shift-Tab, the view will ask the window to change the first responder.

NSResponder (from which **NSView** inherits) has a method called **interpretKeyEvents:**. For most key events, it just tells the view to insert the text. For events that might do something else (like Tab or Shift-Tab), it calls methods on itself.

In **keyDown:**, you simply call **interpretKeyEvents:**

```
- (void)keyDown:(NSEvent *)event
{
    [self interpretKeyEvents:[NSArray arrayWithObject:event]];
}
```

Then you need to override the methods that **interpretKeyEvents:** will call:

```
- (void)insertText:(NSString *)input
{
    // Set string to be what the user typed
    [self setString:input];
}

- (void)insertTab:(id)sender
{
    [[self window] selectKeyViewFollowingView:self];
}

- (void)insertBacktab:(id)sender
{
    [[self window] selectKeyViewPrecedingView:self];
}
```

Of course, you want to be a tidy programmer, so you will be sure to release your instance variables when the view is deallocated:

```
// release instance variables
- (void)dealloc
{
    [string release];
    [bgColor release];
    [super dealloc];
}
@end
```

Build and run your program. You should see that your view becomes the first responder. While it is first responder, it should take keyboard events and log them to the terminal. Also, note that you can Tab and Shift-Tab between the views (Figure 16.15).

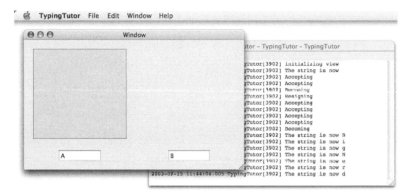

Figure 16.15   Completed Application

For the More Curious: Rollovers

Three mouse events were not discussed in Chapter 15: **mouseMoved:**, **mouseEntered:**, and **mouseExited:**.

```
- (void)mouseMoved:(NSEvent *)event
```

To receive **mouseMoved:**, the view's window needs to accept "mouse-moved" events. If it does, the **mouseMoved:** message is sent to the window's first responder. To set the window to get mouse-moved events, you send it the message **setAcceptsMouseMovedEvents:**

```
[[self window] setAcceptsMouseMovedEvents:YES];
```

At this point, the view will be sent the message every time the mouse moves. This is a lot of events. When people ask me about mouse-moved events, I ask them why they want it. They usually say, "Uh, rollovers."

Rollovers are very popular in Web browsers. As you roll over a region, its appearance changes to make it clear that if you clicked now, that region would accept the click. Bookmarks in Safari, for examples, become highlighted when you roll over them.

To do rollovers, you don't typically use **mouseMoved:**. Instead, you set up a tracking rect and override **mouseEntered:** and **mouseExited:**. When you create a tracking rect, you are given a number (called the tag) that identifies it. You can use the tag to remove the tracking rect when you are finished with it.

The tricky part is keeping the tracking rect up-to-date as the view is moved, resized, and transferred from one window onto another. Assuming that your view has an integer instance variable called rolloverTrackingRectTag, here is the code that will take care of that for you:

```
- (void)resetTrackingRect
{
    // Clear out the old tracking rect
    [self clearTrackingRect];

    // Create a new tracking rect
    rolloverTrackingRectTag = [self addTrackingRect:[self visibleRect]
                                       owner:self
                                    userData:NULL
                                assumeInside:NO];
    }
}

- (void)clearTrackingRect
{
    // If we have a tracking rect, then remove it
    if (rolloverTrackingRectTag > 0) {
        [self removeTrackingRect:rolloverTrackingRectTag];
        rolloverTrackingRectTag = 0;
    }
}

// This is called automatically
// after a view is moved,
// resized, or scrolled

- (void)resetCursorRects
{
    [super resetCursorRects];
    [self resetTrackinRect];
}
```

Then, you change the appearance when **mouseEntered:** and **mouseExited:** are called. Assuming you have a variable called isHighlighted of type BOOL, here is the code:

```
- (void)mouseEntered:(NSEvent *)theEvent
{
    isHighlighted - YES;
    [self setNeedsDisplay:YES];
}

- (void)mouseExited:(NSEvent *)theEvent
{
    isHighlighted = NO;
    [self setNeedsDisplay:YES];
}
```

You would then check isHighlighted in your **drawRect:** method and draw the view appropriately.

If your view has several different tracking rects, in the **mouseEntered:** method you can ask the event for the tag of the rect that was entered:

```
- (int)trackingNumber
```

Chapter 17

Working with Fonts and NSAttributedString

The next step is to get the string to appear in our view. At the end of the chapter, your application will look like Figure 17.1. The character being displayed will change as you type.

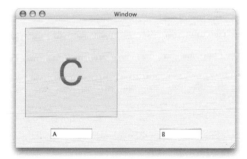

Figure 17.1   Completed Application

NSFont

Overall, the class **NSFont** has basically only two types of methods:

- Class methods for getting the font you want
- Methods for getting metrics on the font, such as letter height

Commonly Used Methods in NSFont

```
+ (NSFont *)fontWithName:(NSString *)fontName size:(float)fontSize
```

This method returns a font object. fontName is a family-face name, such as "HelveticaBoldOblique" or "Times-Roman." If you use a fontSize of 0.0, this method uses the default User Font size.

```
+ (NSFont *)userFixedPitchFontOfSize:(float)fontSize
+ (NSFont *)userFontOfSize:(float)fontSize
+ (NSFont *)messageFontOfSize:(float)fontSize
+ (NSFont *)toolTipsFontOfSize:(float)fontSize
+ (NSFont *)titleBarFontOfSize:(float)fontSize
```

These methods return the user's default font for the corresponding string types. Once again, a size of 0.0 will get a font of the default size.

NSAttributedString

Sometimes you want to display a string that has certain attributes for a range of characters. As an example, suppose you want to display the string "Big Nerd Ranch," and you want the letters 0 through 2 to be underlined, the letters 0 through 7 to be green, and the letters 9 through 13 to be subscripts.

When dealing with a range of numbers, Cocoa uses the struct NSRange. NSRange has two members: location and length are both integers. The location is the index of the first item, and the length is the number of items in the range. You can use the function **NSMakeRange()** to create an NSRange.

To create strings with attributes that remain in effect over a range of characters, Cocoa has **NSAttributedString** and **NSMutableAttributedString**. Here is how you could create the **NSAttributedString** just described:

```
NSMutableAttributedString *s;
s = [[NSMutableAttributedString alloc]
        initWithString:@"Big Nerd Ranch"];

[s addAttribute:NSFontAttributeName
        value:[NSFont userFontOfSize:22]
        range:NSMakeRange(0, 14)];

[s addAttribute:NSUnderlineStyleAttributeName
        value:[NSNumber numberWithInt:1]
        range:NSMakeRange(0,3)];

[s addAttribute:NSForegroundColorAttributeName
        value:[NSColor greenColor]
        range:NSMakeRange(0, 8)];
```

```
[s addAttribute:NSSuperscriptAttributeName
        value:[NSNumber numberWithInt:-1]
        range:NSMakeRange(9,5)];
```

Once you have an attributed string, you can do lots of stuff with it.

```
[s drawInRect:[self bounds]];

// Put it in a text field
[textField setAttributedStringValue:s];

// Put it on a button
[button setAttributedTitle:s];
```

Figure 17.2 shows the result of this code's execution.

Figure 17.2   Using the Attributed String

Here are the names of the global variables for the most commonly used attributes and what they mean:

NSFontAttributeName	A font object. By default, 12-point Helvetica.
NSForegroundColorAttributeName	A color. By default, black.
NSBackgroundColorAttributeName	A color. By default, no background drawn.
NSUnderlineColorAttributeName	A color. By default, the same as the foreground.
NSUnderlineStyleAttributeName	A number. By default, 0 (which means no underline).
NSSuperscriptAttributeName	A number. By default, 0 (which means no superscripting or subscripting).
NSShadowAttributeName	An **NSShadow** object. By default, nil (no shadow).

A list of all the attribute names can be found in <AppKit/NSAttributedString.h>.

The easiest way to create attributed strings is from a file. **NSAttributedString** can read and write the following file formats:

- *A string*: You read a text file.
- *RTF*: Rich Text Format is a standard for text with multiple fonts and colors. In this case, You will read and set the contents of the attributed string with an instance of **NSData**.
- *RTFD*: This is RTF with attachments. Besides the multiple fonts and colors of RTF, you can have images.
- *HTML*: The attributed string can do basic HTML layout, but you probably want to use the **WebView** for best quality. **NSAttributedString** reads HTML, but does not write it.
- *Word*: The attributed string can read and write simple .doc files.

When you read a document in, you may want to know some things about it, such as the paper size. If you supply a place where the method can put a pointer to a dictionary, the dictionary will have all the extra information that it could get from the data. For example:

```
NSDictionary *myDict;
NSData *data = [NSData dataWithContentsOfFile:@"myfile.rtf"];
NSAttributedString *aString;
aString = [[NSAttributedString alloc] initWithRTF:data
                                documentAttributes:&myDict];
```

If you don't care about the document attributes, just supply NULL.

Drawing Strings and Attributed Strings

Both **NSString** and **NSAttributedString** have methods that cause them to be drawn onto a view. **NSAttributedString** has the following methods:

- (void)**drawAtPoint:**(NSPoint)aPoint

Draws the receiver. aPoint is the lower-left corner of the string.

- (void)**drawInRect:**(NSRect)rect

Draws the receiver. All drawing occurs inside rect. If rect is too small for the string to fit, the drawing is clipped to fit inside rect.

- (NSSize)**size**

Returns the size that the receiver would be if drawn.

NSString has analogous methods. With **NSString**, you need to supply a dictionary of attributes to be applied for the entire string.

```
- (void)drawAtPoint:(NSPoint)aPoint
    withAttributes:(NSDictionary *)attribs
```

Draws the receiver with the attributes in `attribs`.

```
- (void)drawInRect:(NSRect)aRect
    withAttributes:(NSDictionary *)attribs
```

Draws the receiver with the attributes in `attribs`.

```
- (NSSize)sizeWithAttributes:(NSDictionary *)attribs
```

Returns the size that the receiver would be if drawn with the atttibutes in `attribs`.

Making Letters Appear

Open `BigLetterView.h`. Add an instance variable to hold the attributes dictionary. Declare the methods that you are about to implement:

```
#import <Cocoa/Cocoa.h>

@interface BigLetterView : NSView
{
    NSColor *bgColor;
    NSString *string;
    NSMutableDictionary *attributes;
}
- (void)prepareAttributes;
- (void)drawStringCenteredIn:(NSRect)bounds;
- (void)setBgColor:(NSColor *)c;
- (void)setString:(NSString *)c;
- (NSString *)string;

@end
```

Open BigLetterView.m. Create a method that creates the attributes dictionary with a font and a foreground color:

```
- (void)prepareAttributes
{
  attributes = [[NSMutableDictionary alloc] init];

  [attributes setObject:[NSFont fontWithName:@"Helvetica"
                             size:75]
              forKey:NSFontAttributeName];

  [attributes setObject:[NSColor redColor]
              forKey:NSForegroundColorAttributeName];
}
```

In the **initWithFrame:** method, call the new method:

```
- (id)initWithFrame:(NSRect)rect
{
    if (self = [super initWithFrame:rect]) {
      NSLog(@"initializing view");
      [self prepareAttributes];
      [self setBgColor:[NSColor yellowColor]];
      [self setString:@" "];
    }
    return self;
}
```

In the **setString:** method, tell the view that it needs to redisplay itself:

```
- (void)setString:(NSString *)c
{
    c = [c copy];
    [string release];
    string = c;
    NSLog(@"The string: %@", string);
    [self setNeedsDisplay:YES];
}
```

Create a method that will display the string in the middle of a rectangle:

```
- (void)drawStringCenteredIn:(NSRect)r
{
    NSPoint stringOrigin;
    NSSize stringSize;

    stringSize = [string sizeWithAttributes:attributes];
    stringOrigin.x = r.origin.x + (r.size.width - stringSize.width)/2;
    stringOrigin.y = r.origin.y + (r.size.height - stringSize.height)/2;
```

```
        [string drawAtPoint:stringOrigin withAttributes:attributes];
}
```

Call that method from inside your **drawRect:** method:

```
- (void)drawRect:(NSRect)rect
{
    NSRect bounds = [self bounds];
    [bgColor set];
    [NSBezierPath fillRect:bounds];

    [self drawStringCenteredIn:bounds];
    if ([[self window] firstResponder] == self) {
        [[NSColor keyboardFocusIndicatorColor] set];
        [NSBezierPath setDefaultLineWidth:4.0];
        [NSBezierPath strokeRect:bounds];
    }
}
```

Make sure you release the `attributes` dictionary in the **dealloc** method:

```
- (void)dealloc
{
    [string release];
    [attributes release];
    [bgColor release];
    [super dealloc];
}
```

Build and run the application. Note that keyboard events go to your view unless they trigger a menu item. Try pressing Command-w. It should close the window (even if your view is the first responder for the key window).

Getting Your View to Generate PDF Data

All of the drawing commands can be converted into PDF by the AppKit framework. The PDF data can be sent to a printer or to a file. Note that the PDF will always look as good as possible on any device, because it is resolution independent.

You have already created a view that knows how to generate PDF data to describe how it is supposed to look. Getting the PDF data into a file is really quite easy. **NSView** has the following method:

```
- (NSData *)dataWithPDFInsideRect:(NSRect)aRect
```

This method creates a data object and then calls **drawRect:**. The drawing commands that would usually go to the screen instead go into the data object. Once you have this data object, you simply save it to a file.

Open BigLetterView.m and add a method that will create a save panel as a sheet:

```
- (IBAction)savePDF:(id)sender
{
    NSSavePanel *panel = [NSSavePanel savePanel];
    [panel setRequiredFileType:@"pdf"];
    [panel beginSheetForDirectory:nil
                             file:nil
                   modalForWindow:[self window]
                    modalDelegate:self
                   didEndSelector:
                     @selector(didEnd:returnCode:contextInfo:)
                      contextInfo:NULL];
}
```

When the user has chosen the filename, the method **didEnd:returnCode: contextInfo:** will be called. Implement this method in BigLetterView.m:

```
- (void)didEnd:(NSSavePanel *)sheet
    returnCode:(int)code
   contextInfo:(void *)contextInfo
{
    NSRect r;
    NSData *data;

    if (code == NSOKButton) {
      r = [self bounds];
      data = [self dataWithPDFInsideRect:r];
      [data writeToFile:[sheet filename] atomically:YES];
    }
}
```

Also, declare these methods in the BigLetterView.h file:

```
- (IBAction)savePDF:(id)sender;

- (void)didEnd:(NSSavePanel *)sheet
    returnCode:(int)code
   contextInfo:(void *)contextInfo;
```

Open the nib file. Drag in BigLetterView.h so that **savePDF:** will appear as one of the actions. Select the Save As... item under the File menu. Relabel it Save PDF.... (You may delete all of the other menu items from the menu, if you wish.) Make the Save PDF... menu item trigger the **BigLetterView**'s **savePDF:** method (Figure 17.3).

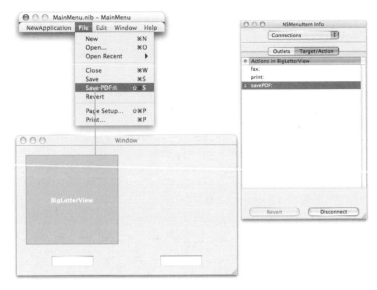

Figure 17.3   Connect Menu Item

Save and build the application. You should be able to generate a PDF file and view it in Preview (Figure 17.4).

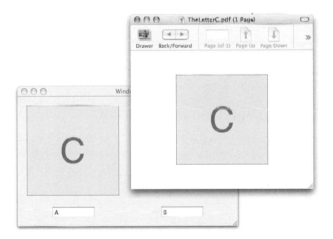

Figure 17.4   Completed Application

You will notice that multi-keystroke characters (like "é") are not handled by your **BigLetterView**. To make this possible, you would need to add several methods that the **NSInputManager** uses. This topic is beyond the scope of this book (I just wanted to show you how to get keyboard events), but you can learn about it in Apple's discussion of **NSInputManager** (/Developer/Documentation/ Cocoa/Conceptual/InputManager/index.html).

For the More Curious: NSFontManager

Sometimes you will have a font that is good but would be perfect if it were bold or italicized or condensed. **NSFontManager** can be used to make this sort of conversion. You can also use a font manager to change the size of the font.

For example, imagine you have a font and would like a similar font, but bold. Here is the code:

```
fontManager = [NSFontManager sharedFontManager];
boldFont = [fontManager convertFont:aFont toHaveTrait:NSBoldFontMask];
```

Challenge 1

Give the letter a shadow. The **NSShadow** class has the following methods:

```
- (id)init;
- (void)setShadowOffset:(NSSize)offset;
- (void)setShadowBlurRadius:(float)val;
- (void)setShadowColor:(NSColor *)color;
```

Challenge 2

Add the Boolean variables: bold and italic to your **BigLetterView**. Add check boxes that toggle these variables. If bold is YES, make the letter appear in boldface; if italic is YES, make the letter appear in italics.

Chapter 18

PASTEBOARDS AND NIL-TARGETED ACTIONS

There is a process running on your Mac called the pasteboard server (/System/Library/CoreServices/pbs). Applications use the **NSPasteboard** class to write data into that process and to read data from that process. The pasteboard server makes operations like copying, cutting, and pasting between applications possible.

An application can copy the same data onto the pasteboard in several formats. For example, an image can be copied onto the pasteboard as a PDF document and as a bitmapped image. Then the application that reads the data can choose the format that it likes most.

When putting data on the pasteboard, your application typically declares the types it will put on the pasteboard and then immediately copies those data to the pasteboard. The receiving application will first ask the pasteboard what types are available and then read the data in its preferred format.

You can also copy data to the pasteboard in a lazy manner. To do so, simply declare all the types of data you could put on the pasteboard and then supply the data when it is requested. We will talk about lazy copying at the end of the chapter.

Multiple pasteboards are available. There is a pasteboard for copy and paste operations and another for drag-and-drop tasks. There is a pasteboard that stores the last string that the user searched for. There is a pasteboard for copying rulers and another pasteboard for copying fonts.

In this section, you will add cut, copy, and paste capabilities to your **BigLetterView**. First, you will implement the methods that will read from and write to the pasteboard. Then we will discuss how those methods get called.

NSPasteboard

As mentioned earlier, the **NSPasteboard** class acts as an interface to the pasteboard server. Following are some of the commonly used methods of **NSPasteboard**:

+ (NSPasteboard *)**generalPasteboard**

Returns the general **NSPasteboard**. You will use this pasteboard to copy, cut, and paste.

+ (NSPasteboard *)**pasteboardWithName:**(NSString *)name

Returns the pasteboard identified by name. Here are the global variables that contain the names of the standard pasteboards:

NSGeneralPboard

NSFontPboard

NSRulerPboard

NSFindPboard

NSDragPboard

- (int)**declareTypes:**(NSArray *)types **owner:**(id)theOwner

Clears whatever was on the pasteboard before and declares the types of data that theOwner will put on the pasteboard. Here are the global variables for the standard types:

NSColorPboardType

NSFileContentsPboardType

NSFilenamesPboardType

NSFontPboardType

NSPDFPboardType

NSPICTPboardType

NSPostScriptPboardType

NSRulerPboardType

NSRTFPboardType

NSRTFDPboardType

NSStringPboardType

NSTabularTextPboardType

NSVCardPboardType

NSTIFFPboardType

NSURLPboardType

You can also create your own pasteboard types.

- (BOOL)**setData:**(NSData *)aData **forType:**(NSString *)dataType

- (BOOL)**setString:**(NSString *)s **forType:**(NSString *)dataType

Write data to the pasteboard.

- (NSArray *)**types**

Returns an array containing the types of data that are available to be read from the pasteboard.

- (NSString *)**availableTypeFromArray:**(NSArray *)types

Returns the first type found in types that is available for reading from the pasteboard. types should be a list of all types that you would be able to read.

- (NSData *)**dataForType:**(NSString *)dataType

- (NSString *)**stringForType:**(NSString *)dataType

Read data from the pasteboard.

Add Cut, Copy, and Paste to BigLetterView

You will create methods named **cut:**, **copy:**, and **paste:** in the **BigLetterView** class. To make these methods easier to write, you will first create methods for putting data onto and reading data off of a pasteboard. Add these methods to BigLetterView.m:

```
- (void)writeStringToPasteboard:(NSPasteboard *)pb {
    // Declare types
    [pb declareTypes:
            [NSArray arrayWithObject:NSStringPboardType]
                owner:self];
    // Copy data to the pasteboard
```

```
        [pb setString:string forType:NSStringPboardType];
    }

    - (BOOL)readStringFromPasteboard:(NSPasteboard *)pb {
        NSString *value;
        NSString *type;

        // Is there a string on the pasteboard?
        type = [pb availableTypeFromArray:
                    [NSArray arrayWithObject:NSStringPboardType]];
        if (type) {
            // Read the string from the pasteboard
            value = [pb stringForType:NSStringPboardType];
            // Our view can handle only one letter
            if ([value length] == 1) {
                [self setString:value];
                return YES;
            }
        }
        return NO;
    }
```

Add **cut:**, **copy:**, and **paste:** to BigLetterView.m:

```
- (IBAction)cut:(id)sender
{
    [self copy:sender];
    [self setString:@" "];
}

- (IBAction)copy:(id)sender
{
    NSPasteboard *pb = [NSPasteboard generalPasteboard];
    [self writeStringToPasteboard:pb];
}

- (IBAction)paste:(id)sender
{
    NSPasteboard *pb = [NSPasteboard generalPasteboard];
    if(![self readStringFromPasteboard:pb]) {
        NSBeep();
    }
}
```

Declare these methods in BigLetterView.h:

```
#import <Cocoa/Cocoa.h>

@interface BigLetterView : NSView
{
    NSColor *bgColor;
```

```
        NSString *string;
        NSMutableDictionary *attributes;
}
- (void)prepareAttributes;
- (IBAction)savePDF:(id)sender;
- (void)didEnd:(NSSavePanel *)sheet
     returnCode:(int)code
   contextInfo:(void *)contextInfo;
- (void)drawStringCenteredIn:(NSRect)bounds;
- (void)setBgColor:(NSColor *)c;
- (NSColor *)bgColor;
- (void)setString:(NSString *)c;
- (NSString *)string;
- (IBAction)cut:(id)sender;
- (IBAction)copy:(id)sender;
- (IBAction)paste:(id)sender;
- (void)writeStringToPasteboard:(NSPasteboard *)pb;
- (BOOL)readStringFromPasteboard:(NSPasteboard *)pb;

@end
```

Nil-Targeted Actions

How is the right view sent the **cut:**, **copy:**, or **paste:** message? After all, there are many, many views. If you select a text field, it should get the message. When you select another view and then choose the Copy or Paste menu item, the message should go to the newly selected view.

To solve this problem, the clever engineers at NeXT came up with *nil-targeted actions*. If you set the target of a control to nil, the application will try to send the action message to several objects until one of them responds. The application first tries to send the message to the first responder of the key window. This is exactly the behavior that you want for Cut and Paste. You can have several windows, each of which can have several views. The active view on the active window gets sent the cut-and-paste messages.

The beauty of targeted actions doesn't end there. **NSView**, **NSApplication**, and **NSWindow** all inherit from **NSResponder**. **NSResponder** has an instance variable called nextResponder. If an object doesn't respond to a nil-targeted action, its nextResponder gets a chance. The nextResponder for a view is usually its superview. The nextResponder of the content view of the window is the window. Thus the responders are linked together in what we call the *responder chain*.

Note that nextResponder has nothing to do with nextKeyView.

For example, one menu item closes the key window. It has a target of `nil`. The action is **performClose:**. None of the standard objects respond to **performClose:** except **NSWindow**. Thus the selected text field, for example, refuses to respond to **performClose:**. Then the superview of the text field refuses, and on up the view hierarchy. Ultimately, the window (the key window) accepts the **performClose:** method. So, to the user, the "active" window is closed.

As was mentioned in Chapter 7, a panel can become the key window but not the main window. If the key window and the main window are different, both windows get a chance to respond to the nil-targeted action.

Your question at this point should be: In what order will the objects be tested before a nil-targeted action is discarded?

1. The `firstResponder` of the `keyWindow` and its responder chain. The responder chain would typically include the superviews and, finally, the key window.
2. The `delegate` of the key window.
3. If it is a document-based application, the **NSWindowController** and then **NSDocument** object for the key window.
4. If the main window is different from the key window, it then goes through the same ritual with the main window:
   - The `firstResponder` of the main window and its responder chain (including the main window itself)
   - The main window's `delegate`.
   - The **NSWindowController** and then **NSDocument** object for the main window.
5. The instance of **NSApplication**.
6. The `delegate` of the **NSApplication**.
7. The **NSDocumentController**.

This series of objects is known as the *responder chain*. Figure 18.1 presents an example. The numbers indicate the order in which the objects would be asked if they respond to the nil-targeted action.

Note that in document-based applications (such as RaiseMan), the **NSDocument** object gets a chance to respond to the nil-targeted action. It receives the messages from the following menu items: Save, Save As..., Revert To Saved, Print..., and Page Layout....

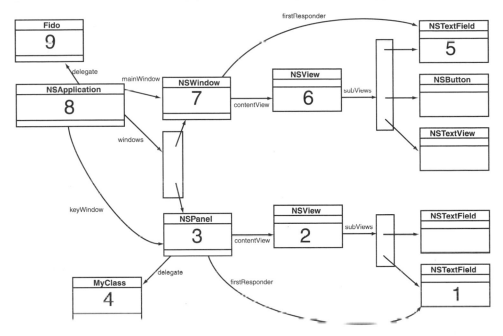

Figure 18.1   An Example of the Order in Which Responders Get a Chance to Respond

Looking at the Nib File

Open the nib file. Notice that the cut, copy, and paste items are connected to the icon that is labeled First Responder. The First Responder icon represents nil. It gives you something to drag to when you want an object to have a nil target (Figure 18.2).

The actions that appear in the inspector when you drag to the First Responder are in the class browser in Interface Builder. If you want an action to appear there, simply add it in the class browser.

Build and run your application. Note that cut, copy, and paste now work with your view. The keyboard equivalents also work. You can only copy strings that have one character into the **BigLetterView**.

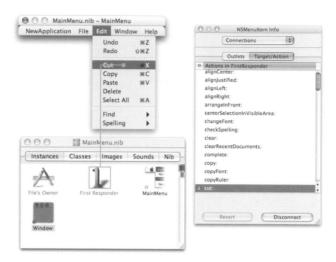

Figure 18.2   Check Menu Item

For the More Curious: Which Object Really Sends the Action Message?

The target on the cut, copy, and paste menu items is nil. We know that sending a message to nil will not do anything. Actually, all target-action messages are handled by **NSApplication**. It has the following method:

- (BOOL)**sendAction:**(SEL)anAction **to:**(id)aTarget **from:**(id)sender

When the target is nil, **NSApplication** knows to try to send messages to the objects in the responder chain.

For the More Curious: Lazy Copying

An application can implement copying to a pasteboard in a lazy manner. For example, imagine a graphics application that copies large images to the pasteboard in several formats: PICT, TIFF, PDF, and so on. You can imagine that copying all these formats onto the pasteboard would be hard on the application and the pasteboard server. Instead, such an application might do a lazy copy. That is, it will declare all the types that it could put on the pasteboard but will put off actually copying those data until another application asks for them.

Essentially, the application puts an "IOU" (instead of the data) on the pasteboard and gives an object that will provide the data when they are needed. When another application actually asks for the data, the pasteboard server calls back for the data.

The declaration works the same as earlier:

```
- (int)declareTypes:(NSArray *)types owner:(id)theOwner
```

But theOwner must implement the following method:

```
- (void)pasteboard:(NSPasteboard *)sender
         provideDataForType:(NSString *)type
```

When another application needs the data, this method will be called. At that point, the application must copy the data it promised onto the supplied pasteboard.

As you can imagine, a problem would arise if the pasteboard server asked for the data after the application had terminated. When the application is terminating, if it has an "IOU" currently on the pasteboard, it will be asked to supply all the data that were promised before terminating. Thus, it is not uncommon for an "IOU" owner to be sent **pasteboard:provideDataForType:** several times while the application is in the process of terminating.

The trickiest part of a lazy copy is that when the user copies data to the pasteboard and later pastes it into another application, he doesn't want the most recent state of the data. Rather, the user wants it *the way it was when the user copied it*. Most developers when implementing a lazy copy will take some sort of a snapshot of the information when declaring the types. When providing the data, the developer will copy the snapshot, instead of the current state, onto the pasteboard.

Challenge

You are putting the string on the pasteboard. Create the PDF for the view and put that on the pasteboard, too. Now you will be able to copy the image of the letter into graphics programs. Test it using Preview's New from Clipboard menu item.

Chapter 19
CATEGORIES

Although the engineers at Apple are very wise, one day you will think, "Golly, if only they had put that method on that class, my life would be so much easier." When this happens, you will want to create a *category*. A category is simply a collection of methods that you would like added to an existing class. The category concept is very useful, and I find it surprising that so few object-oriented languages include this powerful idea.

Creating categories is easier than talking about them. In Chapter 18, you added pasting capabilities to your **BigLetterView**. Notice, however, that if the string on the pasteboard has more than one letter, the paste attempt will fail, because **BigLetterView** is capable of displaying only one letter at a time. Let's extend the example to take just the first letter of the string instead of failing.

Add a Method to NSString

It would be nice if every **NSString** object had a method that returned its first letter. It does not, so you will use a category to add it.

Open your project and create a new file of type Objective-C class. You are not really creating a class, but this is a good starting place for the creation of a category (Figure 19.1).

Name the file **FirstLetter.m**. Also create **FirstLetter.h** (Figure 19.2).

Change FirstLetter.h to declare your category. Here is what it looks like:

```
#import <Foundation/Foundation.h>

@interface NSString (FirstLetter)

- (NSString *)firstLetter;

@end
```

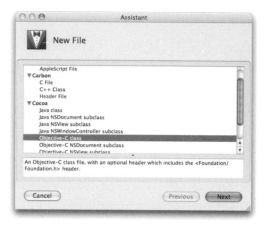

Figure 19.1   Choose File Type

Figure 19.2   Name File

You appear to be declaring the class **NSString**, but you are not giving it any instance variables or a superclass. Instead, you are naming the category **FirstLetter** and declaring a method. A category cannot add instance variables to the class, only methods.

Now implement the method **firstLetter** in the file FirstLetter.m. Make the file look like this:

```
#import "FirstLetter.h"

@implementation NSString (FirstLetter)
```

```
- (NSString *)firstLetter
{
    NSRange r;
    if ([self length] < 2) {
        return self;
    }
    r.location = 0;
    r.length = 1;
    return [self substringWithRange:r];
}
@end
```

Now you can use this method as if it were part of **NSString**. In BigLetter-View.m, change **readStringFromPasteboard:** to look like this:

```
- (BOOL)readStringFromPasteboard:(NSPasteboard *)pb
{
    NSString *value;
    NSString *type = [pb availableTypeFromArray:
                        [NSArray arrayWithObject:NSStringPboardType]];
    if (type) {
        value = [pb stringForType:NSStringPboardType];
        [self setString:[value firstLetter]];
        return YES;
    }
    return NO;
}
```

At the beginning of the BigLetterView.m, import FirstLetter.h.

Build and run your application. You will be able to copy strings with more than one letter into **BigLetterView**. Only the first letter of the string will actually be copied.

In this example, you added only one method, but note that you can add as many methods to the class as you wish. Also, you used only the methods of the class here, but you can also access the class's instance variables directly.

Warning: If you use a lot of categories, your code may become difficult for others to read and maintain. Some large teams discourage the use of categories for this reason.

Cocoa itself has many categories. For example, **NSAttributedString** is part of the Foundation framework. However, **NSAttributedString**'s **drawInRect:** method is part of a category from the AppKit framework. As a result, the documentation for the methods on **NSAttributedString** are distributed between the two frameworks. There are also separate header files for **NSAttributedString** and its categories, which tends to cause some confusion.

For the More Curious: Declaring Private Methods

Often, you will have methods defined in your .m file that you do not want to advertise by declaring them in your .h file. These are known as *private methods*.

If you call a private method before you declare or define it, you will get a warning from the compiler. One common technique to prevent these warnings is to declare the private methods in a category at the beginning of the .m file:

```
#import "Megatron.h"

// Declare the private methods
@interface Megatron (PrivateAPI)
- (void)blowTheLidOff;
- (void)putTheLidBackOn;
@end

@implementation Megatron

...actually implement all the private and public methods...

@end
```

Also, categories are used to declare methods that are not implemented. For example, in NSSpeechSynthesizer.h, the delegate methods are declared as if they are a category on **NSObject**:

```
@interface NSObject (NSSpeechSynthesizerDelegate)

- (void)speechSynthesizer:(NSSpeechSynthesizer *)sender
        didFinishSpeaking:(BOOL)finishedSpeaking;
- (void)speechSynthesizer:(NSSpeechSynthesizer *)sender
             willSpeakWord:(NSRange)characterRange
                  ofString:(NSString *)string;
- (void)speechSynthesizer:(NSSpeechSynthesizer *)sender
          willSpeakPhoneme:(short)phonemeOpcode;
@end
```

These methods are not actually implemented anywhere in the Cocoa frameworks, but this is a good way to let the compiler and other users know about the methods and their signatures.

Chapter 20
DRAG-AND-DROP

Drag-and-drop is little more than a flashy copy-and-paste. When the drag starts, some data are copied onto the dragging pasteboard. When the drop occurs, the data are read off the dragging pasteboard. The only thing that makes this technique trickier than copy-and-paste is that users need feedback: an image that appears as they drag, a view that becomes highlighted when they drag into it, and maybe a big gulping sound when they drop the image.

Several different things can happen when data are dragged from one application to another: Nothing may happen, a copy of the data may be created, or a link to the existing data may be created. Constants represent these operations:

```
NSDragOperationNone
NSDragOperationCopy
NSDragOperationLink
```

There are several other operations that you see less frequently:

```
NSDragOperationGeneric
NSDragOperationPrivate
NSDragOperationMove
NSDragOperationDelete
NSDragOperationEvery
```

Both the source and the destination must agree on the operation that will occur when the user drops the image.

When you add drag-and-drop to a view, there are two distinct parts of the change:

- Make it a drag source.
- Make it a drag destination.

Let's take these steps separately. First, you will make your view be a drag source. When that is working, you will make it be a drag destination.

Make BigLetterView Be a Drag Source

When you finish this section, you will be able to drag a letter off the **BigLetterView** and drop it into any text editor. It will look like Figure 20.1.

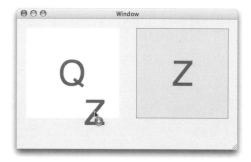

Figure 20.1   Completed Application

To be a drag source, your view must implement **draggingSourceOperationMask ForLocal:**. This method declares what operations the view is willing to participate in as a source. Add the following method to your BigLetterView.m:

```
- (unsigned int)draggingSourceOperationMaskForLocal:(BOOL)isLocal
{
    return NSDragOperationCopy;
}
```

This method is automatically called twice: once with isLocal as YES, which determines what operations it is willing to participate in for destinations within your application, and a second time with isLocal as NO, which determines what operations it is willing to participate in for destinations in other applications.

To start a drag operation, you will use a method on **NSView**:

```
- (void)dragImage:(NSImage *)anImage
               at:(NSPoint)imageLoc
           offset:(NSSize)mouseOffset
            event:(NSEvent *)theEvent
       pasteboard:(NSPasteboard *)pboard
           source:(id)sourceObject
        slideBack:(BOOL)slideBack
```

You will supply it with the image to be dragged and the point at which you want the drag to begin. The documentation says to include the mouseDown event, but a mouseDragged event works well, too. The offset seems to be completely ignored. The pasteboard is usually the standard drag pasteboard. If the drop does not occur, you can choose whether the icon should slide back to the place from which it came.

You will also need to create an image to drag. You can draw on an image just as you can on a view. To make the drawing appear on the image instead of the screen, you must first lock focus on the image. When the drawing is complete, you must unlock the focus.

Here is the whole method to add to `BigLetterView.m`:

```
- (void)mouseDragged:(NSEvent *)event
{
    NSRect imageBounds;
    NSPasteboard *pb;
    NSImage *anImage;
    NSSize s;
    NSPoint p;

    // Get the size of the string
    s = [string sizeWithAttributes:attributes];

    // Create the image that will be dragged
    anImage = [[NSImage alloc] initWithSize:s];

    // Create a rect in which you will draw the letter
    // in the image
    imageBounds.origin = NSMakePoint(0,0);
    imageBounds.size = s;

    // Draw the letter on the image
    [anImage lockFocus];
    [self drawStringCenteredIn:imageBounds];
    [anImage unlockFocus];

    // Get the location of the drag event
    p = [self convertPoint:[event locationInWindow] fromView:nil];

    // Drag from the center of the image
    p.x = p.x - s.width/2;
    p.y = p.y - s.height/2;

    // Get the pasteboard
    pb = [NSPasteboard pasteboardWithName:NSDragPboard];

    // Put the string on the pasteboard
    [self writeStringToPasteboard:pb];

    // Start the drag
    [self dragImage:anImage
```

```
        at:p
        offset:NSMakeSize(0, 0)
        event:event
        pasteboard:pb
        source:self
        slideBack:YES];
    [anImage release];
}
```

That's it. Build and run the application. You should be able to drag a letter off the view and into any text editor. (Try dragging it into Xcode.)

After the Drop

When a drop occurs, the drag source will be notified if you implement the following method:

```
- (void)draggedImage:(NSImage *)image
            endedAt:(NSPoint)screenPoint
          operation:(NSDragOperation)operation;
```

For example, to make it possible to clear the **BigLetterView** by dragging the letter to the trashcan in the dock, advertise your willingness in **draggingSource-OperationMaskForLocal:**

```
- (unsigned int)draggingSourceOperationMaskForLocal:(BOOL) is Local
{
    return NSDragOperationCopy | NSDragOperationDelete;
}
```

Then implement **draggedImage:endedAt:operation:**

```
- (void)draggedImage:(NSImage *)image
            endedAt:(NSPoint)screenPoint
          operation:(NSDragOperation)operation
{
    if (operation == NSDragOperationDelete) {
        [self setString:@" "];
    }
}
```

Build and run the application. Drag a letter into the trashcan. It should disappear from the view.

Make BigLetterView Be a Drag Destination

There are several parts to being a drag destination. First, you need to declare your view to be a destination for the dragging of certain types. **NSView** has a method for this purpose:

```
- (void)registerForDraggedTypes:(NSArray *)pboardTypes
```

You typically call this method in your **initWithFrame:** method.

Then you need to implement six methods. (Yes, six!) All six methods have the same argument: an **NSDraggingInfo** object. It has the dragging pasteboard. The six methods are invoked as follows:

- As the image is dragged into the destination, the destination is sent a **draggingEntered:** message. Often, the destination view updates its appearance. For example, it might highlight itself.
- While the image remains within the destination, a series of **draggingUpdated:** messages are sent. Implementing **draggingUpdated:** is optional.
- If the image is dragged outside the destination, **draggingExited:** is sent.
- If the image is released on the destination, either it slides back to its source (and breaks the sequence) or a **prepareForDragOperation:** message is sent to the destination, depending on the value returned by the most recent invocation of **draggingEntered:** (or **draggingUpdated:** if the view implemented it).
- If the **prepareForDragOperation:** message returns YES, then a **performDragOperation:** message is sent. This is typically where the application actually reads data off the pasteboard.
- Finally, if **performDragOperation:** returned YES, **concludeDragOperation:** is sent. The appearance may change. This is where you might generate the big gulping sound that implies a successful drop.

registerForDraggedTypes

Add a call to **registerForDraggedTypes:** to the **initWithFrame:** method in BigLetterView.m:

```
- (id)initWithFrame:(NSRect)rect
{
    if (self = [super initWithFrame:rect]) {
      NSLog(@"initializing view");
      [self prepareAttributes];
      [self setBgColor:[NSColor yellowColor]];
```

```
        [self setString:@" "];
        [self registerForDraggedTypes:
            [NSArray arrayWithObject:NSStringPboardType]];
    }
    return self;
}
```

Add Highlighting

To signal the user that the drop is acceptable, your view will highlight itself. Add a highlighted instance variable to BigLetterView.h:

```
@interface BigLetterView : NSView
{
    NSColor *bgColor;
    NSString *string;
    NSMutableDictionary *attributes;
    BOOL highlighted;
}
...
```

Add highlighting to **drawRect:**.

```
- (void)drawRect:(NSRect)rect
{
    NSRect bounds = [self bounds];

    // Draw white background if highlighted
    if (highlighted) {
        [[NSColor whiteColor] set];
    } else {
        [bgColor set];
    }
    [NSBezierPath fillRect:bounds];

    // Draw the string
    [self drawStringCenteredIn:bounds];

    // Draw blue rectangle if first responder
    if ([[self window] firstResponder] == self) {
        [[NSColor keyboardFocusIndicatorColor] set];
        [NSBezierPath setDefaultLineWidth:4.0];
        [NSBezierPath strokeRect:bounds];
    }
}
```

Implement the Dragging Destination Methods

So far, we have seen two ways to declare a pointer to an object. If the pointer can refer to any type of object, we would declare it like this:

```
id foo;
```

If the pointer should refer to an instance of a particular class, we can declare it like this:

```
MyClass *foo;
```

A third possibility also exists. If we have a pointer that should refer to an object that conforms to a particular protocol, we can declare it like this:

```
id <MyProtocol> foo;
```

NSDraggingInfo is actually a protocol, not a class. All of the dragging destination methods expect an object that conforms to the **NSDraggingInfo** protocol.

Add the following methods to BigLetterView.m:

```
- (unsigned int)draggingEntered:(id <NSDraggingInfo>)sender
{
    NSLog(@"draggingEntered:");
    if ([sender draggingSource] != self) {
        NSPasteboard *pb = [sender draggingPasteboard];
        NSString *type = [pb availableTypeFromArray:
                    [NSArray arrayWithObject:NSStringPboardType]];
        if (type != nil) {
            highlighted = YES;
            [self setNeedsDisplay:YES];
            return NSDragOperationCopy;
        }
    }
    return NSDragOperationNone;
}

- (void)draggingExited:(id <NSDraggingInfo>)sender
{
    NSLog(@"draggingExited:");
    highlighted = NO;
    [self setNeedsDisplay:YES];
}

- (BOOL)prepareForDragOperation:(id <NSDraggingInfo>)sender
{
    return YES;
```

```
}

- (BOOL)performDragOperation:(id <NSDraggingInfo>)sender
{
    NSPasteboard *pb = [sender draggingPasteboard];
    if(![self readStringFromPasteboard:pb]) {
        NSLog(@"Error: Could not read from dragging pasteboard");
        return NO;
    }
    return YES;
}

- (void)concludeDragOperation:(id <NSDraggingInfo>)sender
{
    NSLog(@"concludeDragOperation:");
    highlighted = NO;
    [self setNeedsDisplay:YES];
}
```

Testing

Open the nib file, and add another **BigLetterView** to the window. Delete the text fields. Make sure to set the nextKeyView for each **BigLetterView** so that you can tab between them (Figure 20.2).

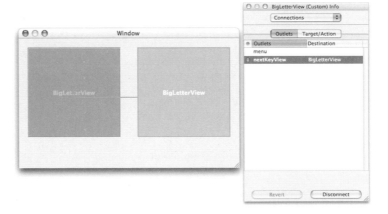

Figure 20.2   Set nextKeyView for Each BigLetterView

Build and run the application. Note that you can drag characters between the views and from other applications.

Chapter 21
NSTIMER

An instance of **NSButton** has a target and a selector (the action). When the button is clicked, the action message is sent to the target. Timers work in a similar way. A timer is an object that has a target, a selector, and a delay, which is given in seconds (Figure 21.1). After the delay, the selector message is sent to the

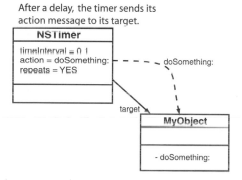

Figure 21.1   NSTimer

target. The timer sends itself as an argument to the message. The timer can also be set to send the message repeatedly.

To play with timers a bit, you will create a typing tutor application. The application will have two **BigLetterView** objects. One will display what the user should type, and the other will display what the user has typed (Figure 21.2). An **NSProgressIndicator** will display how much time is left. When 2 seconds has passed, the application will beep to indicate that the user took too long. Then the user is given 2 more seconds.

You will create an **AppController** class. When the user clicks the Go button, an instance of **NSTimer** will be created. The timer will send a message every 0.2 second. The method triggered will check whether the two views match. If so, the user is given a new letter to type. Otherwise, the progress indicator is incremented. If the user pauses the application, the timer is invalidated.

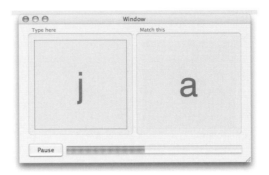

Figure 21.2   Completed Application

Figure 21.3 shows the object diagram.

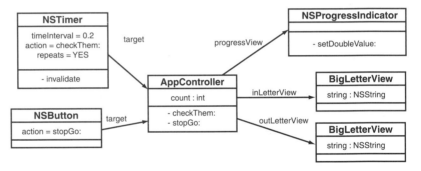

Figure 21.3   Object Diagram

Lay Out the Interface

Go back to your TypingTutor project. Open the `MainMenu.nib`.

Create a new subclass of **NSObject** called **AppController**. Add three outlets to **AppController**: `inLetterView`, `outLetterView`, and `progressView`. `inLetterView` and `outLetterView` will refer to BigLetterView objects. `progressView` will refer to an NS ProgressIndicator. Add one action: **stopGo:** (Figure 21.4).

Create the files for **AppController**. Create an instance of **AppController**.

Select the **BigLetterView** on the left. From the Layout menu, choose the Make subviews -> Box menu item. Relabel the box Type here. Group the other **BigLetterView** in a box, and relabel that box Match this.

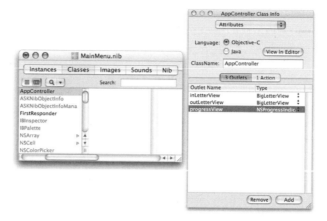

Figure 21.4   AppController's Actions and Outlets

Drop an **NSProgressIndicator** on the window. Use the inspector to make it not indeterminate. Set its range to be 0 to 100 (Figure 21.5).

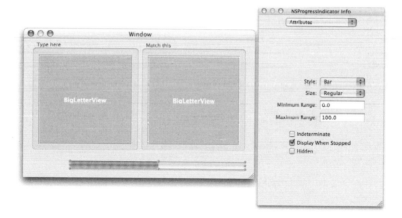

Figure 21.5   Inspect the Progress Indicator

Put a button on the window. Using the inspector, set its title to Go and its alternate title to Pause. Make the button type Rounded Bevel Button, and set its behavior to Toggle. Also, set it to have no icon (Figure 21.6).

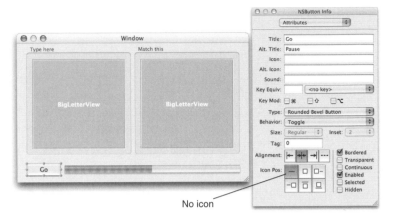

Figure 21.6   Inspect the Button

Make Connections

Control-drag from the button to the **AppController** object. Set the action to be **stopGo:** (Figure 21.7).

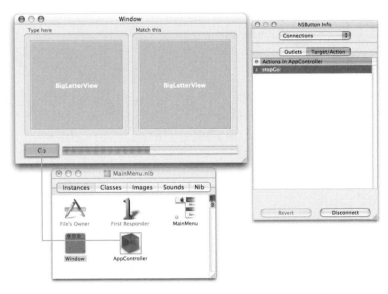

Figure 21.7   Connect the Button to the AppController

Control-drag from the **AppController** to the **NSProgressIndicator**, and set the progressView outlet.

Control-drag from the **AppController** to the **BigLetterView** on the left, and set the inLetterView outlet (Figure 21.8).

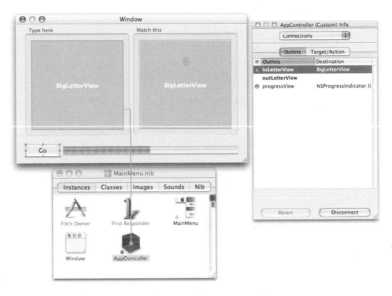

Figure 21.8   Connect the inLetterView Outlet

Control-drag from the **AppController** to the **BigLetterView** on the right, and set the outLetterView outlet (Figure 21.9).

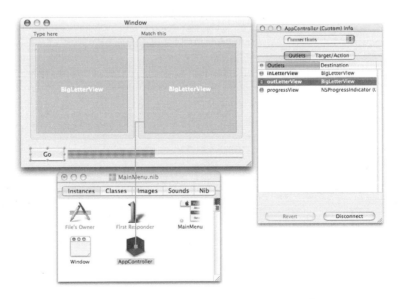

Figure 21.9   Connect the outLetterView Outlet

Adding Code to AppController

Add the following instance variables and methods to `AppController.h`:

```
#import <Cocoa/Cocoa.h>
@class BigLetterView;

@interface AppController : NSObject
{
    IBOutlet BigLetterView *inLetterView;
    IBOutlet BigLetterView *outLetterView;
    IBOutlet NSProgressIndicator *progressView;
    int count;              // How many times has the timer gone off?
    NSTimer *timer;
    NSArray *letters;  // The array of letters that the user will type
    int lastIndex;     // The index in the array of the
                       // letter the user is trying to type
}
- (void)showAnotherLetter;
- (IBAction)stopGo:(id)sender;
@end
```

Implement the following methods in `AppController.m`:

```
#import "AppController.h"
#import "BigLetterView.h"

// Number of times the timer will fire
#define TICKS 10

@implementation AppController

- (id)init
{
    if (self = [super init]) {

        // Create an array of letters
        letters = [[NSArray alloc] initWithObjects:@"a", @"s",
                    @"d",@"f", @"j", @"k", @"l", @";",nil];
        lastIndex = 0;
        // Seed the random number generator
        srandom(time(NULL));
    }
    return self;
}

- (void)awakeFromNib
{
    [self showAnotherLetter];
}
```

```objc
- (void)showAnotherLetter
{
    int x;
    //Choose random numbers until you get a different
    // number than last time
    x = lastIndex;
    while (x == lastIndex){
        x = random() % [letters count];
    }
    lastIndex = x;
    [outLetterView setString:[letters objectAtIndex:x]];

    [progressView setDoubleValue:0.0];
    count = 0;
}

- (IBAction)stopGo:(id)sender
{
    if ([sender state] == 1) {
        NSLog(@"Starting");

        // Create a timer
        timer = [[NSTimer scheduledTimerWithTimeInterval:0.2
                                      target:self
                                      selector:@selector(checkThem:)
                                      userInfo:nil
                                      repeats:YES] retain];
    } else {
        NSLog(@"Stopping");

        // Invalidate and release the timer
        [timer invalidate];
        [timer release];
    }
}

- (void)checkThem:(NSTimer *)aTimer
{
    if ([[inLetterView string] isEqual:[outLetterView string]]) {
        [self showAnotherLetter];
    }
    count++;
    if (count > TICKS){
        NSBeep();
        count = 0;
    }
    [progressView setDoubleValue:(100.0 * count) / TICKS];
}
@end
```

Build and run your application.

Note, once again, that we have separated our classes into views (**BigLetterView**) and controllers (**AppController**). If I were creating a full-featured application, I would probably also create model classes like **Lesson** and **Student**.

For the More Curious: NSRunLoop

NSRunLoop is an object that waits. It waits for events to arrive and then forwards them to **NSApplication**. It waits for timer events to arrive and then forwards them to **NSTimer**. You can even attach a network socket to the run loop, and it will wait for data to arrive on that socket.

Most Cocoa applications have only one thread. This is possible because the one thread is controlled by the run loop. Many people who think they need to create a multithreaded application later realize that their application would have been more efficient and easier to write if they had used the run loop more wisely. It is rarely necessary to create multithreaded applications.

Challenge

Change your ImageFun application so that autoscrolling is timer driven. Delete your **mouseDragged:** method from **StretchView**. In **mouseDown:**, create a repeating timer that invokes a method in the view every tenth of a second. In the invoked method, autoscroll using the current event. To get the current event, use **NSApplication**'s **currentEvent** method:

```
NSEvent *e = [NSApp currentEvent];
```

(Remember that NSApp is a global variable that points to the instance of **NSApplication**.) Invalidate and release the timer in **mouseUp:**. Note that the autoscrolling becomes much smoother and more predictable.

Chapter 22
SHEETS

A sheet is simply an instance of **NSWindow** that is attached to another window. The sheet comes down over the window, and the window stops getting events until the sheet is dismissed. Typically, you will compose a sheet as an off-screen window in your nib file.

NSApplication has several methods that make sheets possible:

```
// Start a sheet
- (void)beginSheet:(NSWindow *)sheet
   modalForWindow:(NSWindow *)docWindow
    modalDelegate:(id)modalDelegate
   didEndSelector:(SEL)didEndSelector
      contextInfo:(void *)contextInfo;

// End the sheet
- (void)endSheet:(NSWindow *)sheet returnCode:(int)returnCode;
```

Besides the sheet window and the window to which it is attached, you supply a modal delegate, a selector, and a pointer when you start the sheet. The modalDelegate will be sent the didEndSelector, and the sheet, its return code, and the contextInfo will be sent as arguments. Thus, the method triggered by the didEndSelector should have a signature like this:

```
- (void)rex:(NSWindow *)sheet
       fido:(int)returnCode
      rover:(void *)contextInfo;
```

The dog names are used here to indicate that you could name the method anything you wish. Most programmers name the method something more meaningful, like **sheetDidEnd:returnCode:contextInfo:**.

Adding a Sheet

You are going to add a sheet that will allow the user to adjust the speed of the TypingTutor application. You will bring up the sheet when the user selects the Adjust speed... menu item. You will end the sheet when the user clicks the OK button. The final application will look like Figure 22.1.

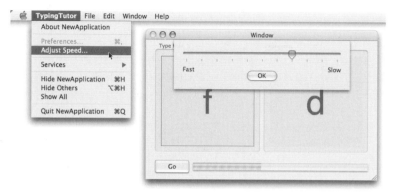

Figure 22.1   Completed Application

Your **AppController** will control the slider and the window, so you will need to add outlets for them. Also, your **AppController** will be sent a message when the user selects the Adjust speed... menu item or clicks the OK button, so you will need to add two action methods to the **AppController**.

Figure 22.2 presents the object diagram.

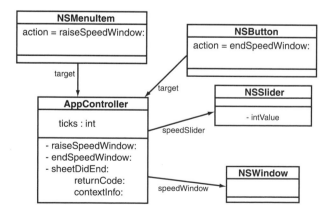

Figure 22.2   Object Diagram

Add Outlets and Actions

Edit AppController.h as follows:

```objc
#import <Cocoa/Cocoa.h>
@class BigLetterView;

@interface AppController : NSObject
{
    int count;          // How many times has the timer fired?
    int ticks;          // How high can "count" go?
    IBOutlet NSWindow *speedWindow;
    IBOutlet NSSlider *speedSlider;
    IBOutlet BigLetterView *inLetterView;
    IBOutlet BigLetterView *outLetterView;
    IBOutlet NSProgressIndicator *progressView;
    NSTimer *timer;
    NSArray *letters;   // The array of letters that the user will type
    int lastIndex;      // The index in the array of the
                        // letter the user is trying to type
}
- (void)showAnotherLetter;
- (IBAction)stopGo:(id)sender;
- (IBAction)raiseSpeedWindow:(id)sender;
- (IBAction)endSpeedWindow:(id)sender;
- (void)sheetDidEnd:(NSWindow *)sheet
        returnCode:(int)returnCode
        contextInfo:(void *)contextInfo;
@end
```

Save the file.

Open MainMenu.nib and drag AppController.h into it.

Lay Out the Interface

Add a menu item to the main menu for your application (Figure 22.3).

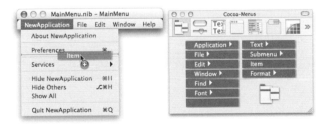

Figure 22.3 Add a Menu Item

Change the title of the menu item to Adjust Speed.... Control-drag from the menu item to the **AppController**. Set the action to be **raiseSpeedWindow:** (Figure 22.4).

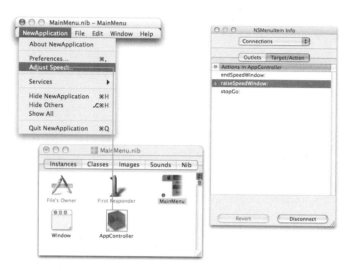

Figure 22.4 Connect the Menu Item

Create a new window by dragging one off the palette. Disable resizing for the window. Put a slider on the new window. To label the left end of the slider as "Fast" and the right end as "Slow," drop two uneditable text fields onto the window. Add a button and change its title to "OK." Inspect the slider and set its range to be 5.0 to 40.0 (Figure 22.5).

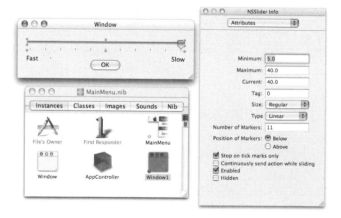

Figure 22.5 Inspect Slider

When the user clicks the OK button, the button should send a message
to the **AppController** that will end the sheet. Control-drag from the button to
the **AppController** to set the `target`. Choose **endSpeedWindow:** as the action
(Figure 22.6).

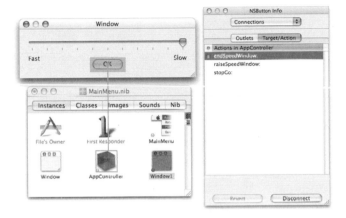

Figure 22.6   Set the Target of the Button

To raise the window as a sheet, your **AppController** must have a pointer to it.
Control-drag from the **AppController** to the icon that represents the new
window. Set it to be the `speedWindow` outlet (Figure 22.7).

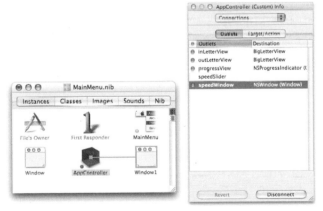

Figure 22.7   Connect speedWindow Outlet

For the **AppController** to read the slider, it must have a pointer to it. Control-drag from the **AppController** to the slider and set the speedSlider outlet (Figure 22.8).

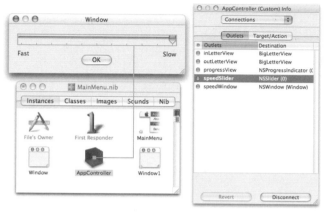

Figure 22.8   Connect speedSlider Outlet

Save and close the nib file.

Add Code

In AppController.m, you defined a constant called TICKS. In the last section, the user got 10 ticks of the timer before the beep was issued. In this section, you will make the number of ticks be a variable. If the user is playing "Fast," he will get fewer ticks than if the user is playing "Slow." You will read the number of ticks from the speedSlider. The first step, then, is to go through AppController.m and replace the constant TICKS with the variable ticks. Delete the line that defines the constant TICKS. In the **init** method, initialize ticks to be 10:

```
- (id)init
{
    if (self = [super init]) {
      ticks = 10;
      letters = [[NSArray alloc] initWithObjects:@"a", @"s",
                    @"d",@"f", @"j", @"k", @"l", @";",nil];
      lastIndex = 0;
      // Seed the random number generator
      srandom(time(NULL));
    }
    return self;
}
```

When the user chooses the Adjust Speed... menu item, the speedSlider will be set so that it reflects the value of ticks and the sheet will run. Add the following method to AppController.m:

```
- (IBAction)raiseSpeedWindow:(id)sender
{
    [speedSlider setIntValue:ticks];
    [NSApp beginSheet:speedWindow
        modalForWindow:[inLetterView window]
        modalDelegate:self
        didEndSelector:@selector(sheetDidEnd:returnCode:contextInfo:)
        contextInfo:NULL];
}
```

Notice that you are attaching the sheet to the window that the inLetterView is on. The **AppController** is the modalDelegate, and it will be sent **sheetDidEnd:returnCode:contextInfo:** when the sheet is dismissed.

The sheet will end when the user clicks the OK button. Add the following method to AppController.m.

```
- (IBAction)endSpeedWindow:(id)sender
{
  // Hide the sheet
  [speedWindow orderOut:sender];

  // Return to normal event handling
  [NSApp endSheet:speedWindow returnCode:1];
}
```

You could have also read the slider's new value in **endSpeedWindow:**, but you know that **sheetDidEnd:returnCode:contextInfo:** is going to be called. You will read the new value in that method. Add the following method to AppController.m:

```
- (void)sheetDidEnd:(NSWindow *)sheet
        returnCode:(int)returnCode
        contextInfo:(void *)contextInfo
{
  // Read the slider's value
  ticks = [speedSlider intValue];

  // Reset the count
  count = 0;

  NSLog(@"sheetDidEnd: Return code = %d", returnCode);
}
```

Build and run your application.

For the More Curious: contextInfo

The contextInfo parameter is a pointer to some data. You can supply it when you start the sheet, and the delegate will get the pointer when you end the sheet. For example, here the developer has started a sheet and inserted a phone number for the context info:

```
[NSApp beginSheet:aWindow
    modalForWindow:someOtherWindow
     modalDelegate:self
    didEndSelector:@selector(didEnd:returnCode:phone:)
        contextInfo:@"703-555-6513"];
```

Later, in the **didEnd:returnCode:phone:** method, the phone number will be supplied as the third argument:

```
- (void)didEnd:(NSWindow *)sheet
    returnCode:(int)returnCode
          phone:(NSString *)phoneNumber
{
  // Read the slider's value
  NSLog(@"sheetDidEnd: Phone number = %@", phoneNumber);
}
```

Notice that the context info and the **NSNotification**'s user info dictionary serve similar purposes.

For the More Curious: Modal Windows

When a sheet is active, the user is prevented from sending events to the window to which it is attached. When an alert panel is run, it is modal—that is, the user is prevented from sending events to any other window.

To make a window modal, use the following method of NSApp:

- (int)**runModalForWindow:**(NSWindow *)aWindow

Only events destined for aWindow will actually make it through this method. When you are ready to make the aWindow nonmodal, send this message to the **NSApplication** object:

- (void)**stopModalWithCode:**(int)returnCode

At that point **runModalForWindow:** will end and return returnCode.

For the More Curious: Alert Sheets

In Chapter 12, you learned how to make alert panels that ran modally. Now that you know about sheets and their modal delegates, we can discuss how to run an alert sheet.

A simple way to create an alert sheet is with the following C function:

```
void NSBeginAlertSheet(NSString *title,
                       NSString *defaultButton,
                       NSString *alternateButton,
                       NSString *otherButton,
                       NSWindow *docWindow,
                             id  modalDelegate,
                            SEL  didEndSelector,
                            SEL  didDismissSelector,
                           void *contextInfo,
                       NSString *msg, ...);
```

Here `title` is the string that will appear at the top of the sheet. The button names come next. The sheet is attached to the docWindow window. The `modalDelegate` object will be sent the `didEndSelector` and the `didDismissSe-lector`. The `contextInfo` pointer points to anything that you would like passed to the didEnd method and the didDismiss method. The `msg` text will appear under the title; it can contain tokens to be substituted in the message. The values to be substituted in come last.

Once again, if you need more control, you can use the class **NSAlert**. Once you have created an instance of **NSAlert**, you send it this message to run it as a sheet:

```
- (void)beginSheetModalForWindow:(NSWindow *)window
             modalDelegate:(id)delegate
            didEndSelector:(SEL)didEndSelector
               contextInfo:(void *)contextInfo;
```

For the More Curious: NSDrawer

A drawer is similar to a sheet in several ways: It is attached to a window, users can open and close it, and it has a content view that can be configured in Interface Builder (Figure 22.9).

Figure 22.9   Example Drawer

A drawer differs from a sheet in that it is not a window: There is a class **NSDrawer**. Also, a sheet disables the window underneath, whereas a drawer simply augments the window to which it is attached. Finally, creating a drawer is done differently than creating a sheet. In creating a drawer, there are three major players: the instance of **NSDrawer**, the content view of the drawer, and the window to which the drawer is attached. You will typically also have a button or menu item for opening and closing the drawer. **NSDrawer** has an action method **toggle:** that will open the drawer if it is closed and close it if it is open (Figure 22.10).

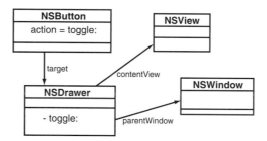

Figure 22.10   NSDrawer

Interface Builder includes a palette item that will create an **NSDrawer**, its parent window, and the drawer's content view, all of which will be connected correctly. In Figure 22.11, I've added a button to the parent window and a matrix of buttons to the content view of the drawer.

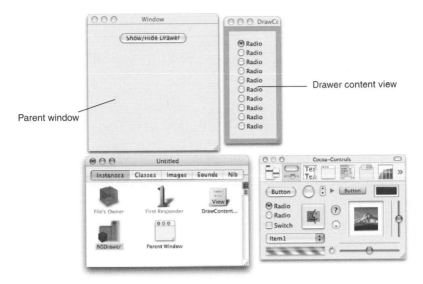

Parent window

Drawer content view

Figure 22.11   Example Drawer as Nib

Sometimes you will wonder whether a sheet or a drawer is more appropriate for your interface. Usually when a sheet is visible, the window beneath it is disabled. A drawer, on the other hand, is an extension to the window that the user may not always want to see.

Challenge

Put the speed adjustment on a drawer instead of a sheet.

Chapter 23
CREATING NSFORMATTERS

A formatter takes a string and makes another object, typically so that the user can type something that is more than just a string. For example, the **NSDateFormatter**, when passed a string like "August 17, 1967", converts it into an **NSCalendarDate** object that represents the seventeenth day of August in the year 1967 (Figure 23.1).

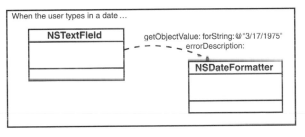

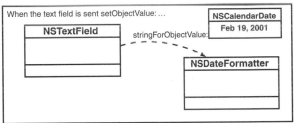

Figure 23.1 NSDateFormatter

Also, a formatter can take an object and create a string for the user to see. For example, imagine a text field that has an **NSDateFormatter**. When the text field is sent **setObjectValue:** with an **NSCalendarDate** object, the date formatter will create a string that represents that date. The user will then see that string.

All formatters are subclasses of the **NSFormatter** class. Two of these subclasses come with Cocoa: **NSDateFormatter** and **NSNumberFormatter**. You used **NSNumberFormatter** in Chapter 6 to format the expected raise as a percentage.

The most basic formatter will implement two methods:

```
- (BOOL)getObjectValue:(id *)anObject
              forString:(NSString *)aString
        errorDescription:(NSString **)errorPtr
```

This message is sent by the control (like a text field) to the formatter when it has to convert aString into an object. aString is the string that the user typed in. The formatter can return YES and set anObject to point to the new object. If the formatter returns NO, it indicates the string could not be converted and the errorPtr is set to indicate what went wrong. Note that errorPtr is a pointer to a pointer; that is, it is a location where you can put a pointer to the string. anObject is also a pointer to a pointer.

```
- (NSString *)stringForObjectValue:(id)anObject
```

This message is sent by the control to the formatter when it has to convert anObject into a string. The control will display the string that is returned for the user (Figure 23.2).

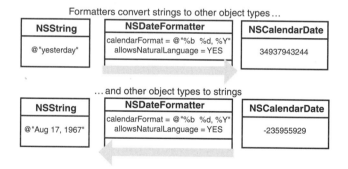

Figure 23.2   NSFormatter

Often the object that is created from the string is also a string. For example, you might have a **TelephoneNumberFormatter** that properly inserts the parentheses and dashes into a telephone number.

A Basic Formatter

In this chapter, you will write your own formatter class. You will create a formatter that allows the user to type in the name of a color, and the formatter will in turn create the appropriate **NSColor** object. Then you will set the background of the **BigLetterView** with that color object. Figure 23.3 shows what the application will look like when you are done.

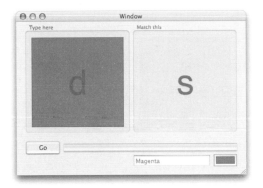

Figure 23.3   Completed Application

Edit the Interface File for the AppController Class

First you will add outlets and actions to your **AppController**. You will add a text field and a color well to the window. You will have outlets so that your **AppController** can send messages to the text field and the color well. You will have actions in **AppController** that will be triggered by the text field and the color well. Alter your AppController.h file to look like this:

```
#import <Cocoa/Cocoa.h>
@class BigLetterView;

@interface AppController : NSObject
{
    IBOutlet NSWindow *speedWindow;
    IBOutlet NSSlider *speedSlider;
    int count;
    int ticks;
    IBOutlet BigLetterView *inLetterView;
    IBOutlet BigLetterView *outLetterView;
    IBOutlet NSProgressIndicator *progressView;
    NSTimer *timer;
    NSArray *letters;
    int lastIndex;
    IBOutlet NSColorWell *colorWell;
    IBOutlet NSTextField *textField;
}
- (void)showAnotherLetter;
- (IBAction)stopGo:(id)sender; // Triggered by text field
- (IBAction)takeColorFromTextField:(id)sender; // Triggered by colorwell
```

```
- (IBAction)takeColorFromColorWell:(id)sender;
- (IBAction)raiseSpeedWindow:(id)sender;
- (IBAction)endSpeedWindow:(id)sender;
- (void)sheetDidEnd:(NSWindow *)sheet
        returnCode:(int)returnCode
        contextInfo:(void *)contextInfo;
@end
```

Edit the Nib File

Open MainMenu.nib. Drag the new AppController.h file into the nib file. Interface Builder will parse the file and add the actions and outlets to the AppController object (Figure 23.4).

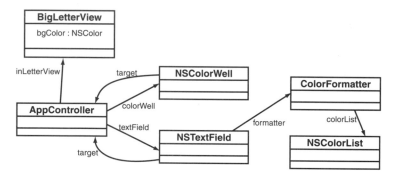

Figure 23.4   Object Diagram

Add a text field and a color well to the window. Set the target of each to the AppController object. The action for the color well will be **takeColor FromColorWell:**. The action for the text field will be **takeColorFrom TextField:**. Set the **AppController**'s textField outlet to the text field. Set the **AppController**'s colorWell outlet to the color well (Figure 23.5).

NSColorList

For this exercise, you will use an **NSColorList**. An **NSColorList** is a dictionary of color objects that maps a name to an instance of **NSColor** objects. Several color lists come standard with Mac OS X. In particular, the color list named "Apple" includes many of the standard colors, such as "Purple" and "Yellow."

NSColorList is not a particularly useful class, but it makes this exercise very elegant. We will not spend much time discussing it.

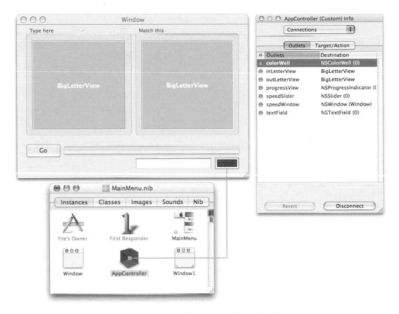

Figure 23.5   Set colorWell Outlet

Searching Strings for Substrings

When you have a string like "dakakookookakoo" and you are searching through it for a shorter string like "ka," the result will be an NSRange. The location is the first letter of the matching substring in the longer string. The length is the length of the substring.

Of course, there are a couple of options that you might want to set. For example, you might want to do a case-insensitive search. Or you might want to do a backward search (from the end of the string instead of the beginning). To search backward for the string "KA" in "dakakookookakoo" in a case-insensitive manner, you would use the following code:

```
NSRange aRange;
NSString *big = @"dakakookookakoo";
NSString *small = @"KA";

aRange = [big rangeOfString:small
                options:(NSCaseInsensitiveSearch | NSBackwardsSearch)];
```

After this code executes, aRange.location would be 10 and aRange.length would be 2.

If the substring is not found, the length will be 0.

Create a Subclass of NSFormatter

In Xcode, create a new Objective-C class named **ColorFormatter**. Make **ColorFormatter** be a subclass of **NSFormatter**. Give the class an instance variable of type **NSColorList**. Call the variable colorList.

```
#import <Cocoa/Cocoa.h>

@interface ColorFormatter : NSFormatter {
    NSColorList *colorList;
}
@end
```

Edit ColorFormatter.m to look like this:

```
#import <Cocoa/Cocoa.h>
#import "ColorFormatter.h"

@interface ColorFormatter (Private API)
- (NSString *)firstColorKeyForPartialString:(NSString *)string
@end

@implementation ColorFormatter

- (id)init
{
    if (self = [super init]) {
      colorList = [[NSColorList colorListNamed:@"Apple"] retain];
    }
    return self;
}

// A private method
- (NSString *)firstColorKeyForPartialString:(NSString *)string
{
    NSArray *keys = [colorList allKeys];
    NSString *key;
    NSRange whereFound;
    int i, keyCount;
    keyCount = [keys count];

    // Loop through the color list
    for (i = 0; i< keyCount; i++) {
        key = [keys objectAtIndex: i];
        whereFound = [key rangeOfString:string
                            options:NSCaseInsensitiveSearch];
        // Does the string match the beginning of the color name?
        if ((whereFound.location == 0) && (whereFound.length > 0)) {
            return key;
        }
    }
```

```
        // If no match is found, return nil
        return nil;
}

- (NSString *)stringForObjectValue:(id)obj
{
        // Find a string for the color "obj"
        float red, green, blue, alpha;
        float red2, green2, blue2, alpha2;
        NSColor *color2;
        NSString *key, *closestKey;
        float howClose, distance;
        int i, keyCount;
        NSArray *keys;
        closestKey = nil;
        // Is this a color object?
        if ([obj isKindOfClass: [NSColor class]]) {

            // Get the color components
            [obj getRed:&red
                  green:&green
                   blue:&blue
                  alpha:&alpha];
            keys = [colorList allKeys];
            keyCount = [keys count];

            // Initialize howClose to something large
            howClose = 3;

            // Loop through all the colors looking for closest
            for (i = 0; i< keyCount; i++) {
                key = [keys objectAtIndex: i];
                color2 = [colorList colorWithKey:key];

                // Find the color components of the current color
                [color2 getRed:&red2
                         green:&green2
                          blue:&blue2
                         alpha:&alpha2];

                // How far is it from obj?
                distance = fabs(red2 - red) +
                           fabs(green2 - green) +
                           fabs(blue2 - blue);

                // Is this the closest yet?
                if (distance < howClose) {
                    howClose = distance;
                    closestKey = key;
                }
            }

            // Return the name of the closest color
            return closestKey;
        } else {
```

```
            // If not a color, return nil
            return nil;
        }
    }
    - (BOOL)getObjectValue:(id *)obj
                forString:(NSString *)string
          errorDescription:(NSString **)errorString
    {
        // Look up the color for 'string'
        NSString *matchingKey = [self firstColorKeyForPartialString:string];
        if (matchingKey) {
            *obj = [colorList colorWithKey:matchingKey];
            return YES;
        } else {
            // Occasionally, 'errorString' is NULL
            if (errorString != NULL) {
                *errorString = @"No such color";
            }
            return NO;
        }
    }
    - (void)dealloc
    {
        [colorList release];
        [super dealloc];
    }
    @end
```

You will need to attach the formatter to your text field. Do so in the
awakeFromNib method of **AppController**:

```
- (void)awakeFromNib
{
    ColorFormatter *colorFormatter = [[ColorFormatter alloc] init];
    [textField setFormatter:colorFormatter];
    // The formatter is retained by the text field
    [colorFormatter release];
    [textField setObjectValue:[inLetterView bgColor]];
    [colorWell setColor:[inLetterView bgColor]];
    [self showAnotherLetter];
}
```

Also in **AppController**, create the action methods:

```
- (IBAction)takeColorFromTextField:(id)sender
{
    NSColor *c = [sender objectValue];
    NSLog(@"taking color from text field");
    [inLetterView setBgColor:c];
    [colorWell setColor:c];
}
```

```
- (IBAction)takeColorFromColorWell:(id)sender
{
    NSColor *c = [sender color];
    NSLog(@"taking color from color well");
    [inLetterView setBgColor:c];
    [textField setObjectValue:c];
}
```

Be sure to import `ColorFormatter.h` at the beginning at `AppController.m`.

Build and run your application. You should be able to type in color names and see the background of the **BigLetterView** change accordingly. Also, if you use the color well, you should see the name of the color change in the text field.

The Delegate of the NSControl

You are probably wondering where the error string goes. The control can have a delegate. If the formatter decides the string is invalid, the delegate is sent the error message.

```
- (BOOL)control:(NSControl *)control
          didFailToFormatString:(NSString *)string
               errorDescription:(NSString *)error
```

The delegate can override the opinion of the formatter. If it returns YES, the control displays the string as is. If it returns NO, it means that the delegate agrees with the formatter: The string is invalid.

Implement the following method in `AppController.m`:

```
- (BOOL)control:(NSControl *)control
     didFailToFormatString:(NSString *)string
          errorDescription:(NSString *)error
{
    NSLog(@"AppController told that formatting of %@ failed: %@",
              string, error);
    return NO;
}
```

Now open the nib file and make the **AppController** the delegate of the text field (Figure 23.6).

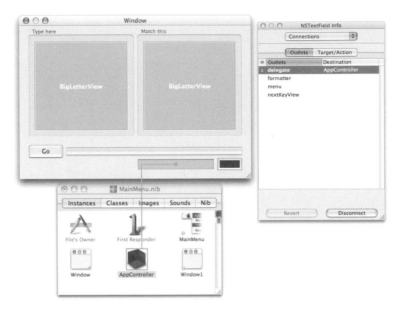

Figure 23.6   Connect the Text Field's delegate Outlet

Build and run your application. When validation fails, you will see a message on the console indicating what the string was and why it failed.

Checking Partial Strings

You might want to create a formatter that prevents the user from typing letters that are not part of a color name. To make the formatter check the string after every keystroke, implement the following method:

```
- (BOOL)isPartialStringValid:(NSString *)partial
          newEditingString:(NSString **)newString
          errorDescription:(NSString **)errorString
```

Here partial is the string, including the last keystroke. If your formatter returns NO, it indicates that the partial string is not acceptable. Also, if your formatter returns NO, it can supply the newString and an errorString. The newString will appear in the control. The errorString should give the user an idea of what she or he did wrong. If your formatter returns YES, the newString and the errorString are ignored.

Add the following method to your ColorFormatter.m:

```
- (BOOL)isPartialStringValid:(NSString *)partial
           newEditingString:(NSString **)newString
           errorDescription:(NSString **)error
{
    NSString *match;
    if ([partial length] == 0){
        return YES;
    }
    match = [self firstColorKeyForPartialString:partial];
    if (match) {
        return YES;
    } else {
        *error = @"No such color";
        return NO;
    }
}
```

Build and run your application. You will not be able to type in anything except the color names.

Notice something annoying about this app: You can't see what color would be chosen if you simply tabbed out of the field. What you would like is a formatter that does autocompletion. To enable autocompletion, you need to control the range of the selection as well. Delete the **isPartialStringValid:newEditing-String:errorDescription:** method and replace it with this method:

```
- (BOOL)isPartialStringValid:(NSString **)partialPtr
        proposedSelectedRange:(NSRange *)proposedSelPtr
               originalString:(NSString *)orig
        originalSelectedRange:(NSRange)origSel
             errorDescription:(NSString **)error
{
    NSString *match;
    // Zero-length strings are fine
    if ([*partialPtr length] == 0) {
        return YES;
    }
    match = [self firstColorKeyForPartialString:*partialPtr];

    // No color match?
    if (!match) {
        return NO;
    }

    // If this would not move the cursor forward, it
    // is a delete
    if (origSel.location == proposedSelPtr->location) {
        return YES;
    }
```

```
        // If the partial string is shorter than the
        // match, provide the match and set the selection
        if ([match length] != [*partialPtr length]) {
            proposedSelPtr->location = [*partialPtr length];
            proposedSelPtr->length = [match length] -
                                                [*partialPtr length];

            *partialPtr = match;
            return NO;
        }
        return YES;
}
```

Build and run your application. Your formatter will now autocomplete color names as you type them.

Formatters That Return Attributed Strings

Sometimes it is nice for the formatter to define not only the string that is to be displayed, but also the attributes of that string. For example, a number formatter might print the number in red if it is negative. For this purpose, you will use **NSAttributedString**.

Your formatter can implement the following method:

```
- (NSAttributedString *)attributedStringForObjectValue:(id)anObj
                    withDefaultAttributes:(NSDictionary *)aDict
```

If the method exists, it will be called instead of **stringForObjectValue:**. The dictionary that you are passed contains the default attributes for the view where the data will be displayed. It is a good idea to merge the dictionary with your added attributes. For example, use the font from the text field where the data will be displayed, but make the foreground color red to show that the profits are negative.

Implement the following method to display the name of the color in that color:

```
- (NSAttributedString *)attributedStringForObjectValue:(id)anObject
                    withDefaultAttributes:(NSDictionary *)attributes
{
    NSColor *fgColor;
    NSAttributedString *atString;
    NSMutableDictionary *md = [attributes mutableCopy];
    NSString *match = [self stringForObjectValue:anObject];
    if (match) {
```

```
        fgColor = [colorList colorWithKey:match];
        [md setObject:fgColor forKey:NSForegroundColorAttributeName];
    }
    atString = [[NSAttributedString alloc] initWithString:match
                                        attributes:md];
    [md release];
    [atString autorelease];
    return atString;
}
```

Build and run the application. Note that the text field will not change colors until it gives up first-responder status.

Challenge

Color objects come from particular color spaces. Asking for the red, green, and blue components is possible only if the color is from an RGB-based color space, like NSCalibratedRGBColorSpace. Thus, if the user uses the color panel's CMYK view or Black/White view to choose a color, your formatter will fail to name the resulting color. Fix this problem.

NSColor has the following methods:

- (NSString *)**colorSpaceName**

Returns the name of the receiver's color space.

- (NSColor *)**colorUsingColorSpaceName:**(NSString *)spaceName

Returns a similar color from the color space named spaceName.

Chapter 24
PRINTING

Code to handle printing is always relatively hard to write. There are many factors at play: pagination, margins, and page orientation (landscape versus portrait). This chapter is designed to get you started on your journey toward the perfect printout.

Compared to most operating systems, Mac OS X makes writing print routines considerably easier. After all, your views already know how to generate PDF, and Mac OS X knows how to print PDF. If you have a document-based application and a view that knows how to draw itself, you just implement **printShowingPrintPanel:**. In this method, you create an **NSPrintOperation** object and run it. The code would look like this:

```
- (void)printShowingPrintPanel:(BOOL)flag
{
    NSPrintInfo *printInfo = [self printInfo];
    NSPrintOperation *printOp;

     printOp = [NSPrintOperation printOperationWithView:aView
                                            printInfo:printInfo];
    [printOp setShowPanels:flag];
    [self runModalPrintOperation:printOp
                    delegate:nil
                didRunSelector:NULL
                    contextInfo:NULL];
}
```

Adding Printing to TypingTutor

If your application is not document based, you will implement a **print:** method in the target of the menu item. For example, add the following method to the **AppController** class in your TypingTutor project:

```
- (IBAction)print:(id)sender
{
```

```
    NSPrintInfo *printInfo = [NSPrintInfo sharedPrintInfo];
    NSPrintOperation *printOp;
    printOp = [NSPrintOperation printOperationWithView:inLetterView
                                             printInfo:printInfo];

    [printOp setShowPanels:YES];
    [printOp runOperation];
}
```

Declare the method in AppController.h. Drag AppController.h into the nib
file. Select the menu item called Print.... In the connections inspector, disconnect
its target outlet. Make the **AppController** be the target of the menu item, and
set the action to **print:** (Figure 24.1).

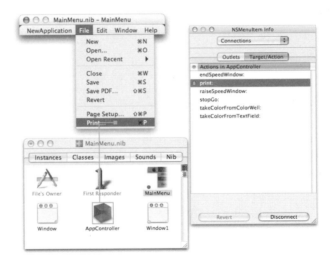

Figure 24.1   Connect Menu Item

Build the project and confirm that printing works. Unless you have a printer set
up, you will only be able to preview what would have been printed (Figure 24.2).

To print all the views on the window, simply change the **print:** method to use
the window's content view:

```
- (IBAction)print:(id)sender
{
    NSPrintInfo *printInfo = [NSPrintInfo sharedPrintInfo];
    NSPrintOperation *printOp;
    NSView *v = [[inLetterView window] contentView];
    printOp = [NSPrintOperation printOperationWithView:v
                                             printInfo:printInfo];

    [printOp setShowPanels:YES];
    [printOp runOperation];
}
```

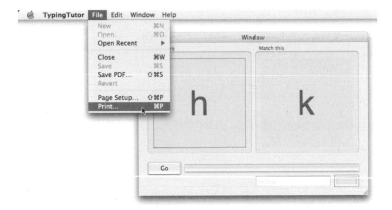

Figure 24.2   Completed Application

Dealing with Pagination

What about multiple pages? A view, after all, has only a single page. How will you get a view to print multiple page documents? Off-screen, you will make a huge view that can display all the pages of the document simultaneously (Figure 24.3). The print system will ask the view how many pages it is displaying. Then it will ask the view where each page can be found in the view.

Figure 24.3   Each Page Is a Rectangle on the View

Your view, then, must override two methods:

```
// How many pages?
- (BOOL)knowsPageRange:(NSRange *)rptr;

// Where is each page?
- (NSRect)rectForPage:(int)pageNum;
```

As an example, you will add printing to the RaiseMan application. You will print the name and expected raise for as many people as will fit on the paper size that the user selected from the print panel (Figure 24.4).

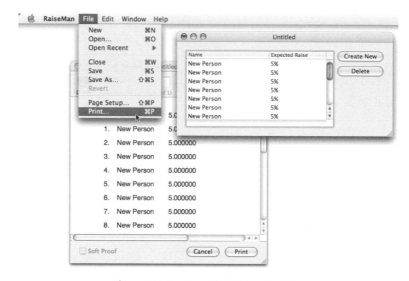

Figure 24.4   Completed Application

To do so, you will create a view that does the printing. The view will be big enough to display all of the people simultaneously, but for each page there will be a rectangle that contains the information for the people that will be printed on that page. The view will be called **PeopleView** (Figure 24.5).

The code in MyDocument.m is actually pretty simple:

```
- (void)printShowingPrintPanel:(BOOL)flag
{
    NSPrintInfo *printInfo = [self printInfo];
    NSPrintOperation *printOp;
    PeopleView *view;
    // End editing
    [personController commitEditing];
```

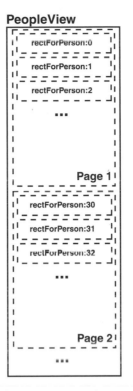

Figure 24.5   PeopleView

```
view = [[PeopleView alloc] initWithPeople:employees
                            printInfo:printInfo];
printOp = [NSPrintOperation printOperationWithView:view
                            printInfo:printInfo];

[printOp setShowPanels:flag];
[self runModalPrintOperation:printOp
            delegate:nil
        didRunSelector:NULL
            contextInfo:NULL];

[view release];
}
```

You will have to import `PeopleView.h`. This is not so different from the TypingTutor example, but there are some minor differences:

- **NSDocument** implements **printDocument:** to call [self printShowingPrint Panel:YES], so your subclass of **NSDocument** is implementing **printShowing PrintPanel:** instead of **print:**.

- The view that does the printing needs to be created. Usually you will create a view by calling **initWithFrame:**. In **PeopleView**, you will create another constructor that takes the array of people and the print info object. The print info object knows the paper size. Using the array of people and the print info object, you can figure out how big the frame should be.
- **NSDocument** has a method **printInfo** that returns the instance of **NSPrintInfo** for that document.

In the MainMenu.nib file, make sure the Print... menu item is nil-targeted and has set its action to **printDocument** (Figure 24.6).

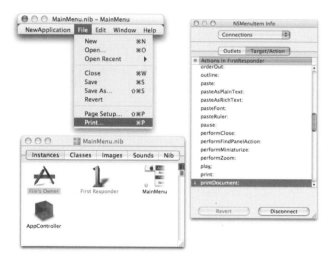

Figure 24.6   Connect Menu Item

Create a class called **PeopleView** that is a subclass of **NSView**. PeopleView.h would look like this:

```
#import <Cocoa/Cocoa.h>

@interface PeopleView : NSView {
    NSArray *people;
    NSMutableDictionary *attributes;
    NSSize paperSize;
    float leftMargin;
    float topMargin;
}
- (id)initWithPeople:(NSArray *)array printInfo:(NSPrintInfo *)pi;
- (NSRect)rectForPerson:(int)index;
- (int)peoplePerPage;

@end
```

In `PeopleView.m`, you will implement the **initWithPeople:printInfo:** method. This initializer will call **NSView**'s **initWithFrame:** method.

```
#import "PeopleView.h"
#import "Person.h"
#define VSPACE 30.0

@implementation PeopleView

- (id)initWithPeople:(NSArray *)array printInfo:(NSPrintInfo *)pi
{
    NSRange pageRange;
    NSRect frame;

    // Get the useful data out of the print info
    paperSize = [pi paperSize];
    leftMargin = [pi leftMargin];
    topMargin = [pi topMargin];

    people = [array retain];

    // Get the number of pages
    [self knowsPageRange:&pageRange];

    // The view must be big enough to hold the first and last pages
    frame = NSUnionRect([self rectForPage:pageRange.location],
                        [self rectForPage:NSMaxRange(pageRange)-1]);

    // Call the superclass's designated initializer
    [super initWithFrame:frame];

    // The attributes of the text to be printed
    attributes = [[NSMutableDictionary alloc] init];
    [attributes setObject:[NSFont fontWithName:@"Helvetica" size:15.0]
                   forKey:NSFontAttributeName];
    return self;
}

// The origin of the view is at the upper-left corner
- (BOOL)isFlipped
{
    return YES;
}

- (NSRect)rectForPage:(int)page
{
    NSRect result;
    result.size = paperSize;

    // Page numbers start at 1
    result.origin.y = (page - 1) * paperSize.height;
    result.origin.x = 0.0;
    return result;
}
```

```
- (int)peoplePerPage
{
    float ppp = (paperSize.height - (2.0 * topMargin)) / VSPACE;
    return (int)ppp;
}

- (BOOL)knowsPageRange:(NSRange *)r
{
    int peoplePerPage = [self peoplePerPage];

    // Page counts start at 1
    r->location = 1;
    r->length = ([people count] / peoplePerPage);
    if ([people count] % peoplePerPage > 0) {
        r->length = r->length + 1;
    }
    return YES;
}

- (NSRect)rectForPerson:(int)i
{
    NSRect result;
    int peoplePerPage = [self peoplePerPage];
    result.size.height = VSPACE;
    result.size.width = paperSize.width - (2 * leftMargin);
    result.origin.x = leftMargin;
    int page = i / peoplePerPage;
    int indexOnPage = i % peoplePerPage;
    result.origin.y = (page * paperSize.height) + topMargin +
                                        (indexOnPage * VSPACE);
    return result;
}

- (void)drawRect:(NSRect)r
{
    int count, i;
    count = [people count];
    for (i=0; i<count; i++) {
        NSRect personRect = [self rectForPerson:i];
        if (NSIntersectsRect(r, personRect)) {
            Person *p = [people objectAtIndex:i];
            NSString *dataString;
            dataString = [NSString stringWithFormat:@"%d.\t%@\t\t%f",
                                    i, [p personName],
                                    [p expectedRaise]];
            [dataString drawInRect:personRect
                    withAttributes:attributes];
        }
    }
}
```

```
- (void)dealloc
{
    [attributes release];
    [people release];
    [super dealloc];
}
```

```
@end
```

Build and run the application. Notice that multiple-pages-per-sheet setup (4-up, for example) works. Notice that you can change the paper size and more or less people subsequently appear on each page.

For the More Curious: Am I Drawing to the Screen?

Often in an application, you will want to draw things differently on screen than on the printer. For example, in a drawing program, the view might show a grid on-screen, but not when printed on paper.

In your **drawRect:** method, you can ask the current graphics context if it is currently drawing to the screen:

```
if ([[NSGraphicsContext currentContext] isDrawingToScreen]) {
    ...draw grid...
}
```

Using ObjectAlloc

Apple supplies developers with a very handy tool for hunting down memory leaks—an application called ObjectAlloc. To see how it works, create a memory leak by commenting out the line that releases **PeopleView** in MyDocument.m:

```
[self runModalPrintOperation:printOp
                    delegate:nil
              didRunSelector:NULL
                 contextInfo:NULL];
    //[view release];
```

Recompile your app. In the Debug menu, you will find the Launch Using Performance Tool submenu. Choose ObjectAlloc.

When ObjectAlloc starts, you will be presented with a window that displays the number of instances of each class that is created in your application. Click the run button as shown in Figure 24.7.

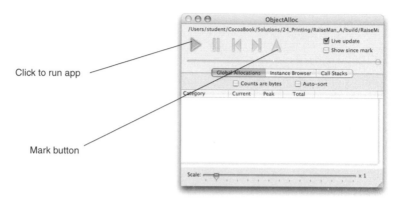

Figure 24.7   Run Application in ObjectAlloc

When the sheet appears, check Also record CF & ObjC reference counting as shown in Figure 24.8.

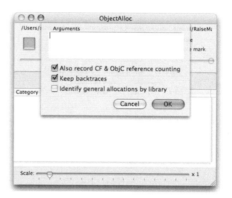

Figure 24.8   Record Reference Counting

As your application runs, you will see three numbers for each class:

- Current: how many objects of this class are in memory right now
- Peak: the maximum number of objects of this class that have been in memory at the same time
- Total: the total number of instances that have been created

Check the box labeled Show since mark.

In RaiseMan, create a new document. In ObjectAlloc, click the mark button. Create some **Person** objects and note their existence in ObjectAlloc. In RaiseMan, close the document. In ObjectAlloc, notice that the **Person** objects are deallocated.

Create another new document. Print/preview it three times. Notice that the **PeopleView** objects are not deallocated correctly.

Change to the Instance Browser tab of ObjectAlloc. Find an instance of **PeopleView**, and look at its allocation event. (A panel will appear asking whether it is okay to pause the app; it is.) You should see the state of the stack as it was when the **PeopleView** object was allocated (Figure 24.9).

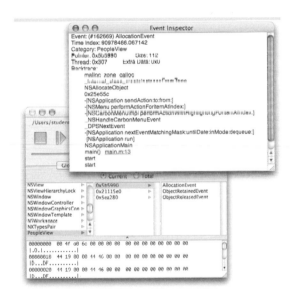

Figure 24.9   State of the Stack

Using ObjectAlloc, you can hunt down many types of memory leaks.

Challenge

Add page numbers to the printout.

Chapter 25

UPDATING MENUS

In many applications, it is necessary to enable and disable menu items as the user interacts with the application. In particular, as the first responder changes, a menu item that is nil-targeted will need to be disabled if the responder chain does not respond to its action. By default, this activity is handled for you. When displaying itself, the menu item will automatically figure out if the current target has the appropriate action. If it does not, the menu item will be disabled.

When a menu item is deciding whether it should be enabled, it will ask its target if it implements `validateMenuItem:`. If so, the target is sent `validateMenuItem:`. If the target returns YES, the menu item is enabled.

To enable and disable menu items, you will implement the following method:

```
- (BOOL)validateMenuItem:(NSMenuItem *)menuItem;
```

It will return YES if the menu item should be enabled.

Note that for nil-targeted actions, the member of the responder chain that would respond to the action is asked to validate it. For example, the window will be asked to validate **performClose:** (a window without a close button will invalidate this menu item). If a text field is selected, it will be asked to validate the **copy:** menu item. As the first responder changes, the new chain is asked to validate the respective menu items (Figure 25.1).

To review, a menu item will automatically enable or disable itself. First, it checks whether its target implements the action. If not, the menu item is disabled. Otherwise, it asks the target whether it responds to **validateMenuItem:**. If not, the menu item is enabled. Otherwise, it is enabled if and only if the target validates the menu item.

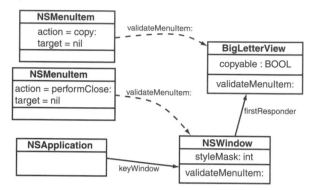

Figure 25.1 The Target Validates the Menu Item

Making a BigLetterView Uncopyable

Your TypingTutor program currently allows the user to simply drag or copy/paste the letter from the "Match this" **BigLetterView** to the "Type here" **BigLetterView**. This behavior would be cheating, and you should prevent it (Figure 25.2).

Figure 25.2 Completed Application

You will add a BOOL instance variable called copyable to the **BigLetterView** class. If copyable is NO, you will prevent the user from dragging or copying from the view. Start by editing the BigLetterView.h file to add the following instance variable:

```
@interface BigLetterView : NSView
{
    NSColor *bgColor;
    NSString *string;
    NSMutableDictionary *attributes;
    BOOL highlighted;
    BOOL copyable;
}
...
```

Next, add accessor methods for the variable in BigLetterView.m:

```
- (void)setCopyable:(BOOL)yn
{
    copyable = yn;
}
- (BOOL)copyable
{
    return copyable;
}
```

Also, declare these methods in BigLetterView.h.

In **initWithFrame:**, make the view copyable by default:

```
- initWithFrame:(NSRect)rect
{
    if (self = [super initWithFrame:rect]) {
      NSLog(@"initWithFrame:");
      [self prepareAttributes];
      [self setBgColor:[NSColor yellowColor]];
      [self setString:@" "];
      [self setCopyable:YES];
      [self registerForDraggedTypes:
              [NSArray arrayWithObject:NSStringPboardType]];
    }
    return self;
}
```

Make the "Match this" **BigLetterView** uncopyable in **AppController**'s **awakeFromNib** method:

```
- (void)awakeFromNib
{
```

```
    ColorFormatter *colorFormatter = [[ColorFormatter alloc] init];
    [textField setFormatter:colorFormatter];
    [colorFormatter release];
    [textField setObjectValue:[inLetterView bgColor]];
    [colorWell setColor:[inLetterView bgColor]];
    [outLetterView setCopyable:NO];
    [self showAnotherLetter];
}
```

In **BigLetterView**'s **mouseDragged:** method, start the drag operation only if the view is copyable:

```
- (void)mouseDragged:(NSEvent *)event
{
    NSRect imageBounds;
    NSPasteboard *pb;
    NSImage *anImage;
    NSSize s;
    NSPoint p;

    if (!copyable) {
        NSLog(@"Drag not permitted");
        return;
    }

    // Get the size of the string
    s = [string sizeWithAttributes:attributes];

    // Create the image that will be dragged
    anImage = [[NSImage alloc] initWithSize:s];

    // Create a rect in which you will draw the letter
    // in the image
    imageBounds.origin = NSMakePoint(0,0);
    imageBounds.size = s;
    [anImage setSize:s];

    // Draw the letter on the image
    [anImage lockFocus];
    [self drawStringCenteredIn:imageBounds];
    [anImage unlockFocus];

    // Get the location of the drag event
    p = [self convertPoint:[event locationInWindow] fromView:nil];

    // Drag from the center of the image
    p.x = p.x - s.width/2;
    p.y = p.y - s.height/2;

    // Get the pasteboard
    pb = [NSPasteboard pasteboardWithName:NSDragPboard];
```

```
    // Put the string on the pasteboard
    [self writeStringToPasteboard:pb];

    // Start the drag
    [self dragImage:anImage
                 at:p
             offset:NSMakeSize(0, 0)
              event:event
         pasteboard:pb
             source:self
          slideBack:YES];
    [anImage release];
}
```

If you build and run the application now, the Copy and Cut menu items will still be enabled. To disable them appropriately, add a **validateMenuItem:** method:

```
- (BOOL)validateMenuItem:(NSMenuItem *)menuItem
{
    NSString *selectorString;
    selectorString = NSStringFromSelector([menuItem action]);
    NSLog(@"validateCalled for %@", selectorString);

    // By using the action instead of the title, we do not
    // have to worry about whether the menu item is localized
    if (([menuItem action] == @selector(copy:)) ||
        ([menuItem action] == @selector(cut:))){
        return copyable;
    } else {
        return YES;
    }
}
```

Build and run your application. Note that the Copy and Cut menu items are disabled when the uncopyable **BigLetterView** is selected.

For the More Curious: Menu Delegates

Sometimes, as an application is running, the menus need to be updated. In this chapter, we have discussed how to enable and disable items. If you wish to make more substantial changes to the menu, there are a few ways to do so.

First, you can obtain a pointer to the menu and explicitly add or remove items. This technique works well for infrequent changes. For example, when a new plug-in is loaded, it might add a few menu items this way.

Second, you can create a delegate for your app that is sent the following message before the menu is displayed:

```
- (void)menuNeedsUpdate:(NSMenu *)menu
```

This approach is a good way to deal with tasks like changing the title of the menu item depending on which view is currently the first responder.

Third, you can create a delegate for your app that refills the entire menu each time. This strategy suffices for things like a list of menu items that is always changing, such as a buddy list in a chat program. For this sort of menu, you would implement the following two methods:

```
- (int)numberOfItemsInMenu:(NSMenu *)menu
```

This method returns the number of items that should appear in the menu. The menu immediately creates this many menu items and calls the next method for each.

```
- (BOOL)menu:(NSMenu *)menu
  updateItem:(NSMenuItem *)item
     atIndex:(int)x
shouldCancel:(BOOL)shouldCancel
```

This method gives you a chance to update the new menu item at index x with a title, target, action, key equivalent, and its enabled status. Return YES to continue filling in more items. Return NO to stop the process. The shouldCancel parameter is pretty silly. I suggest you just ignore it. (If you want the specific silliness, refer to the documentation.)

The menu is what makes key equivalents work. Thus, if you are generating a menu dynamically, you need to take responsibility for the key equivalents. You should implement the following method:

```
- (BOOL)menuHasKeyEquivalent:(NSMenu *)menu
                    forEvent:(NSEvent *)event
                      target:(id *)target
                      action:(SEL *)action
```

If one of the menu items that you would create has a key equivalent, return YES and fill in the target and action pointers.

If the delegate exists but doesn't implement this method, the menus are created and checked for keyboard equivalents.

Often, a dynamically created menu will not contain any key equivalents. You can then avoid the pointless creation and recreation of the menu by simply implementing this method to return NO:

```
- (BOOL)menuHasKeyEquivalent:(NSMenu *)menu
                     forEvent:(NSEvent *)event
                       target:(id *)target
                       action:(SEL *)action
{
    return NO;
}
```

Chapter 26

WORKING WITH NSTextView

NSTextView is a very smart class. It is basically a word processor. It deals with fonts, justification, rulers, graphics, spell-check, undo, drag-and-drop, and copy-and-paste. We could spend days discussing the text system. For many uses of an NSTextView, however, you merely need to read data from the view and insert data into the view.

When we talk about NSTextView, we are actually talking about a whole team of objects that make NSTextView work: An NSTextStorage (which inherits from NSMutableAttributedString) tracks changes to the text and informs the NSLayoutManager. The NSLayoutManager lays out the text in a region that is defined by an NSTextContainer. The NSTextView is the view in which the text is rendered. You don't need to know anything about NSTextContainer or NSLayoutManager unless you are working on a project where you need *a lot* of control over the text and its layout.

The class called NSText is the superclass of NSTextView. It is terribly confusing to beginners, because no one ever uses NSText. NSText existed before NSTextView, and it continues to exist to support people who might have used it at that time.

NSTextView

Here are some of the commonly used methods on NSTextView:

- (NSString *)string

Presents the text view's contents as a string.

- (void)setString:(NSString *)aString

Replaces the contents of the text view with aString.

- (NSRange)**selectedRange**

Returns the range of the current selection.

- (void)**setSelectedRange:**(NSRange)charRange

Sets the selection to the characters in charRange.

- (void)**scrollRangeToVisible:**(NSRange)aRange

Scrolls the text view in its enclosing scroll view until the first characters of aRange are visible.

- (void)**replaceCharactersInRange:**(NSRange)aRange
              withString:(NSString *)aString

Replaces the characters in aRange with aString.

- (void)**replaceCharactersInRange:**(NSRange)aRange
              withRTF:(NSData *)rtfData

Replaces the characters in aRange with RTF text interpreted from rtfData.

- (void)**replaceCharactersInRange:**(NSRange)aRange
              withRTFD:(NSData *)rtfdData

Replaces the characters in aRange with RTFD text interpreted from rtfdData.

- (NSData *)**RTFFromRange:**(NSRange)aRange

Returns an **NSData** object that contains an RTF stream aRange.

- (NSData *)**RTFDFromRange:**(NSRange)aRange

Returns an **NSData** object that contains an RTFD stream from aRange.

- (NSTextStorage *)**textStorage**

Returns the text storage object that is the mutable attributed string that you see in the text view.

At heart, the text view is just a view that displays an attributed string. Thus, everything you learned in Chapter 17 about attributed strings is useful when thinking about **NSTextView**.

Messages the Delegate Will Be Sent

The delegate of the **NSTextView** is informed about many things:

- (BOOL)**textShouldBeginEditing:**(NSText *)aTextObject

Sent the first time the user tries to edit the text in the text view after it has become the first responder. If the delegate returns NO, the user will be unable to edit the text.

- (void)**textDidBeginEditing:**(NSNotification *)aNotification

Sent after the first change that the user makes after the view has become the first responder.

- (void)**textDidChange:**(NSNotification *)aNotification

Sent each time the user changes the text in the text view.

- (BOOL)**textShouldEndEditing:**(NSText *)aTextObject

Sent when the text view is asked whether it resigns as the first responder. If the delegate returns NO, the text view refuses to give up its first-responder status.

- (void)**textDidEndEditing:**(NSNotification *)aNotification

Sent when the text view has given up its first-responder status.

- (NSRange)**textView:**(NSTextView *)aTextView
    willChangeSelectionFromCharacterRange:(NSRange)oldSelRange
                    toCharacterRange:(NSRange)newSelRange

Sent before the text view changes the selection. The delegate can return a new selection that will become the active selection.

- (void)**textViewDidChangeSelection:**(NSNotification *)aNotification

Sent after the selection has changed.

- (BOOL)**textView:**(NSTextView *)aTextView
        shouldChangeTextInRange:(NSRange)affectedCharRange
            replacementString:(NSString *)replacementString

Sent before the user is allowed to replace the text in some range with another string.

Build the Editor with Which This Book Was Written

This book was originally written in XML. Before marking up a document with XML, you must decide on a *DTD*. A DTD (document type definition) determines which tags may be used in the markup. A common DTD for technical documents is DocBook. This book was originally a DocBook document.

Before writing this book, I needed an editor. The exercise for this section is to write a simplified version of the DocBook editor with which this book was written (Figure 26.1).

Figure 26.1   Completed Application

Read, Write, and Edit Text Files

The first step is to write a simple text editor, like Apple's TextEdit. Create a new project of type Cocoa Document-based Application called DocBooker. This effort will create the skeleton of an application that can have multiple documents open at the same time.

Open MyDocument.h, and add an outlet for the text view and a variable for the string it is displaying:

```
#import <Cocoa/Cocoa.h>

@interface MyDocument : NSDocument
{
    NSString *string;
    IBOutlet NSTextView *textView;
}
@end
```

Open MyDocument.nib, and drop MyDocument.h into it. Delete the text field in the middle of the document window that says Your document contents here.

Drop a text view on the window, and resize it to fill the window. In the attributes inspector, disable Multiple fonts allowed and enable Undo allowed. Also, set it not to do Continuous Spell Checking and to hide the scroller when not necessary (Figure 26.2).

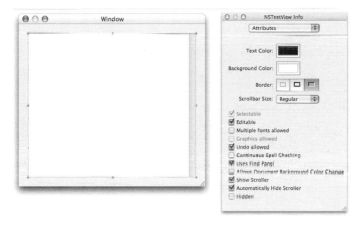

Figure 26.2 Inspect the TextView

In the size inspector, make the text view resize with the window (you are really setting the resize characteristics of the scroll view that the text view is inside), as shown in Figure 26.3.

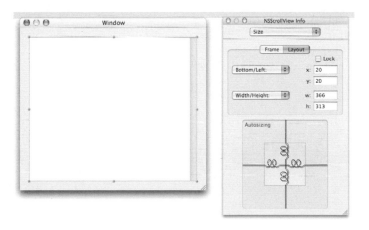

Figure 26.3 Make the Scroll View Resizable

Your **MyDocument** object will need to send messages to the text view to implement loading and saving. Set the textView outlet of the File's Owner to be the text view (Figure 26.4).

Figure 26.4   Set the textView Outlet

Save and close the nib file.

Change the code in MyDocument.m as follows:

```
#import "MyDocument.h"

@implementation MyDocument

- (NSString *)string
{
    return string;
}

- (void)setString:(NSString *)value
{
    [value retain];
    [string release];
    string = value;
}

- (void)updateString
{
```

```objc
    [self setString:[textView string]];
}

- (void)updateView
{
    [textView setString:[self string]];
}

- (NSString *)windowNibName
{
    return @"MyDocument";
}

- (void)windowControllerDidLoadNib:(NSWindowController *) aController
{
    [super windowControllerDidLoadNib:aController];
     if (!string) {
        [self setString:@""];
    }
    [self updateView];
}

- (NSData *)dataRepresentationOfType:(NSString *)aType
{
    [self updateString];
    return [string dataUsingEncoding:NSUTF8StringEncoding];
}

  (BOOL)loadDataRepresentation:(NSData *)data ofType:(NSString *)aType
{
    NSString *aString = [[NSString alloc] initWithData:data
                                  encoding:NSUTF8StringEncoding];
    if (aString == nil) {
        return NO;
    }
    [self setString:aString];
    [aString release];
    [self updateView];
    return YES;
}

- (void)dealloc
{
    [string release];
    [super dealloc];
}
@end
```

Now you have a perfectly good text editor. Build and run the application. Create a new file, edit it, save it, close it, and open it again. The undo, redo, cut, copy, and paste operations should all work correctly. Try control-clicking on the text view to bring up the standard text view menu. In the next section, you will replace that menu (Figure 26.5).

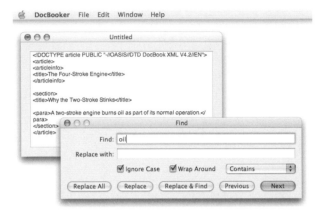

Figure 26.5 A Perfectly Good Text Editor

Note that because you haven't set the document types for your application, all of the files will be saved with the ???? extension. This is fine for now.

Also, note that spell-checking and the find panel work correctly.

Add a Context-Sensitive Menu

On Mac OS X, every view can have a menu associated with it. To get this menu, the user control-clicks on the view. By default, the text view has a menu with standard text operations like cut, copy, and paste.

You will now add a second menu of tags. When the user control-clicks on the view, if the selection has a nonzero length, you will show the tags menu. If the selection has zero length, you will show the standard menu.

What will the tags menu do? When marking up an XML document, you will wrap text in tags like this: <title>My Autobiography</title>. It would be convenient to be able to select a range of text and then control-click to bring up a menu of tags that it could be wrapped in. When the user chooses a tag, the open tag will appear before the selection, and the close tag will appear after it.

You are going to create a subclass of **NSTextView**. The object diagram is shown in Figure 26.6.

Open MyDocument.nib. Create a subclass of **NSTextView** called **XMLEditView**. Add an action called **wrap:** (Figure 26.7); it will be the action for all menu items. Create the files XMLEditView.m and XMLEditView.h, and add them to your project.

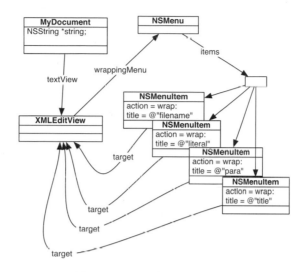

Figure 26.6   Object Diagram

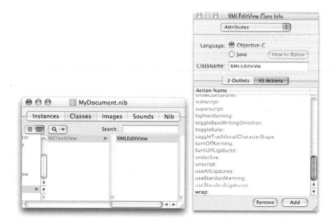

Figure 26.7   Add wrap Action to XMLEditView

Select the **NSTextView** object. In the inspector, set its custom class to **XMLEditView** (Figure 26.8).

You could build and run your application, but because you haven't overridden any methods in **XMLEditView**, it will act just like an instance of **NSTextView**.

Figure 26.8   Change Class of Text View

Adding the Menu

A dazzling array of DocBook tags exists, but you will use only a few of my favorites. You could add them to the menu, one by one, but it will be much easier to create a property list containing them and then to read them at runtime.

Developers often want to create a text file that represents a list or dictionary. You can create a file called a *property list* (or plist), which represents any combination of **NSDictionary**, **NSArray**, and **NSString**. (In fact, there is a developer application called PropertyListEditor for creating and editing plists. You will not use it in this exercise, though.) Plists come in two styles: old-school and XML. In this exercise, you will create an XML property list.

In an old-school plist, a dictionary appears in curly braces, an array appears in parentheses, and strings appear in quotes if they contain any white space. Below is a dictionary with two keys—one bound to a string, the other to an array of strings:

```
{
    pet = Rex;
    parents = ("Tom Hillegass", "Suzanna Hillegass");
}
```

In an XML plist, each token is wrapped in tags. Here is the same plist in XML format:

```
<?xml version="1.0" encoding="UTF-8"?>
<!DOCTYPE plist PUBLIC "-//Apple Computer//DTD PLIST 1.0//EN">
```

```
<plist version="1.0">
<dict>
<key>pet</key>
<string>Rex</string>
<key>parents</key>
<array>
<string>Tom Hillegass</string>
<string>Suzanna Hillegass</string>
</array>
</dict>
</plist>
```

If you were creating this plist in PropertyListEditor, it would look like Figure 26.9.

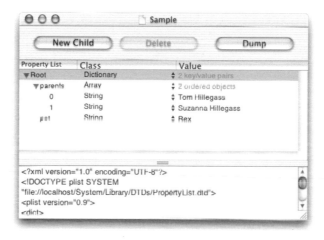

Figure 26.9 Property List Editor

Property lists are nice, because they are easy to edit with a text editor and are easy to read in. To create a dictionary from a plist, you would use the following line of code:

```
NSDictionary *dict;
dict = [NSDictionary dictionaryWithContentsOfFile:@"/tmp/m.plist"];
```

Create a new empty file called Tags.plist (Figure 26.10) that represents an array of strings. Add a plist containing my favorite DocBook tags to Tags.plist:

```
<?xml version="1.0" encoding="UTF-8"?>
<!DOCTYPE plist PUBLIC "-//Apple Computer//DTD PLIST 1.0//EN">
<plist version="1.0">
<array>
    <string>para</string>
    <string>filename</string>
    <string>literal</string>
    <string>title</string>
</array>
</plist>
```

Putting typos into a plist is sadly common. Fortunately, you can check the formatting of your plist using Xcode's Parse File As Property List menu item in the Format menu.

Figure 26.10   Create a New File

Creating the NSMenu

You need a variable to hold your new menu. Add it to XMLEditView.h:

```
#import <Cocoa/Cocoa.h>

@interface XMLEditView : NSTextView
{
    NSMenu *wrappingMenu;
}
- (IBAction)wrap:(id)sender;
@end
```

Here is the code for reading in an array from a property list, sorting the array, and creating a menu from it. Add this code to your XMLEditView.m file.

```objc
- (void)awakeFromNib
{
    int i;
    NSString *path;
    NSArray *tagArray;

    // Read and sort the plist
    path = [[NSBundle mainBundle] pathForResource:@"Tags"
                                           ofType:@"plist"];
    tagArray = [NSArray arrayWithContentsOfFile:path];
    tagArray = [tagArray sortedArrayUsingSelector:
                         @selector(caseInsensitiveCompare:)];
    NSLog(@"tags = %@", tagArray);

    // Create the menu
    wrappingMenu = [[NSMenu alloc] initWithTitle:@"Wrap in"];
    for (i = 0; i < [tagArray count]; i++) {
        NSMenuItem *item;
        NSString *title = [tagArray objectAtIndex:i];
        item = [[NSMenuItem alloc] initWithTitle:title
                                          action:@selector(wrap:)
                                   keyEquivalent:@""];
        [wrappingMenu addItem:item];
        // item is retained by menu
        [item release];
    }
}
```

Don't forget to clean up after yourself. Add a **dealloc** method to XMLEditView.m:

```objc
- (void)dealloc
{
    [wrappingMenu release];
    [super dealloc];
}
```

How do you control which menu is returned? The **menuForEvent:** method is called on the view when the user control-clicks. The menu returned from this method is the one that the user sees. Override the method in XMLEditView.m:

```objc
- (NSMenu *)menuForEvent:(NSEvent *)e
{
    NSRange selection = [self selectedRange];
    if (selection.length > 0) {
        return wrappingMenu;
    } else {
        return [self menu];
    }
}
```

Add a **wrap:** method that just prints out the name of the menu item that the user chose:

```
- (IBAction)wrap:(id)sender
{
    NSString *title = [sender title];
    NSLog(@"The user chose %@", title);
}
```

Build and run your application. Make a selection and control-click. If the selection has zero length, you should see the standard text menu (Figure 26.11).

Figure 26.11   Menu for Zero-Length Selection

If the selection has a nonzero length, you should see the wrapping menu (Figure 26.12). When you choose an item from the menu, you should see a log statement in the run log.

Figure 26.12   Menu for Nonzero-Length Selection

Replace the Selection

Now implement the **wrap:** method. It needs to find the selection and replace it with a string that includes the opening and closing tags.

```
- (IBAction)wrap:(id)sender
{
    NSString *title = [sender title];
    NSRange selection = [self selectedRange];
    NSString *wholeThing = [self string];

    NSString *oldString = [wholeThing substringWithRange:selection];
    NSString *newString = [NSString stringWithFormat:@"<%@>%@</%@>",
                                            title, oldString, title];
    [self insertText:newString];
}
```

Build and run the application. You should be able to select text and wrap it in DocBook tags. Notice that you can undo these wrappings.

Before you give the app to your friends, be sure to set its document information. Select the target DocBooker and open the info panel in Xcode. Inspect the DocBooker target, select the Properties tab, set the name of the document type to be XML Document, and set extensions to be xml (Figure 26.13).

Figure 26.13 Set the Document Type Information

For the More Curious: The Field Editor

It takes a lot of smarts to lay out the characters in a text field. If every text field on a window had this kind of smarts, your application would take up a lot of unnecessary memory. After all, only one text field gets edited at a time. For efficiency reasons, all text fields on a window share one field editor. The field editor is an instance of **NSTextView**.

When a user selects and begins to edit a text field, the field editor takes over the processing of the events and drawing for that view. The field editor makes the text field become its delegate (Figure 26.14).

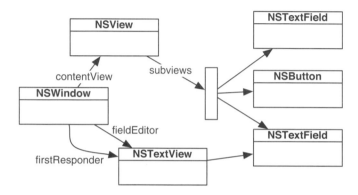

Figure 26.14   Field Editor

What happens if you want to create a delegate of the text field? For example, suppose you want to receive the **textShouldEndEditing:** message from the field editor for a text field so that you can prevent the user from tabbing to another field (Figure 26.15).

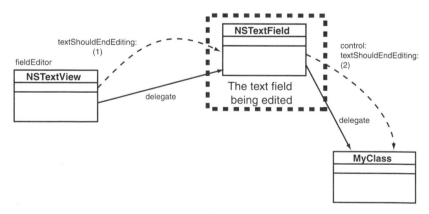

Figure 26.15   The Delegate of an NSControl

When the user tries to change the first responder to another view, the field editor will send **textShouldEndEditing:** to its delegate (the text field). If the text field has a delegate, it will send the message to that delegate.

```
- (BOOL)control:(NSControl *)textField
    textShouldEndEditing:(NSText *)fieldEditor
```

The delegate object can return NO, which will prevent the user from changing the first responder.

Here are a few other messages forwarded by the text field:

```
- (BOOL)control:(NSControl *)control
         textShouldBeginEditing:(NSText *)fieldEditor;
- (void)controlTextDidBeginEditing:(NSNotification *)aNotification;
- (void)controlTextDidChange:(NSNotification *)aNotification;
- (void)controlTextDidEndEditing:(NSNotification *)aNotification;
```

Challenge

Save the data for the RaiseMan application in a plist. This is not so tricky: **employees**, after all, is basically an array of dictionaries containing strings and numbers.

Of course, you will have to convert **Person** objects into **NSDictionary** objects. As part of key-value coding, **NSObject** has the following method:

```
(NSDictionary *)dictionaryWithValuesForKeys:(NSArray *)keys;
```

If you pass it an array of keys, it will return a dictionary containing the data for those keys. For example, if I had a **Person** object, I could get its contents as a dictionary like this:

```
NSArray *keys;
keys = [NSArray arrayWithObjects:@"expectedRaise", @"personName", nil];
myDict = [myPerson dictionaryWithValuesForKeys:keys];
```

If you create an array of dictionaries in this manner, you can write the array out to a file. **NSArray** has the following method:

```
- (BOOL)writeToFile:(NSString *)path
         atomically:(BOOL)useAuxiliaryFile;
```

The first argument is the full path to where you would like the plist written. The second argument determines whether the data are written to another file and then moved into place. This atomic operation would prevent incomplete saves from corrupting the existing data file.

Reading in a file is done with the following **NSArray** class method:

```
+ (id)arrayWithContentsOfFile:(NSString *)path;
```

Chapter 27

CREATING INTERFACE BUILDER PALETTES

Interface Builder includes several standard palettes. The palettes allow the user to drag objects off the palette and drop them into a nib file. They also allow the user to inspect and edit the attributes of that object. Finally, the palette allows the user to put the interface into test mode. The user interface (UI) objects come alive and act as they would in an application.

When you save a nib file, you are archiving objects into a file. When you load a nib file into your application, you are unarchiving those objects. Some of the objects in the nib file are just placeholders. File's Owner, for example, is a placeholder for the object that will be supplied when the nib file is read in. Other objects, like the text fields, are actually archived into the file.

Until this chapter, all the instances of your custom classes have just been placeholders. When the nib file is read in, these instances are created with **alloc** and **init**. Then their outlets are set. On the other hand, when an instance of **NSTextField** is read in from the nib file, it is created with **alloc** and **initWithCoder:** because it was actually archived in the nib file.

In creating a palette, you are creating a collection of classes that know how to archive themselves into a nib file and unarchive themselves when the nib file is read into the application. In addition, you will frequently create inspectors for these objects. Inspectors allow the developer to set the instance variables of the objects inside Interface Builder.

The point of palettizing, then, is to make it easy for other people to use your classes in Interface Builder. For example, imagine you are the smartest programmer at the local nuclear power plant. You create a custom view class called **DangerMeter**. All the other programmers would like to use your **DangerMeter** in their nib files. They would like to be able to select the view and set the minRads and maxRads for the view in the inspector. If you are a kind programmer, you will palettize your view and create an inspector for it. While you are at it, you should also put **MeltdownTimer** and **ExposureWarningView** in the palette. You can create inspectors for these classes, too.

Note that a palette is a type of bundle. The bundle contains some compiled code that will be dynamically linked into Interface Builder. It also includes a couple of nib files: one for the palette and one for each of the inspectors. In addition, you can have sounds and images in a palette.

Now that you have created a nifty view like **BigLetterView**, it is time to palettize it so that it will be easy for other people to use. This chapter will teach you how to do so. Notice from the description that you will have to do several things:

- Teach your object to archive and unarchive itself. This is how it will get in and out of the nib file.
- Create an inspector object for the view. For **BigLetterView**, you are going to let the user change the background color of the view and determine whether the view is copyable.
- Create two nib files: the one from which the user will drag the **BigLetterView**, and the nib for the inspector (Figure 27.1).

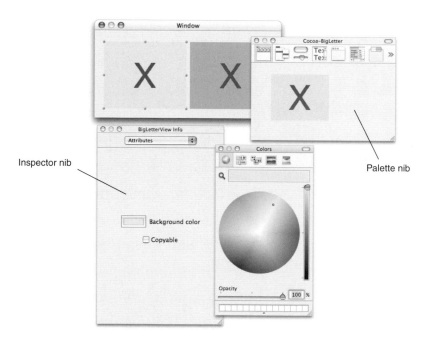

Figure 27.1   Completed Palette

For your object to "come alive" in test mode, Interface Builder must dynamically link in the code for your objects. Loading code into a running application is somewhat dangerous, and until your project is bug free, you may crash Interface Builder a few times. This is expected. Also, once your code has been linked in, it cannot be unlinked. You will have to restart Interface Builder to test each new version of your palette. As you might imagine, debugging a palette can be a time-consuming process.

One palette can make several classes available to the user. Each of these classes will be represented by a view on the palette nib, and each of may have a corresponding inspector. Each palette is controlled by a subclass of **IBPalette**. Each inspector is controlled by a subclass of **IBInspector**.

Add NSCoding Methods to BigLetterView

For your object to be saved to and read from a nib file, it must have coding methods. Luckily, **NSView** has already taken care of most of the hard stuff. You will simply extend **NSView**'s **encodeWithCoder:** and **initWithCoder:** methods.

Add the following methods to your BigLetterView.m file. You may notice that **initWithCoder:** and **initWithFrame:** have several similarities. When the view comes from a nib file, **initWithCoder:** will be called instead of **initWith-Frame:**.

```
- (void)encodeWithCoder:(NSCoder *)coder
{
    // Call NSView's encodeWithCoder: method
    [super encodeWithCoder:coder];
    if ([coder allowsKeyedCoding]) {
        [coder encodeObject:bgColor forKey:@"bgColor:"];
        [coder encodeObject:string forKey:@"string"];
        [coder encodeBool:copyable forKey:@"copyable"];
    } else {
        [coder encodeObject:bgColor];
        [coder encodeObject:string];
        [coder encodeValueOfObjCType:@encode(BOOL) at:&copyable];
    }
}
```

```
- (id)initWithCoder:(NSCoder *)coder
{
    if (self = [super initWithCoder:coder]) {
      [self registerForDraggedTypes:
        [NSArray arrayWithObject:NSStringPboardType]];
                                      [self prepareAttributes];
        if ([coder allowsKeyedCoding]) {
          [self setBgColor:[coder decodeObjectForKey:@"bgColor"]];
          [self setString:[coder decodeObjectForKey:@"string"]];
          [self setCopyable:[coder decodeBoolForKey:@"copyable"]];
        } else {
          [self setBgColor:[coder decodeObject]];
          [self setString:[coder decodeObject]];
          [self setCopyable:[coder decodeValueOfObjCType:@encode(BOOL)
                                          at:&copyable]];
        }
    }
    return self;
}
```

(Notice that these coding methods are compatible with non-keyed archivers. In Interface Builder, this is called "Pre-10.2 Format". Honestly, not that many people still use Pre-10.2 format, but as long as Interface Builder supports it, your palettized objects should too.)

Make sure the project will compile. Close the project.

Create a Palette Project

In Xcode, create a new project of type IBPalette (Figure 27.2). Name it BigLetter.

Figure 27.2   Select Project Type

The new project is created assuming that the palette will have one view subclass, **BigLetter**. Although a palette can have many classes, yours will have only the class **BigLetterView**. The new project assumes that you will also have one inspector class, **BigLetterInspector**. The new project assumes that you are creating one palette class, **BigLetterPalette**.

Select and delete the files BigLetter.h and BigLetter.m. Notice that two nib files were created automatically: one for the palette and one for the inspector.

Delete the line that imports BigLetter.h from BigLetterPalette.h and BigLetterInspector.m.

BigLetterPalette.h declares a category on the class **BigLetter**. Change it to be a category on **BigLetterView**:

```
#import <InterfaceBuilder/InterfaceBuilder.h>
#import "BigLetterView.h"

@interface BigLetterPalette : IBPalette
{
}
@end

@interface BigLetterView (BigLetterPaletteInspector)
- (NSString *)inspectorClassName;
@end
```

Also change it in BigLetterPalette.m.:

```
@implementation BigLetterView (BigLetterPaletteInspector)

- (NSString *)inspectorClassName
{
    return @"BigLetterInspector";
}

@end
```

Drag BigLetterView.h, BigLetterView.m, FirstLetter.h, and FirstLetter.m into the new project from the Finder (Figure 27.3).

Figure 27.3   Add the BigLetterView Class and FirstLetter Category

Edit the Nib File for Your Palette

Double-click on BigLetterPalette.nib to open it in Interface Builder.

Drag BigLetterView.h into the doc window so that Interface Builder will know about your **BigLetterView** class. Drag a custom view onto the palette window and change its class to **BigLetterView** (Figure 27.4).

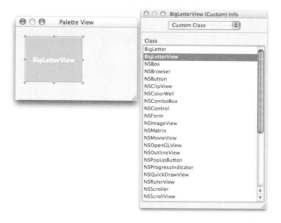

Figure 27.4   Add an Instance of BigLetterView to the Palette Window

Set the File's Owner to be an instance of **BigLetterPalette** (Figure 27.5).

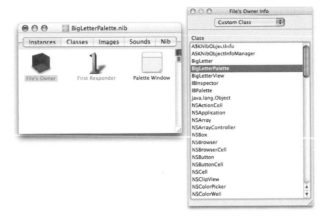

Figure 27.5   Set the File's Owner to be BigLetterPalette

Control-drag from File's Owner to the palette window and set the original window outlet (Figure 27.6).

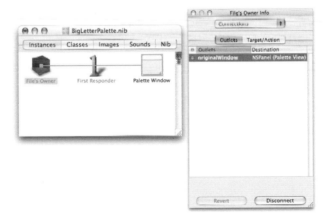

Figure 27.6   Set the originalWindow Outlet

Save and close the nib file.

palette.table

When reading in a palette, Interface Builder will look for a file called palette.table. In this file, the palette declares which subclass of **IBPalette** to use, what nib file to read, and which classes in the palette should appear in the classes browser. You can also specify images and sounds that you are including in the palette. The palette.table file should appear under Resources in Xcode's outline view. Edit the contents of the file to look like this:

```
<?xml version="1.0" encoding="UTF-8"?>
<!DOCTYPE plist SYSTEM
    "file://localhost/System/Library/DTDs/PropertyList.dtd">
<plist version="1.0">
  <dict>
    <key>Class</key> <string>BigLetterPalette</string>
    <key>NibFile</key> <string>BigLetterPalette</string>
    <key>ExportClasses</key>
    <array>
      <string>BigLetterView</string>
    </array>
  </dict>
</plist>
```

Once again, you may want to check the formatting of this file.

Build and Test

Build your palette. Your project directory contains a subdirectory called build. Your palette, BigLetter.palette, is found there. You can load it from the preferences panel of Interface Builder (Figure 27.7).

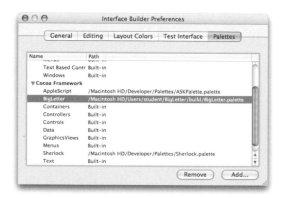

Figure 27.7   Load the Palette

If errors occur when it loads, you can see the messages using the Console application.

After your palette successfully loads, try creating a new nib file with two instances of your **BigLetterView**. Set the nextKeyView of each to the other. Run the application in test mode and see if your view works. Make sure that you can tab between the two views.

Close the new nib file without saving it.

finishInstantiate

Notice that the **BigLetterView** appears without a letter in the palette. The user would guess its purpose more easily if the view drew itself with a letter. After the palette is loaded, the **IBPalette** object (in your case, **BigLetterPalette**) is sent **finishInstantiate**. This would be a good chance to set the string of the **BigLetterView** to be non-nil.

First, you need to add an outlet from the palette controller object (**BigLetterPalette**) to the **BigLetterView**. Add the declaration of an instance variable to BigLetterPalette.h:

```
@interface BigLetterPalette : IBPalette
{
    IBOutlet BigLetterView *view;
}
@end
```

Drag BigLetterPalette.h from Xcode into BigLetterPalette.nib in Interface Builder. Set the outlet to point to the **BigLetterView** in the window (Figure 27.8).

In **BigLetterPalette**'s **finishInstantiate** method, set the view's string:

```
- (void)finishInstantiate
{
    [view setString:@"X"];
    [super finishInstantiate];
}
```

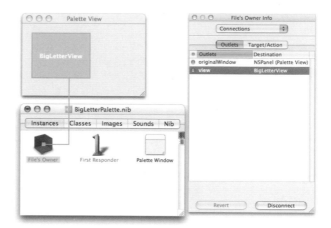

Figure 27.8   Set the View Outlet

Build the application. Quit Interface Builder, and then start it again. Interface Builder will automatically reload the palette. You should see the "X" in the palette (Figure 27.9).

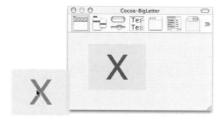

Figure 27.9   Working Palette

Adding an Inspector

It would be nice if anyone using your palette could select an instance of **BigLetterView** in their nib and see an inspector that would allow them to set the background color and copyability of the selected **BigLetterView** (Figure 27.10).

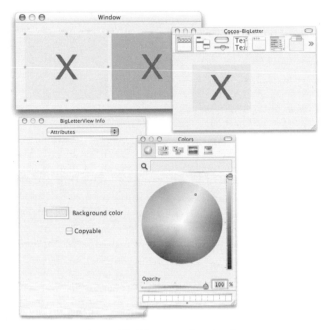

Figure 27.10   Completed Palette

Create a Nib File for Your Inspector

In Xcode, double-click on `BigLetterInspector.nib`. The File's Owner will be an instance of **BigLetterInspector**. This inspector object will take information from the info panel and set the instance variables of your object. It will also read the instance variables and set the UI objects in the info panel. Drop a color well and a check box on the window (Figure 27.11).

Figure 27.11   Completed Interface for Inspector

Your inspector will need outlets for the color well and the check box. Add it to BigLetterInspector.h and name them colorWell and copyableCheckbox:

```
#import <InterfaceBuilder/InterfaceBuilder.h>

@interface BigLetterInspector : IBInspector
{
  IBOutlet NSColorWell *colorWell;
  IBOutlet NSButton *copyableCheckbox;
}
@end
```

Drag the BigLetterInspector.h into the nib file Set the type of the File's Owner to BigLetterInspector (Figure 27.12). Connect the window outlet of the **BigLetterInspector** to the window (Figure 27.13).

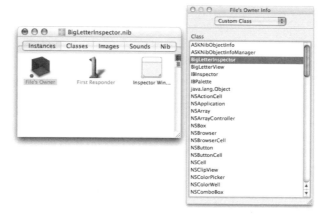

Figure 27.12 Set the Class for the File's Owner

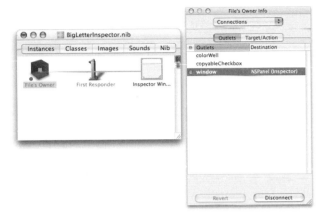

Figure 27.13   Set the Window Outlet

Connect the `colorWell` outlet to the **NSColorWell** object (Figure 27.14).

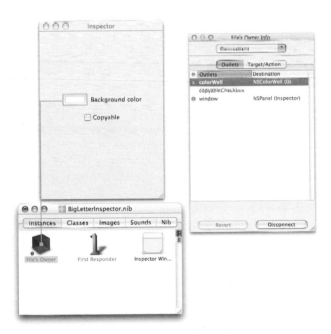

Figure 27.14   Set the colorWell Outlet

Connect the check box (Figure 27.15).

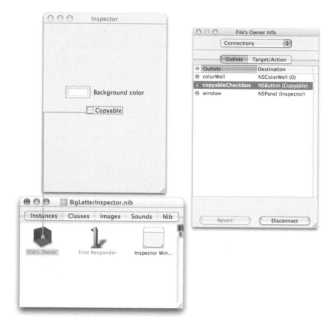

Figure 27.15   Set the copyableCheckbox Outlet

To an inspector, life consists mainly of responding to two messages, **ok:** and **revert:** (Figure 27.16). The **ok:** message tells the inspector to read the objects on the inspector panel and update the instance variables of the inspected object to match. The **revert:** message tells the inspector to read the instance variables of the inspected object and set the objects on the inspector panel to match.

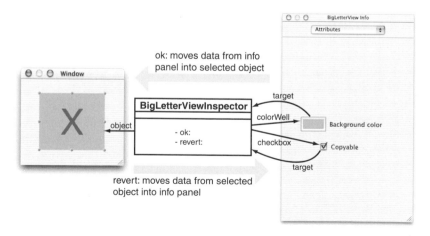

Figure 27.16   The Role of the Inspector

When a user changes the color well in the inspector panel, you will want the inspected object (a **BigLetterView**) to have its instance variable (bgColor) updated. To do so, set the target of the color well to be the File's Owner. The action is **ok:** (Figure 27.17).

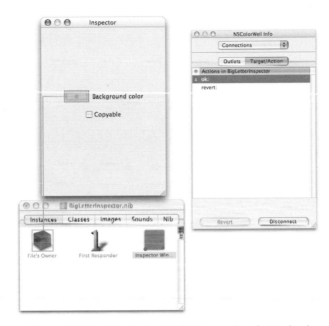

Figure 27.17   The Color Well Triggers the ok: Method

Also, set the target of the check box to be the File's Owner. The action is again **ok:** (Figure 27.18).

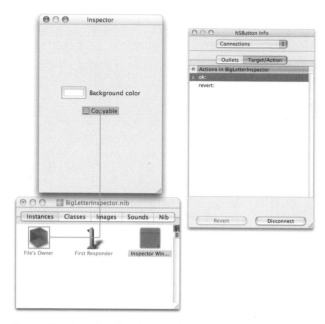

Figure 27.18   The Check Box Also Triggers the ok: Method

Code for an Inspector

Your inspector will have three methods:

- **init** will read the nib file that you just created.
- **ok:** will read the color well and check box and set the bgColor and copyable instance variables of the **BigLetterView**.
- **revert:** will read the bgColor and copyable instance variables of the **BigLetterView** and set the color well and the check box.

Here is what BigLetterInspector.m should look like:

```
#import "BigLetterInspector.h"
#import "BigLetterView.h"

@implementation BigLetterInspector

- (id)init
{
    if (self = [super init]) {
        [NSBundle loadNibNamed:@"BigLetterInspector" owner:self];
    }
    return self;
}
```

```
- (void)ok:(id)sender
{
    BigLetterView *selectedView;
    selectedView = [self object];
    [selectedView setBgColor:[colorWell color]];
    [selectedView setCopyable:[copyableCheckbox state]];
    [super ok:sender];
}

- (void)revert:(id)sender
{
    NSColor *color;
    BigLetterView *selectedView;
    selectedView = [self object];
    [copyableCheckbox setState:[selectedView copyable]];
    color = [selectedView bgColor];
    [colorWell setColor:color];
    [super revert:sender];
}
@end
```

That's it. You have created a palette and an inspector. Compile the palette and restart Interface Builder. It should automatically reload the palette.

Note how the inspector allows you to choose the background color for the selected **BigLetterView**.

Adding Bindings to a Custom View

When an object is selected in Interface Builder and the bindings inspector is opened, the class of the object is asked what its exposed bindings are. To add a binding named budda, add the following method to BigLetterView.m:

```
+ (void)initialize
{
    [self exposeBinding:@"budda"];
}
```

When the user actually chooses a binding, your view will be sent the following method:

```
- (void)bind:(NSString *)binding
    toObject:(id)observable
withKeyPath:(NSString *)keyPath
     options:(NSDictionary *)options
```

This method, which is defined in **NSObject**, seems to do the right thing most of the time. There is seldom any need to override it.

When the controller changes, key-value coding is used to read the value. Implement **setBudda:** and **budda** in BigLetterView.m:

```
- (void)setBudda:(id)x
{
    NSLog(@"setBudda:%@", x);
    [self setString:[x firstLetter]];
}
- (id)budda
{
    return string;
}
```

That's it. Rebuild your palette and restart Interface Builder. You will have a budda binding in the inspector, as shown in Figure 27.19.

Figure 27.19   Your View Has a Custom Binding

To test the application, create a new nib file in Interface Builder. Drop an **NSArrayController** into your doc window. Add a key called fullName to the array controller. Put a **BigLetterView**, a table view with one column, and a button on the window, as shown in Figure 27.20. Control-drag from the button to the array controller, and choose the **insert:** method. In the bindings inspector for the one column of the table view, make it display the fullName attribute of the arranged objects of the array controller. Also, bind the budda binding to the fullName atttribute of the selected object of the array controller.

In test interface mode, add a few rows using the button. Edit the text in the column, and note that the **BigLetterView** always shows the first letter of the selected row.

The bindings will be archived by **NSView**'s **encodeWithCoder:** method.

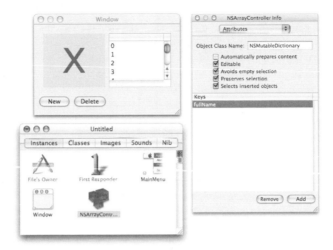

Figure 27.20   Test the Binding with a New Nib File

For the More Curious: How to Palettize Objects That Are Not Views

Views are easy to palettize. If you wanted to palettize something like your **Foo** class from Chapter 2, you would need to associate it with some view for the purpose of dragging. Most developers would use an **NSButton** as the view. It is easy to put an image or label on a button so that it will look like anything you want.

In your subclass of **IBPalette**, you will need an outlet to the button:

```
#import <InterfaceBuilder/InterfaceBuilder.h>

@interface BigLetterPalette : IBPalette
{
    IBOutlet BigLetterView *view;
    IBOutlet NSButton *button;
}

@end
```

In `BigLetterPalette.m`, in **finishInstantiate** you would associate the button with a **Foo** object:

```
- (void)finishInstantiate
{
    [super finishInstantiate];
    [self associateObject:[[Foo alloc] init]
                 ofType:IBObjectPboardType
              withView:button];
}
```

The **finishInstantiate** method will be called automatically when the palette is
loaded.

You will also need **encodeWithCoder:** and **initWithCoder:** methods that
properly encode and decode the textField outlet in Foo.m.

```
{
    [super init];
    if ([coder allowsKeyedCoding]) {
        textField = [[coder decodeObjectForKey:@"textField"] retain];
    } else {
        textField = [[coder decodeObject] retain];
    }
    return self;
}

- (void)encodeWithCoder:(NSCoder *)coder
{
    if ([coder allowsKeyedCoding]) {
        [coder encodeObject:textField forKey:@"textField"];
    } else {
        [coder encodeObject:textField];
    }
}
```

Finally, you would declare that **Foo** implements the **NSCoding** protocol.

```
@interface Foo : NSObject <NSCoding>
```

After building and loading the palette, you could drag from the button to the
nib's doc window. The image of the button would become the symbol
representing the **Foo** object. Just as in Chapter 2, you would make it the target of
two buttons and set the text field outlet. Niftiest of all, your entire RandomApp
application would work in Test Interface mode.

Challenge

Add your formatter to your custom palette. You will need to use the IBFormat-
terPboardType when you associate the formatter with a button. Also, make sure
that **ColorFormatter**'s **initWithCoder:** method properly initializes the
colorList. (It doesn't have to decode it from the coder; just make sure that its
colorList is initialized after calling [super initWithCoder:coder].)

When you have completed this challenge, you will be able to drop your
formatter on text fields and table view columns, just as you did with the number
formatter while creating the RaiseMan application.

Chapter 28
APPLESCRIPT

AppleScript is a language designed to allow normal users to automate repetitive tasks. When an AppleScript script is run, it usually generates some Apple events. Apple events move between applications by way of the Apple event manager and mach messaging.

You can create and run AppleScript scripts using the application /Applications/ AppleScript/Script Editor. The following simple script will bring up a new document containing the words "Share the love" in TextEdit. Type it into Script Editor and try it out:

```
tell application "TextEdit"
    activate
    make new document at the beginning of documents
    set the text of the front document to "Share the love"
end tell
```

As a programmer, I find the AppleScript language to be rather strange and hard to work with, but it has done a great job of helping users to automate common tasks. Instead of writing a script from scratch, I usually search the Internet for one that does almost what I want, and then I tinker with it until it acts in accordance with my wishes.

Executing an AppleScript from a Cocoa application is quite straightforward. If the preceding script was in an **NSString**, you could compile and run it like this:

```
NSAppleScript *appleScript;
NSDictionary  *errorDict;
NSAppleEventDescriptor *ae;
appleScript = [[NSAppleScript alloc] initWithSource:theString];
ae = [appleScript executeAndReturnError:&errorDict];
```

The **NSAppleEventDescriptor** produced has the result that was returned at the end of the script. **NSAppleEventDescriptor** has three methods for reading the result as standard types:

```
- (SInt32)int32Value
- (NSString *)stringValue
- (Boolean)booleanValue
```

(`Boolean`, `BOOL`, and `char` are all the same thing.)

Making an Application AppleScript-able

Making a Cocoa application accessible to AppleScripters is done via key-value coding. Before you begin, you should recognize that the AppleScript system is rather finicky. Your plists must be carefully created, or nothing works. (In fact, an error in your plists can crash Script Editor.)

In Xcode, open the SpeakLine project from Chapter 5.

The first step is to inform the system that your application is AppleScript enabled. The `Info.plist` for SpeakLine contains a dictionary; add the following key and value to that dictionary:

```
<key>NSAppleScriptEnabled</key>
<string>YES</string>
```

By default, your application automatically understands a set of AppleScript commands. To exercise these commands, clean, build, and launch the app. In Script Editor, run a script that uses SpeakLine:

```
tell application "SpeakLine"
    activate
    get name of first window
end tell
```

The title of the main window should appear in the lower pane of Script Editor (Figure 28.1).

Figure 28.1   Getting the Window Name

To see what attributes, relationships, and commands are available, click the Open Dictionary... menu item and look at SpeakLine's AppleScript dictionary. It should look something like Figure 28.2.

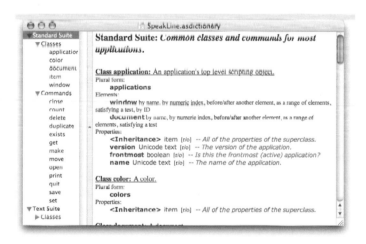

Figure 28.2   Browsing the AppleScript Dictionary

Notice the two suites: Standard and Text. A suite is a collection of AppleScript-able classes and commands. **Window**, for example, is a class. Each class has attributes. A window, for example, has a Boolean attribute `miniaturized`. Some attributes are read-only; others can be set. Classes also have relationships, which come in two varieties: `ToOneRelationship` and `ToManyRelationship`. For example, the application class has a `ToManyRelationship` with its windows. A window has a `ToOneRelationship` with the document it is displaying. Finally, a class has supported commands. For example, a document can handle a `Print` command. These ideas are rendered as a diagram in Figure 28.3.

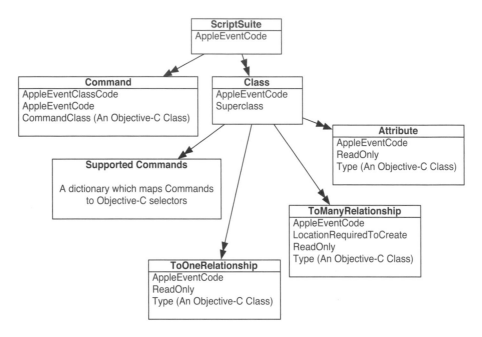

Figure 28.3 What Is an AppleScript Suite?

All of these parts are defined in a `.scriptSuite` file. The examples mentioned previously are all in `/System/Library/Frameworks/Foundation.framework/Resources/NSCoreSuite.scriptSuite`. Open that file in TextEdit and browse it for moment.

Each part in the `.scriptSuite` file has an entry in a corresponding `.scriptTerminology` file that contains the word used for it in a script, its definition, and any synonyms. To review these components, take a look at `/Frameworks/Foundation/Resources/NSCoreSuite.scriptTerminology` in TextEdit.

Thus, the most important part of making your application scriptable is creating good `.scriptSuite` and `.scriptTerminology` files.

Create the Plists

In Xcode, create two new text files in the Resources group: `SpeakLine.scriptSuite` and `SpeakLine.scriptTerminology`. Add a class with a command and an action to the `SpeakLine.scriptSuite`. (The system is very finicky about these files, so type carefully.)

```
<?xml version="1.0" encoding="UTF-8"?>
<!DOCTYPE plist PUBLIC "-//Apple Computer//DTD PLIST 1.0//EN"
"http://www.apple.com/DTDs/PropertyList-1.0.dtd">
<plist version="1.0">
<dict>
    <key>Name</key>
    <string>SpeakLine</string>
    <key>AppleEventCode</key>
    <string>Spkl</string>

    <key>Classes</key>
    <dict>
        <key>MyApplication</key>
        <dict>
            <key>AppleEventCode</key>
            <string>capp</string>
            <key>Attributes</key>
            <dict>
                <key>utterance</key>
                <dict>
                    <key>AppleEventCode</key>
                    <string>Utte</string>
                    <key>Type</key>
                    <string>NSString</string>
                </dict>
            </dict>
            <key>Superclass</key>
            <string>NSCoreSuite.NSApplication</string>
            <key>SupportedCommands</key>
            <dict>
                <key>Utter</key>
                <string>handleUtterScriptCommand:</string>
            </dict>
        </dict>
    </dict>

    <key>Commands</key>
    <dict>
        <key>Utter</key>
        <dict>
            <key>AppleEventClassCode</key>
            <string>Spkl</string>
            <key>AppleEventCode</key>
            <string>Uttr</string>
            <key>CommandClass</key>
            <string>NSScriptCommand</string>
        </dict>
    </dict>
</dict>
</plist>
```

Now edit the SpeakLine.scriptTerminology file:

```xml
<?xml version="1.0" encoding="UTF-8"?>
<!DOCTYPE plist PUBLIC "-//Apple Computer//DTD PLIST 1.0//EN"
"http://www.apple.com/DTDs/PropertyList-1.0.dtd">
<plist version="1.0">
<dict>
      <key>Description</key>
      <string>SpeakLine Script Suite</string>
      <key>Name</key>
      <string>SpeakLine Suite</string>

      <key>Classes</key>
      <dict>
          <key>MyApplication</key>
          <dict>
              <key>Attributes</key>
              <dict>
                  <key>utterance</key>
                  <dict>
                      <key>Description</key>
                      <string>The utterance</string>
                      <key>Name</key>
                      <string>utterance</string>
                  </dict>
              </dict>
              <key>Description</key>
              <string>Speakline App</string>
              <key>Name</key>
              <string>my application</string>
              <key>PluralName</key>
              <string>my applications</string>
          </dict>
      </dict>

      <key>Commands</key>
      <dict>
          <key>Utter</key>
          <dict>
              <key>Description</key>
              <string>Speak the utterance</string>
              <key>Name</key>
              <string>utter</string>
          </dict>
      </dict>
</dict>
</plist>
```

Using ParseFileasPropertyList menu item, make sure that you did not make an error in formatting these plists.

Clean and build your project again. In Script Editor, look at the dictionary for SpeakLine. It should now have a third suite containing your class (with the attribute utterance) and the utter command (Figure 28.4).

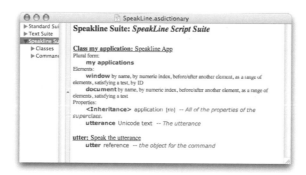

Figure 28.4   Browsing the Updated Dictionary

Handling the Apple Events

Your suite claims that you are going to subclass **NSApplication** and add the utterance attribute and a method called **handleUtterScriptCommand:**   In Xcode, create a new Objective-C class called **MyApplication**. Declare the method to handle the command in MyApplication.h:

```
#import <Cocoa/Cocoa.h>

@interface MyApplication : NSApplication {

}
- (void)handleUtterScriptCommand: (NSScriptCommand *)command;
@end
```

Basically, **MyApplication** plans to pass the responsibility off to the **AppController** class. How will it get a message to the **AppController**? In Interface Builder, you will make **AppController** be the delegate of the **MyApplication** object.

Open MainMenu.nib and control-drag from the File's Owner (which represents the instance of **MyApplication**) to the **AppController**. Set the delegate outlet as shown in Figure 28.5.

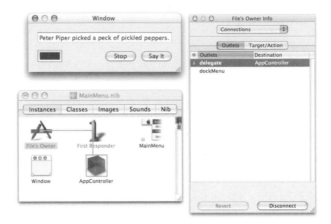

Figure 28.5 Setting the Application's delegate Outlet

Returning to Xcode, implement the method in `MyApplication.m`:

```
- (void)handleUtterScriptCommand:(NSScriptCommand *)command
{
    NSLog(@"handleUtterScriptCommand:%@", command);
    [[self delegate] sayIt:nil];
}
```

Import `AppController.h` at the beginning of `MyApplication.m`.

What about the `utterance` attribute? An application's attributes and relationships can be handled by its delegate. The delegate implements the following method:

```
- (BOOL)application:(NSApplication *)a
  delegateHandlesKey:(NSString *)key
```

For any keys that the delegate can handle, it returns YES. Add the following method to `AppController.m`:

```
- (BOOL)application:(NSApplication *)sender
         delegateHandlesKey:(NSString *)key
{
    NSLog(@"Key checked = %@", key);
    if ([key isEqual:@"utterance"])
        return YES;
    else
        return NO;
}
```

Next, create accessors for that attribute. Of course, you don't actually have an utterance instance variable, so the accessors that are called will access the string in the text field:

```
- (NSString *)utterance
{
    return [textField stringValue];
}
- (void)setUtterance:(NSString *)s
{
    [textField setStringValue:s];
}
```

The final step is to edit the Info.plist so that it uses your subclass instead of **NSApplication** when the application launches. In Xcode, edit the Info.plist:

```
<key>NSPrincipalClass</key>
<string>MyApplication</string>
```

Build and launch your app. In Script Editor, try this AppleScript:

```
tell application "SpeakLine"
    activate
    set utterance to "The rain in spain"
    utter
end tell
```

The utterance should change, and then you should hear it spoken.

The .scriptTerminology file can be localized so that scripters can script in their native language.

Creating these plists so that they are consistent with one another and with the CoreSuite is a tricky business. SuiteModeler is a shareware application created by Don Briggs that takes much of the sweat out of creating these plists. A license for it is less than $50. I use SuiteModeler, and it has saved me a lot of frustration.

Chapter 29

COCOA AND OPENGL

This chapter is not designed to teach you OpenGL. If you want to learn OpenGL, read *The OpenGL Programming Guide*. This chapter is intended to show you how to do drawing with OpenGL in an application that is written using Cocoa. Like all other drawing in Cocoa, OpenGL rendering will be done in a view. Until now, all of your views have used an **NSGraphicsContext** to do drawing with Quartz (via **NSImage**, **NSBezierPath**, and **NSAttributedString**).

NSOpenGLView is a subclass of **NSView** that has an OpenGL drawing context. Just as you needed the focus locked on a view to do drawing with Quartz, so the OpenGL drawing context must be active for any OpenGL drawing commands to have an effect.

Here are some important methods in **NSOpenGLView**:

- (id)**initWithFrame:**(NSRect)frameRect
        pixelFormat:(NSOpenGLPixelFormat *)format

  The designated initializer.

- (NSOpenGLContext*)**openGLContext**

  Returns the views in the OpenGL context.

- (void)**reshape**

  Called when the view is resized. The OpenGL context is active when this method is called.

- (void)**drawRect:**(NSRect)r

  Called when the view needs to be redrawn. The OpenGL context is active when this method is called.

A Simple Cocoa/OpenGL Application

Figure 29.1 shows the application that you will create.

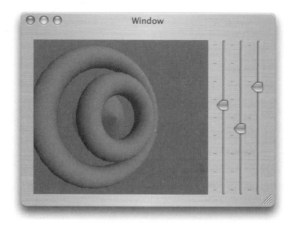

Figure 29.1   Completed Application

Create a new Cocoa Application project and call it Gliss (short for "GL Bliss"). Under the Project menu, use Add Frameworks... to add the frameworks OpenGL.framework and GLUT.framework to the project. You will not be using the GLUT event model—just a couple of convenient functions.

Open MainMenu.nib and create a subclass of **NSOpenGLView** named **GlissView**. Create an outlet called sliderMatrix that will point to an **NSMatrix**. Create an action called **changeParameter:**. Create the files for **GlissView**.

Drag an **NSOpenGLView** onto the window and set its custom class to **GlissView**. Set it to resize with the window, as shown in Figure 29.2.

Drop an **NSSlider** on the window. Configure the slider to be continuous and to allow values other than the markers. Option-drag one corner's resize handles (as if resizing) to make it into a matrix of three slider cells, as shown in Figure 29.3.

 Set the target of the matrix to be the **GlissView** and set the action to be **changeParameter:**. Set the sliderMatrix outlet of the the **GlissView** to point to the matrix. (Be sure to create connections in both directions.)

The first slider will control the X-coordinate of the light. Set its range from -4 to 4 and give it an initial value of 1. It should have a tag of 0. The inspector should look like Figure 29.4.

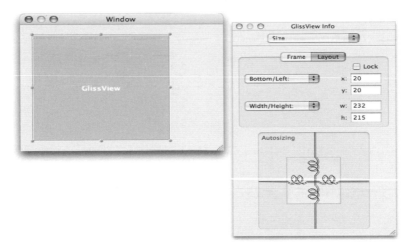

Figure 29.2   Size Inspector for New View

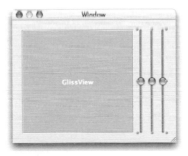

Figure 29.3   Matrix of Sliders

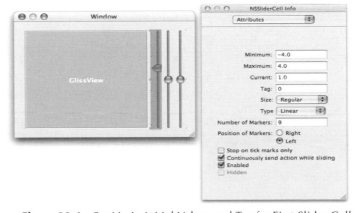

Figure 29.4   Set Limit, Initial Value, and Tag for First Slider Cell

The second slider will control the angle from which the scene is viewed. Set its range from -4 to 4, and give it an initial value of 0. It should have a tag of 1.

The third slider will control from how far the scene is viewed. Set its range from 0.3 to 5, and give it an initial value of 4. It should have a tag of 2.

Select the **GlissView**. In the attributes inspector, set the view to have a 16-bit depth buffer, as shown in Figure 29.5.

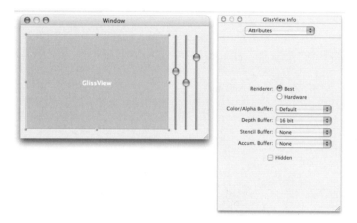

Figure 29.5 Create a 16-Bit Depth Buffer

Inspect the **NSMatrix**. Set it to autosize its cells. In the size inspector, make the matrix cling to the right edge of the window, as shown in Figure 29.6. Save the nib file.

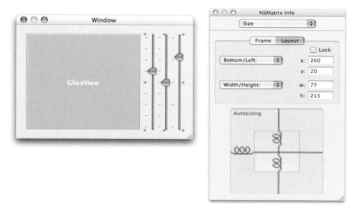

Figure 29.6 Matrix Size Inspector

Edit GlissView.h as follows:

```
#import <Cocoa/Cocoa.h>
#define LIGHT_X_TAG  0
#define THETA_TAG    1
#define RADIUS_TAG   2

@interface GlissView : NSOpenGLView
{
    IBOutlet NSMatrix *sliderMatrix;
    float lightX, theta, radius;
}
- (void)prepare;
- (IBAction)changeParameter:(id)sender;
@end
```

Next, edit GlissView.m:

```
#import "GlissView.h"
#import <GLUT/glut.h>

@implementation GlissView

- (id)initWithFrame:(NSRect)frameRect
        pixelFormat:(NSOpenGLPixelFormat *)pixFmt
{
    self = [super initWithFrame:frameRect pixelFormat:pixFmt];
    [self prepare];
    return self;
}

- (id)initWithCoder:(NSCoder *)c
{
    self = [super initWithCoder:c];
    [self prepare];
    return self;
}

- (void)prepare
{
    NSLog(@"prepare");
    float mat[4];
    NSOpenGLContext *glcontext;
    GLfloat ambient[] = {0.2, 0.2, 0.2, 1.0};
    GLfloat diffuse[] = {1.0, 1.0, 1.0, 1.0};

    // The GL context must be active for these functions to have an effect
    glcontext = [self openGLContext];
    [glcontext makeCurrentContext];
```

```
    // Configure the view
    glShadeModel(GL_SMOOTH);
    glEnable(GL_LIGHTING);
    glEnable(GL_DEPTH_TEST);

    // Add some ambient lighting
    glLightModelfv(GL_LIGHT_MODEL_AMBIENT, ambient);

    // Initialize the light
    glLightfv(GL_LIGHT0, GL_DIFFUSE, diffuse);
    // and switch it on.
    glEnable(GL_LIGHT0);

    // Set the properties of the material under ambient light
    mat[0] = 0.1;
    mat[1] = 0.1;
    mat[2] = 0.7;
    mat[3] = 1.0;
    glMaterialfv(GL_FRONT, GL_AMBIENT, mat);

    // Set the properties of the material under diffuse light
    mat[0] = 0.2;
    mat[1] = 0.6;
    mat[2] = 0.1;
    glMaterialfv(GL_FRONT, GL_DIFFUSE, mat);
}

// Called when the view resizes
- (void)reshape
{
    NSLog(@"reshaping");
    NSRect rect = [self bounds];
    glViewport(0,0, rect.size.width, rect.size.height);
    glMatrixMode(GL_PROJECTION);
    glLoadIdentity();
    gluPerspective(60.0, rect.size.width/rect.size.height, 0.2, 7);
}

- (void)awakeFromNib
{
    [self changeParameter:self];
}

- (IBAction)changeParameter:(id)sender
{
    lightX = [[sliderMatrix cellWithTag:LIGHT_X_TAG] floatValue];
    theta = [[sliderMatrix cellWithTag:THETA_TAG] floatValue];
    radius = [[sliderMatrix cellWithTag:RADIUS_TAG] floatValue];
    [self setNeedsDisplay:YES];
}

- (void)drawRect:(NSRect)r
{
    GLfloat lightPosition[] = {lightX, 1, 3, 0.0};
```

```
    // Clear the background
    glClearColor (0.2, 0.4, 0.1, 0.0);
    glClear(GL_COLOR_BUFFER_BIT |
            GL_DEPTH_BUFFER_BIT);

    // Set the view point
    glMatrixMode(GL_MODELVIEW);
    glLoadIdentity();
    gluLookAt(radius * sin(theta), 0,  radius * cos(theta),
              0, 0, 0,
              0, 1, 0);

    // Put the light in place
    glLightfv(GL_LIGHT0, GL_POSITION, lightPosition);

    // Draw the stuff
    glTranslatef(0, 0, 0);
    glutSolidTorus(0.3, 0.9, 35, 31);
    glTranslatef(0, 0, -1.2);
    glutSolidCone(1, 1, 17, 17);
    glTranslatef(0, 0, 0.6);
    glutSolidTorus(0.3, 1.8, 35, 31);

    // Flush to screen
    glFinish();
}
@end
```

Notice that the OpenGL calls are broken into three parts: **prepare** is all the calls to be sent initially, **reshape** is all the calls to be sent when the view resizes, and **drawRect:** is all the calls to be sent each time the view needs to be redrawn. Build and run the app.

Chapter 30
CREATING FRAMEWORKS

In time, you will develop a collection of classes that are designed to work together. To make reuse of the collection easier, you can compile them into a *framework*. A framework is simply a directory that can include header files, a library of compiled code, and resources. When you create an application that uses this directory, you will link against the framework.

When you link against a framework, its location is recorded in the executable. If the framework is not found in that location when the application runs, the following locations are checked:

- `~/Library/Frameworks`
- `/Library/Frameworks`
- `/Network/Library/Frameworks`
- `/System/Library/Frameworks`

Apple installs all of the standard frameworks in /System/Library/Frameworks/. If your framework is used in several applications, you will typically install it in /Library/Frameworks/. If your framework is used by only one application, you will typically embed it inside that application's app wrapper.

To make your framework easier to use, you should ensure that it includes the headers for all the code that you wish to make public. Typically, you will also create a master header that includes all the other headers. The master header makes imports like the following possible:

```
#import <Foundation/Foundation.h>
```

To speed the launch of applications that link against your framework, make sure that it can be easily prebound into an app.

Create a Framework

In this chapter, you will build a framework that includes the **BigLetterView** class, the **ColorFormatter** class, and the **FirstLetter** category. The name of the framework will be BNRCocoa.

You will install the new framework in your home directory, so in Finder create a ~/Library/Frameworks directory, if one does not already exist (Figure 30.1).

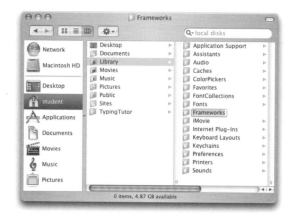

Figure 30.1   Creating the ~/Library/Frameworks Directory

Create a new project of type Cocoa Framework named BNRCocoa. From the Finder, drag the .h and .m files for **BigLetterView**, **FirstLetter**, and **ColorFormatter** into the Classes group of the new project (Figure 30.2). (Check the Copy check box to copy them in.) Delete the file main.c.

Note that the Cocoa framework is already included in the project.

Create a new file in Xcode of type Empty File named BNRCocoa.h. Move it under the top-level group BNRCocoa.

Edit BNRCocoa.h as follows:

```
#import <BNRCocoa/BigLetterView.h>
#import <BNRCocoa/ColorFormatter.h>
#import <BNRCocoa/FirstLetter.h>
```

Figure 30.2 Adding the BigLetterView, ColorFormatter, and FirstLetter Files to the Project

Open the Targets group on the left side of your Xcode window and select the BNRCocoa target. For each header file displayed on the right side of the Xcode window, choose public from the pop-up menu in the second column, as shown in Figure 30.3.

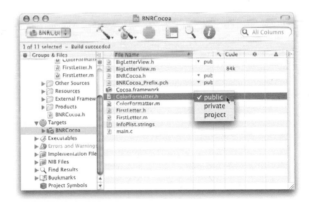

Figure 30.3 Making the Header Files Public

Build the framework. In the Finder, move the BNRCocoa.framework from the build directory of your project directory into ~/Library/Frameworks, as shown in Figure 30.4.

Figure 30.4   Moving BNRCocoa.framework into ~/Library/Frameworks

Open the TypingTutor project. Delete the files for **BigLetterView**, **ColorFormatter**, and **FirstLetter**. Using the Add Frameworks... menu item under the Project menu, add ~/Library/Frameworks/BNRCocoa.framework to the project (Figure 30.5).

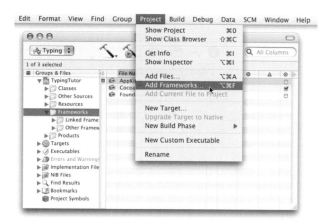

Figure 30.5   Choosing Add Frameworks... from the Project Menu

Import the the master header in AppController.h:

```
#import <BNRCocoa/BNRCocoa.h>
```

Eliminate the lines importing BigLetterView.h and ColorFormatter.h in AppController.m.

Clean, recompile, and run TypingTutor. Ignore any warnings about prebinding. You will take care of those issues soon.

Embed the Framework in an Application

Oddly enough, to embed a framework, both the framework and the application must be compiled in a special manner.

Compile the Framework for Embedding

Switch back to the BNRCocoa project. Click on the BNRCocoa target under the Targets group on the left side of the Xcode window, then choose Get Info from the Project menu to open the info panel (Figure 30.6).

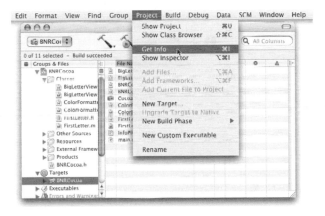

Figure 30.6 Opening the Info Panel for the BNRCocoa Target

Click the Build tab. Scroll down to the build setting named INSTALL_PATH, and change its value to @executable_path/../Frameworks (Figure 30.7).

Close the info panel. Clean and compile the framework.

Figure 30.7   Changing the INSTALL_PATH Build Setting

Compile the Application with the Framework

Open the TypingTutor project. You no longer want to use the framework that is in ~/Library/Frameworks, so delete it from the project. Choose Add Frameworks... from the Project menu, and add the BNRCocoa.framework that is in the build directory of the BNRCocoa project (typically ~/BNRCocoa/build/BNRCocoa.framework).

Expand the TypingTutor target under the Targets group in the left side of the Xcode window to reveal the build phases. Click on the Frameworks & Libraries build phase, then choose New Build Phase from the Project menu and select New Copy Files Build Phase from the submenu (Figure 30.8).

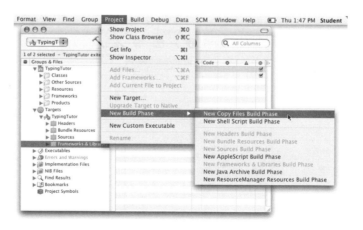

Figure 30.8   Creating a New Copy Files Build Phase

Select the new Copy Files build phase. Choose Get Info from the Project menu to open the info panel. Choose Frameworks from the Destination pop-up menu (Figure 30.9), and then close the info panel.

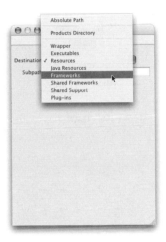

Figure 30.9   Setting the Destination of the Copy Files Build Phase

In the outline view on the left side of the Xcode window, drag the BNRCocoa.framework icon from the Frameworks folder down into the Copy Files build phase you created (Figure 30.10).

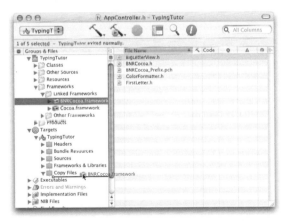

Figure 30.10   Adding BNRCocoa.framework to the Copy Files Build Phase

Clean and build the application. In the Terminal, browse the resulting app wrapper for the BNRCocoa.framework. Note that you can delete the BNRCocoa.framework from ~/Library/Frameworks, and the one in the BNRCocoa project directory and the application will still run because it has copied the framework into the app wrapper.

Prebinding

Libraries are loaded into memory at some location. Apps launch most quickly if the libraries are loaded into non-overlapping addresses. If two libraries try to claim the same space, one is moved, which can slow the launch very slightly.

While compiling an app that uses a framework that has not been "optimized," you may receive warnings. A simple fix is to set the address where the framework is loaded to some random address by passing a flag to the linker. In your framework project, just set the address in the Other linker flags build setting in the Build tab of the target info panel like this (Figure 30.11):

```
-segladdr 0x20000000
```

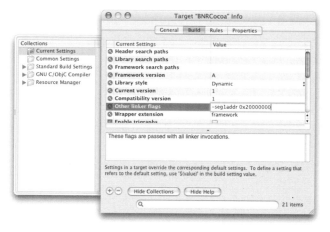

Figure 30.11   Adjusting the Other Linker Flags Build Setting

Non-Apple libraries can use any address in the range 0x00000000 to 0x3FFFFFFF. This choice can eliminate the warning and increase the speed of your launch a tiny bit.

Change the segladdr on your BNRCocoa framework to 0x20000000 and recompile it. Note that prebinding is not disabled.

Zero-Link

Zero-link is a nifty technology that speeds builds while you are doing development. It eliminates the need for your app to be linked every time you build it. Of course, you need to turn off this feature and rebuild the app with true linking before you ship it.

By default, your Cocoa project is created with two build styles: Development and Deployment. You've been using the Development build style throughout this book. The Deployment build style uses true linking and strips the debugging symbols out of the app. If you want to change back and forth between the two build styles, the easiest way is to add the Build Styles pop-up to your toolbar in Xcode.

Chapter 31
GNUstep

Developers often ask me if their Cocoa code can be used on other platforms. My answer is usually, "Well ... eh ... not really." This chapter gives a longer answer to that question.

When NeXT made the OpenStep API (which was later renamed Cocoa) be an open standard, the Free Software Foundation announced that it would provide an open-source implementation of the standard. That was a decade ago, and the group has yet to release a 1.0 version of this implementation called *GNUstep* (http://www.gnustep.org).

GNUstep comprises replacements for Xcode, Interface Builder, and the Cocoa framework. There are also subprojects to create frameworks for Web development and database access. GNUstep should run on all sorts of Unix machines and even Windows, but I've used it only on Linux.

The effort may be a noble one, but using GNUstep is not for the faint of heart:

- GNUstep is difficult to install.
- The tools are buggy and crash regularly.
- Porting your application from Mac OS X is difficult because the file formats for nib files are different under GNUstep. (While the OpenStep API is open, Apple has kept the nib file format closed and proprietary.)
- The interface that GNUstep creates is a decent copy of the NeXT UI. It was a slick look in 1994, but now the look and feel are like neither the Mac nor a normal X11 application.
- Quartz and the Apple Window Server run natively on Mac OS X. GNUstep attempts to graft this graphics model onto whatever back end it is using. (On most systems, X11 serves as the back end.) The performance and aesthetics may disappoint users who are familiar with Mac OS X.

If after reading these warnings you still feel smart enough and determined enough to install and use GNUstep, I'll do my best to show you how to get started.

Creating a System That Will Run GNUstep Applications

Start with a nice, fresh Linux machine. The GNUstep team tends to be fairly aggressive about using the latest gcc, so you'll want to make sure the machine is up-to-date with a recent distribution. Install WindowMaker (http://www.windowmaker.org) as your window manager—the package management system on your machine should make this easy. (Any window manager will work, but the NeXT-style menus and icons look a lot better with WindowMaker.)

You'll also want to download and install ffcall. It is available via anonymous FTP at ftp.gnustep.org.

The easiest way to install GNUstep is to use CVS from the terminal. Log in to the server (just press Enter when asked for a password) and download the entire project:

```
% cvs -d:pserver:anoncvs@subversions.gnu.org:/cvsroot/gnustep login
% cvs -z3 -d:pserver:anoncvs@subversions.gnu.org:/cvsroot/gnustep co
gnustep
```

This will create a directory named gnustep. Inside this directory, you will find a directory called core that has four important parts:

1. make: All of the makefiles needed to build GNUstep applications. It also includes a script called GNUstep.sh, which gives you all of the necessary environment variables. By default, it is installed in /usr/GNUstep/System/Library/Makefiles/.
2. base: The replacement for Foundation.framework.
3. gui: The replacement for Appkit.framework.
4. back: To make it possible to port the AppKit to several different platforms, the system-specific parts have been moved into a carefully delineated back-end, called back.

There is also a script in the core directory called compile-all. This handy script will configure, build, and install the entire core for you. The system, for portability reasons, does not use frameworks. The libraries and headers will be installed in /usr/GNUstep/System.

With the libraries and makefiles installed, you next need to start up some daemons. The gdomap daemon owns port 538 and tracks services that your GNUstep applications create. The gdnc daemon holds the distributed notification center. You should start both when your machine boots:

```
# Setup for the GNUstep environment
if [ -f /usr/GNUstep/System/Makefiles/GNUstep.sh ]; then
  . /usr/GNUstep/System/Makefiles/GNUstep.sh
fi

# Start the GNUstep daemons
if [ -f $GNUSTEP_SYSTEM_ROOT/Tools/gdomap ]; then
    echo -n "Starting GNUstep services... "
    echo -n "gdomap "
    $GNUSTEP_SYSTEM_ROOT/Tools/gdomap
    echo "gdnc "
    $GNUSTEP_SYSTEM_ROOT/Tools/gdnc
fi
```

For each user, you will want to set the necessary environment variables. The easiest way to do so is to add the following lines to your /etc/profile:

```
# Setup for the GNUstep environment
if [ -f /usr/GNUstep/System/Makefiles/GNUstep.sh ]; then
  . /usr/GNUstep/System/Makefiles/GNUstep.sh
fi
```

You'll want to start the pasteboard server when the X server starts. Create a ~/.xinitrc file:

```
$GNUSTEP_SYSTEM_ROOT/Tools/gpbs
exec wmaker
```

At this point, reboot your machine, log in, and start the X server. At a terminal, confirm that the following processes are running:

```
% ps -auxw | grep GNU
root      1782   15:31   0:00 /usr/GNUstep/System/Tools/gdomap
root      1784   15:31   0:00 /usr/GNUstep/System/Tools/gdnc
aaron     1929   15:37   0:00 /usr/GNUstep/System/Tools/gpbs
aaron     1981   15:38   0:00 grep GNU
```

Good. If you have gotten this far, you have a system from which you can now run GNUstep applications. You are not, however, ready to *develop* GNUstep applications.

Building and Starting the Development Tools

In the CVS-created gnustep directory, you will find dev-apps/Gorm. Gorm is the replacement for Interface Builder. At a terminal, issue two commands: make and make install. Gorm will be installed in /usr/GNUstep/System/Applications/Gorm.app.

In dev-apps/ProjectCenter, run make and make install. ProjectCenter is the replacement for Project Builder.

To start ProjectCenter, use WindowMaker's Run... menu item. When the panel appears, type openapp ProjectCenter as shown in Figure 31.1.

Figure 31.1   Start ProjectCenter

Creating the RandomApp with GNUstep

When ProjectCenter has started, create a new project of type GormApplication. Name it RandomApp, as shown in Figure 31.2.

Figure 31.2   Create a New Project

Throughout this process, there are a few things to remember:

- Save often. The tools do crash occasionally.
- Use the option-key to trigger menu items. For example, option-q will trigger the Quit menu item.

A template project will be created for you. Double-click RandomApp.gorm under the Interfaces group as shown in Figure 31.3.

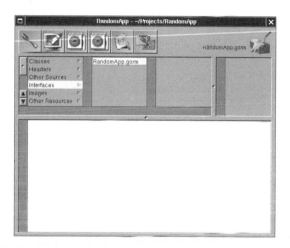

Figure 31.3   New Project

Gorm will start and open the RandomApp.gorm file. Drag a button from the palette window onto your window. Change its title to Seed random number generator, as shown in Figure 31.4.

Drop another button on the window. Change its title to Generate random number. Drag a title text field onto the window. Change its string value to ???.

In the Classes page, select **NSObject**. Create a subclass of **NSObject** and rename it **Foo**. Add two actions, **generate:** and **seed:**, to the class **Foo**, as shown in Figure 31.5. Also add an outlet named textField.

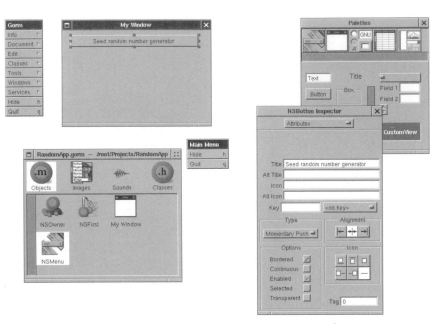

Figure 31.4   Gorm

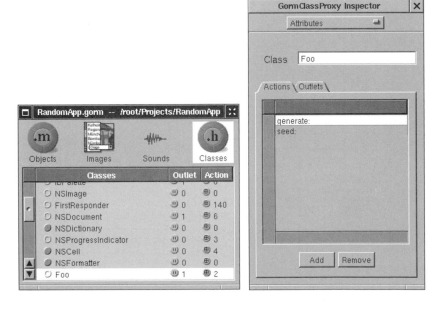

Figure 31.5   Foo

To create the files, use the Create Class Files... menu item in the Classes menu. Save Foo.h and Foo.m in your project directory.

Using the Classes menu, create an instance of **Foo**.

Control-drag from the seed button to the **Foo** object. If you are familiar with Interface Builder, you will be surprised that no line appears. (Intellectual property trivia: Apple has a patent on the window-as-a-thin-line technique.) Instead, a green rectangle will appear around the source of the connection (the **NSButton**) and a purple rectangle will appear around the destination (the **Foo**). In the list of outlets in the connections inspector, choose target and then choose the action **seed:**, as shown in Figure 31.6.

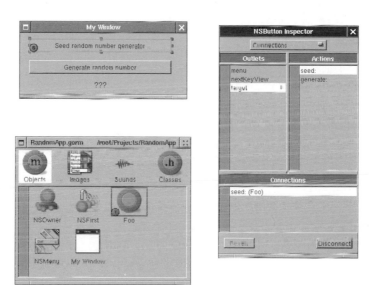

Figure 31.6   Making a Connection

Control-drag from the Generate button to **Foo** and set the action to be **generate:**. Control-drag from **Foo** to the text field and set the textField outlet. Save the Gorm file.

In ProjectCenter, edit Foo.m as follows:

```
#include <AppKit/AppKit.h>
#include "Foo.h"

@implementation Foo
```

```
- (IBAction)generate:(id)sender
{
    // Generate a number between 1 and 100 inclusive
    int generated;
    generated = (random() % 100) + 1;

    // Ask the text field to change what it is displaying
    [textField setIntValue:generated];
}

- (IBAction)seed:(id)sender
{
    // Seed the random number generator with the time
    srandom(time(NULL));
    [textField setStringValue:@"Generator seeded"];
}

@end
```

Notice that GNUstep people do not use #import. The implementation of #import in gcc was quite poor until the most recent release. If GNUstep people do not use #import, how do they prevent the same header file from being included more than once? They use the old #ifndef trick in their header files:

```
#ifndef _MyFramework_H_MyClass
#define _MyFramework_H_MyClass

@class MyClass
...
@end
#endif
```

Another surprising style difference in GNUstep style is the set of macros that is used quite consistently. A Cocoa programmer typically creates an accessor that looks like this:

```
- (void)setRex:(NSCalendarDate *)c
{
    [c retain];
    [rex release];
    rex = c;
}
```

This would work in GNUstep, but GNUstep developers typically use an equivalent macro:

```
- (void)setRex:(NSCalendarDate *)c
{
    ASSIGN(rex, c);
}
```

Here are some of the commonly used macros:

- AUTORELEASE (object): Send an **autorelease** message to the object.
- RELEASE (object): Send a **release** message to the object.
- RETAIN (object): Send a **retain** message to the object.
- DESTROY (variable): Send a **release** message to the object stored in the variable (often an instance variable), and then set the variable to nil.
- ASSIGN (variable, value): Assign a value to a variable (often an instance variable). The macro retains the new value, puts the new value in the variable, and then releases the old value. If the variable already had the new value, the macro does nothing.
- ASSIGN_COPY (variable, value): Same as ASSIGN, but copies the value (instead of retaining it) before assigning it to the variable.

Besides saving a few lines of typing, these macros allow developers to easily substitute the retain count mechanism with automatic garbage collection routines.

Now it is time to build your project. You must make sure that everything is saved: the code, the Gorm file, and the project itself. To see the build panel, click the screwdriver button in ProjectCenter. Click the screwdriver button in the build panel to begin the build, as shown in Figure 31.7.

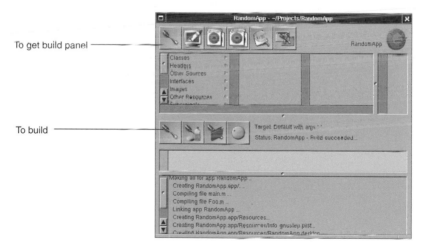

Figure 31.7 Building

To run your program, click the button with the screen and rocket to get the launch panel. Then click the rocket to run it, as shown in Figure 31.8.

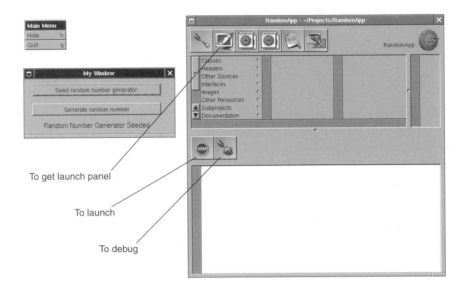

To get launch panel

To launch

To debug

Figure 31.8   Running

Your application should run without a problem. If you click the buttons and nothing happens (or if there are no buttons present), chances are you have forgotten to save something.

That information should suffice to get you started.

The project created in this chapter has a lot of promise, but it is still awkward to use. The frameworks seem further along than the tools, but I wouldn't bet my business on either in their current state. In time, if enough people help, GNUstep will become a great way to run your OpenStep/Cocoa applications on many platforms.

Chapter 32
THE END

When I teach a class, it always ends with the "Feel-Good Talk," which delivers the following messages:

- The knowledge you have received from this experience never comes easy. You have learned a lot of stuff. Be proud.
- The only way to solidify what you have learned is to write applications. The sooner you start, the easier it will be.
- There is still much more to learn, but you have crossed the hump in the learning curve. Matters will be easier from here. Once again, the only way to progress is to write applications.
- As a speaker, I'm available for weddings, parties, bar mitzvahs, and other events. I also offer five-day classes at the Big Nerd Ranch. For a schedule, please see the Big Nerd Ranch Web site (http://www.bignerdranch.com).

The final part of the "Feel-Good Talk" is a listing of resources that will help answer your questions as they arise. As with any programming topic, your answers will be found in a hodgepodge of online documentation, Web sites, and mailing lists.

- If you have a question about Cocoa, the first place to check is in the reference documentation. All of the classes, protocols, functions, and constants are listed there. Look in /Developer/Documentation/Cocoa/Reference/.
- If you have a question about Objective-C, the first place to check is in the Objective-C reference documentation. Look in /Developer/Documentation/Cocoa/ObjectiveC/.
- If you have a question about Xcode or Interface Builder, the first place to check is in the developer tools reference documentation. Look in /Developer/Documentation/DeveloperTools/.
- Mark Dalrymple and I wrote a book on the plumbing of Mac OS X from a developer's point of view. If your code is going to do anything with the operating system (like multithreading or networking), I strongly recommend that you pick up a copy of *Core Mac OS X and Unix Programming*.

- Don't be afraid to experiment—most questions can actually be answered by creating a tiny application. Creating this application will probably take you less than 15 minutes.
- The Web site for this book (`http://www.bignerdranch.com/Book`) has the answers to many questions and several fun examples.
- Two Web sites are frequented by Mac OS X developers: StepWise (`http://www.stepwise.com/`) and CocoaDev Wiki (`http://www.cocoadev.com/`).
- You can search the archives of the MacOSX-dev mailing list at the OmniGroup Web site (`http://www.omnigroup.com/`). It is a very active mailing list, and searching it can be rather tedious. Apple also has a mailing list for Cocoa developers. You can join the cocoa-dev mailing list at Apple's list server (`http://lists.apple.com/`). Both lists are archived at `http://www.cocoabuilder.com/`.
- If you have exhausted all other possibilities, Apple's Developer Technical Support will answer your questions for a fee. The folks there have answered lots of questions for me, and I find them to be consistently knowledgeable and helpful.
- Join the Apple Developer Connection. It will give you access to the latest developer tools and documentation. The ADC Web site is `http://connect.apple.com/`.

Finally, try to be nice. Help beginners. Give away useful applications and their source code. Answer questions in a kind manner. It is a relatively small community, and few good deeds go forever unrewarded.

Thanks for reading my book!

INDEX

Register Your Book

at www.awprofessional.com/register

You may be eligible to receive:

- Advance notice of forthcoming editions of the book
- Related book recommendations
- Chapter excerpts and supplements of forthcoming titles
- Information about special contests and promotions throughout the year
- Notices and reminders about author appearances, tradeshows, and online chats with special guests

Contact us

If you are interested in writing a book or reviewing manuscripts prior to publication, please write to us at:

Editorial Department
Addison-Wesley Professional
75 Arlington Street, Suite 300
Boston, MA 02116 USA
Email: AWPro@aw.com

Addison-Wesley

Visit us on the Web: http://www.awprofessional.com